Anne Hardy

Where to Eat in Canada

FORTY-FOURTH YEAR

14-15

We acknowledge the support of the Government of Canada through the Canada Book Fund for our publishing activities.

ISBN 978 0 7780 1418 8

Front cover by Paul Cézanne

Printed in Canada by Coach House Printing

PUBLISHED IN CANADA BY OBERON PRESS

HOW TO USE THIS GUIDE

The restaurants recommended in this guide have been arranged alphabetically by location, from Abbotsford in British Columbia to Yellowknife in the Northwest Territories. Each entry begins with the name of the city, town or village in which the restaurant is located, followed by the name and address of the restaurant and its telephone number. Next comes the entry itself, printed in roman type, followed by two or three lines, in italic type, indicating the hours during which the restaurant is open for business. The entry ends with a quantity of other useful information: does the restaurant have a full liquor licence or is it licensed for beer and wine only? What credit cards does it take? If the restaurant is in an urban centre, does it have free off-street parking? Do you need to book a table? Is there wheelchair access to the front door and the washrooms?

If you already know what restaurant you want to go to, look up the restaurant in the guide, selecting first the name of the centre and then the name of the restaurant. You will find a heading like this:

LAKE LOUISE, Alberta   **MAP 98**
THE POST HOTEL   ☆☆☆
200 Pipestone Road   **$300 ($650)**
(800) 661-1586

At left, you will find the name, address and telephone number of the restaurant, all arranged under Lake Louise. The first line on the right means that Lake Louise is represented by Map Number 98. Look for Number 98 on the map of Alberta. Once you've found it, consult your road-map for the most convenient route to Lake Louise. Often a quick check of the entry in the guide will help you to find your way.

The second line indicates how many stars the restaurant has earned. The maximum is three, and there are only twenty-three restaurants in the guide that have earned this rating. Ninety-three have earned two stars and 139 have earned one. We consider a further 91 restaurants to be good buys, which doesn't necessarily mean that they are unusually cheap, though it usually does. They are indicated by a pointing finger.

The third line indicates the price. The first (and often the only) figure indicates the average cost of dinner for two with a modest wine, applicable taxes and a tip of 15%. Dinner for two is taken to mean two appetizers, two main courses, one sweet, two coffees and three glasses of an open wine. Where a restaurant has earned two stars, the cost of half a bottle of wine is included. Where a restaurant has earned three stars, the cost of a full bottle is part of the estimated price. The wines chosen are not the cheapest the establishment has to offer, nor are they the most expensive. Where, as in the case of the Post Hotel, a second figure in parentheses follows the first, this second figure indicates the average cost of dinner, bed and breakfast. The presence of this figure means that we recommend not only dinner but also, if convenient, an overnight stay.

If you don't know where you want to go, turn to the maps. Find yourself on the map that shows the province you are in. Select the nearest number and then look it up in the Index. Under the number you'll find all the centres represented by that number. Let's suppose that the nearest number is 202, which stands for the city of Toronto. Look up Toronto in the Index to Southern Ontario and you'll find that there are two other centres with the same number, each enclosed in parentheses. This means that these centres are both in the immediate vicinity of Toronto, too close to be given a number of their own. They are Port Credit and Whitby. Now look up Toronto in the main body of the guide, where you will find all 39 restaurants that we recommend in the city itself. If you then look up both of the other two centres, you will find two more restaurants in the area that are also recomended.

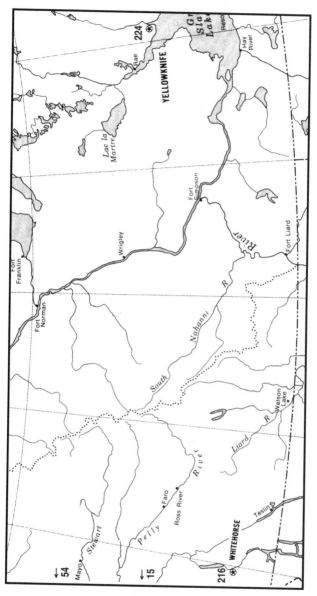

YUKON & NORTHWEST TERRITORIES

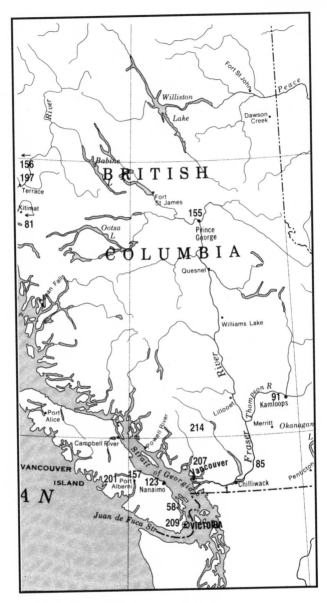

BRITISH COLUMBIA

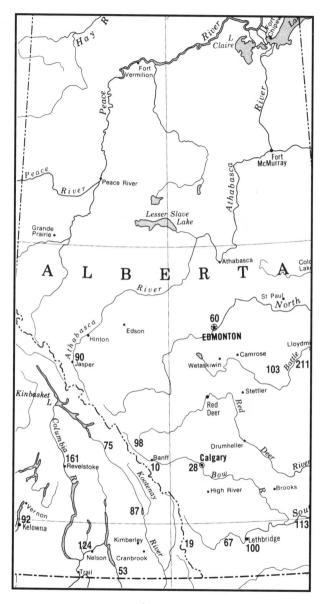

ALBERTA

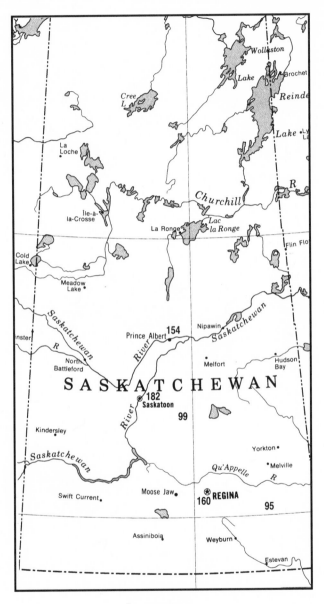

SASKATCHEWAN

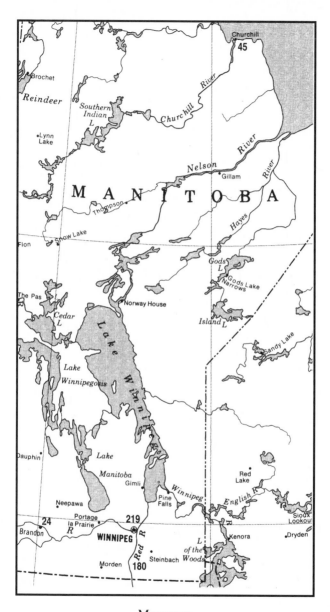

MANITOBA

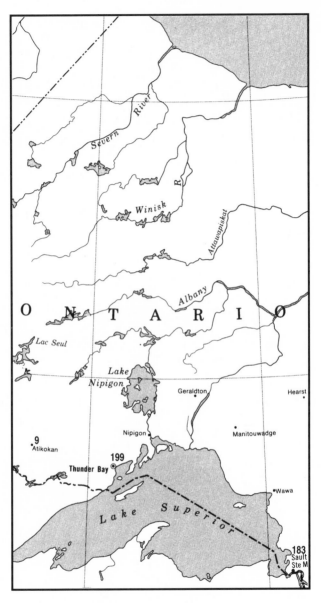

NORTHWESTERN ONTARIO

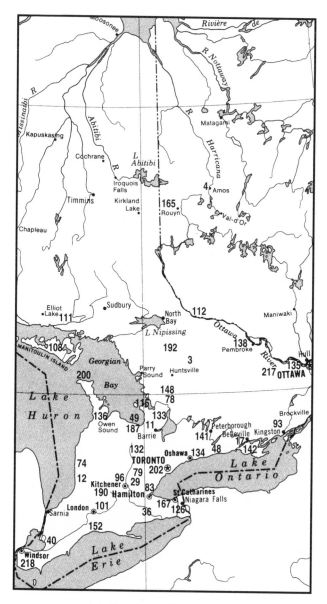

SOUTHERN ONTARIO

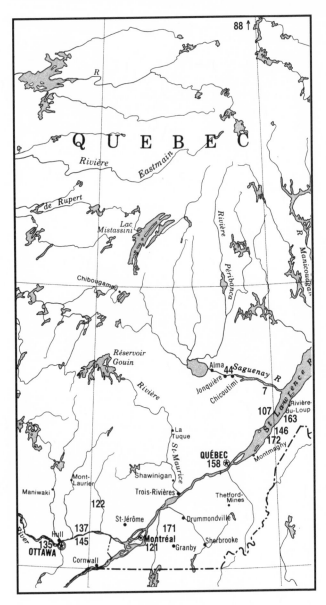

CENTRAL QUEBEC

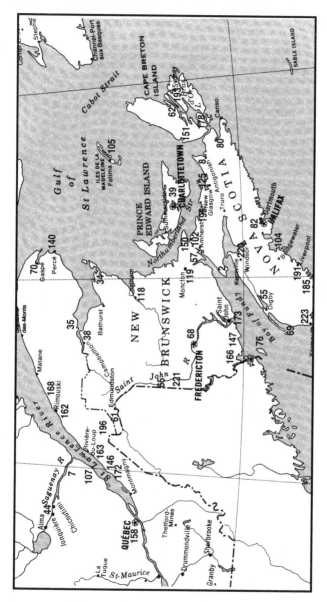

EASTERN QUEBEC & THE MARITIMES

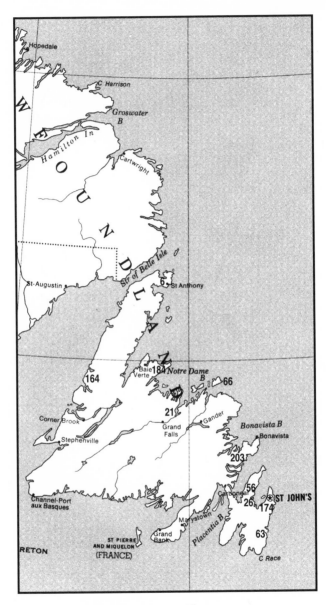

NEWFOUNDLAND & LABRADOR

INDEX TO MAPS

MANITOBA

24 Brandon
45 Churchill
180 St. Pierre-Jolys
219 Winnipeg

NORTHWESTERN ONTARIO

9 Atikokan
183 Sault Ste. Marie
199 Thunder Bay

SOUTHERN ONTARIO

3 Algonquin Park
4 Amos
11 Barrie
12 Bayfield
17 Belleville
(17) Brighton
29 Cambridge
36 Cayuga
40 Chatham
48 Cobourg
49 Collingwood
(49) Thornbury
74 Goderich
78 Gravenhurst
(78) Bracebridge
79 Guelph
(79) Morriston
83 Hamilton
(83) Ancaster
(83) Burlington
(83) Dundas
93 Kingston

(93) Ivy Lea
96 Kitchener
(96) Waterloo
101 London
108 Manitoulin Island
111 Massey
112 Mattawa
115 Midland
(115) Penetang
126 Niagara-on-the-Lake
132 Orangeville
133 Orillia
134 Oshawa
135 Ottawa
(135) Chelsea
136 Owen Sound
138 Pembroke
141 Peterborough
142 Picton
(142) Bloomfield
(142) Wellington
148 Port Carling
152 Port Stanley
165 Rouyn
167 St. Catharines
(167) Beamsville
187 Singhampton
190 Stratford
(190) St. Marys
192 Sundridge
200 Tobermory
202 Toronto
(202) Port Credit
(202) Whitby
217 White Lake
218 Windsor
(218) Kingsville

NEWFOUNDLAND & LABRADOR

ABBOTSFORD, B.C.
CLAYBURN VILLAGE STORE
34810 Clayburn Road
Clayburn
(604) 853-4020

MAP 1

🖐

$50

The Clayburn Village Store is closed for the months of January, May and September. That's when Bryan and Trish Haber take off, perhaps to a food festival in California, perhaps to Betty's Tea-Shop in York, where they buy Tippy Assam tea for the Village Store back home. (Theirs is the only cream tea with clotted cream to be had anywhere this side of Victoria.) They make all their own chutneys, pickles, cheese scones and sticky-toffee puddings. Every year they bring home new soup recipes, and their recipe for carrot-and-coconut soup has been published in *Bon Appetit*. We also like their caramelized onion soup with garlic and parmesan cheese, though many of the customers seem to prefer the Thai coconut-and-squash soup. Bryan Haber is also keen on British ales, which he buys from Samuel Smith's Yorkshire Brewery in Tadcaster. There's Imperial Stout, Nut Brown and Teddy Porter, and he now has an organic ale and an organic cider as well. There's always an assortment of British candies on the candy counter, all sold from big glass jars, just the way they used to be in the nineteen-thirties. They didn't have a frozen-yogurt machine then though; he does.

Open Tuesday to Saturday 10 am to 5 pm. Closed on Sunday and Monday. Licensed. Master Card, Visa. ♿

ADVOCATE HARBOUR, N.S.
WILD CARAWAY
3721 Highway 209
(902) 392-2889

MAP 2

☆☆☆

$95 ($175)

Who would have expected to find one of the best restaurants this side of Halifax in a village of 200 souls like this? But the fact is that a young couple, Andrew Aitken and Sarah Griebel, have restored a mid-Victorian house over looking Cape d'Or, and opened two charming guest-rooms. There's a huge garden behind the house that supplies most of the herbs and vegetables the restaurant needs. When you get there, look for the crisp-fried local squid, the terrine of chicken and wild mushrooms, the pan-fried fillet of char, the pan-roasted fillet of halibut with aged cheddar and buttered cucumber, the seared local scallops with cauliflower and white truffles. The sweets are equally amazing and they make their own rhubarb lemonade and their own ginger beer. They smoke their own seafood and cut their own fries. They start every meal with fresh dulse and caraway buns. Every Sunday there's a fabulous brunch, but the menu is always a surprise.

Open Monday and Wednesday to Saturday 11 am to 8 pm, Sunday 9 am to noon (brunch), 5 pm to 9 pm. Closed on Tuesday. Shorter hours in winter. Licensed. Master Card, Visa. &

ALGONQUIN PARK, Ontario   MAP 3
AROWHON PINES   ☆
Highway 60   **$190 ($575)**
(866) 633-5661

All the recipes at Arowhon Pines were worked out over the years, then put onto a computer in such detail that no hired chef could put a foot wrong. And so it has worked out. Meals are planned a week in advance, which means that nobody ever gets the same meal twice. As you enter the great hexagonal dining-room, you're confronted by a large buffet table, where there are several pâtés and terrines, smoked mousse of lake trout, honey-garlic chicken wings and a wild-rice salad. You can eat as much of any of these as you like. When you sit down at your table—don't try to book a window table, because it's first come first seated—there's a choice of four entrées, one of which will be fish, another a vegetarian dish. The sweets are all famous, so try to save room for one. There's a huge assortment of pies, tarts and cakes, at least one of which will be hot. The coffee is excellent, but you have to bring your own bottle—there's no corkage fee.

Lunch is also served buffet-style on weekends only. The price in parentheses above covers three meals a day for a couple, plus all the recreational facilities on offer. Until 10 July, however, and from 1 September until 13 October, the price goes down to 410.00.

Open daily 12.30 pm to 2 pm, 6.30 pm to 9 pm from 30 May until 13 October. Bring your own bottle. Master Card, Visa. Book ahead. &

ALGONQUIN PARK
MAP 3
BARTLETT LODGE
☆
Highway 60
$175 ($425)
(705) 633-5543

People write to us about the hospitality of the people at Bartlett Lodge. The Lodge is on Cache Lake, which is about fifteen miles from the West Gate. Drive to the far end of the car park, where you'll find a free telephone to the Lodge. A boat will come to pick you up in about two minutes. In fine weather they'll come in a custom-built Giesler; if it's raining they'll come in a covered pontoon boat. On the far side you'll be offered an elaborate dinner for 65.00 a head. Jakob Lutes, the chef from the Atelier in Ottawa, was soon replaced by his sous-chef, Dave Fortune, whose menu changes from day to day. There's usually a soup, followed by a fish or meat course and a sweet. People write to us about the fillet of beef, the lamb shank and the mushroom risotto. The pies are wonderful and coffee is on the house.

Open daily 6 pm to 8 pm from 9 May until 19 October. Bring your own bottle. Master Card, Visa. You must book ahead.

AMHERST, N.S.
See LORNEVILLE.

This is a guide to Canadian restaurants from coast to coast—the first ever published and the only one of its kind on the market today. Every restaurant in the guide has been personally tested. Our reporters are not allowed to identify themselves or to accept free meals.

AMOS, Quebec
LE MOULIN
100 1 Avenue o
(819) 732-8271

MAP 4
★★
$140

Le Moulin has one of the best kitchens in northern Quebec, and it's doing well in spite of its remote location. (It's 50 miles west of Val d'Or and 75 miles northeast of Noranda.) Jean-Victor Flingou is an excellent cook who enjoys his work, but after more than twenty years he's turned the evening meal over to his son, Maxim. He and his son still bring in all their seafood from Montreal, and there's always a surprising variety on the menu: Atlantic salmon, mackerel, grouper, halibut, scallops, mussels and occasionally red tuna. But Flingou cooks what he feels like cooking. It may be lamb (sometimes from Ontario, sometimes from Alberta), veal, sweetbreads, or duck. He's never much liked pork and these days he doesn't serve it at all. He forages himself for mushrooms to go with his provimi veal; when he can't find enough mushrooms he'll just make a blanquette de veau. He's doing more with shrimps nowadays, because there's always a demand for them. Bison is a new favourite. Chicken is often on the menu, because he needs the bones for his stock. Every day there's a menu *du jour* for 20.00 at lunch and 35.00 at dinner. It starts with soup or snails, goes on to duck or salmon and ends with a crème pâtissière with local strawberries.

Open Monday to Friday 11 am to 2 pm, 5 pm to 9 pm, Saturday 5 pm to 9 pm. Closed on Sunday. Licensed. Amex, Master Card, Visa. Book ahead. &

ANCASTER, Ontario
THE MILL
548 Old Dundas Road
(905) 648-1828

(MAP 83)
★
$125

The Mill (which used to be called the Old Mill) is generally considered to be the flagship restaurant of the Land mark Group, which includes Spencer's in Burlington and the Earth-to-Table Bread Bar in Hamilton. At first glance, it appears to be the most traditional and conservative of the three. In fact, however, it's more up-to-date than it looks. Jeff Crump, the chef, has always espoused the merit of local, organic ingredients. His beef is aged for at least 45 days at their farm in Flamborough and his fish all comes from sustainable sources. At dinner you can if you like start with the tuna salad, which is not quite so good as the seared Ahi tuna offered as a main course. So you're probably better to start with the foie gras pâté, the beet-root salad or the beef carpaccio with a truffle aioli. The best of the main courses is certainly the Chilean seabass with cauliflower; the cauliflower and the fish are both handled with real delicacy. They also have some lamb and several steaks. For sweet there's a lovely lemon-thyme pot de crème. This is an impressive kitchen.

Open Tuesday to Saturday 11.30 am to 10 pm, Sunday 9.30 am to 2.30 pm (brunch), 5 pm to 9 pm. Closed on Monday. Licensed. Master Card, Visa. &

L'ANSE-AUX-MEADOWS,	MAP 6
Newfoundland	☆☆
THE NORSEMAN	**$140**
(877) 623-2018	

Newfoundland has changed a lot since this guide first appeared in 1971. But one could hardly have imagined then that a menu like this would appear at the Norseman in less than 50 years. All the big-city fashions appear in a village where only 28 people live. That means chorizo, quinoa, wild mushrooms and so on. You can still have your cod roasted in the old way with pan-fried pork scrunchions. But you can also have it roasted with baby spinach and a pine-nut relish. They like to serve salmon with fresh herbs and infused red cabbage. The lamb is local and so is the beef, the taste of which is said to come from the lichen on which the cattle graze. The fish chowder is head and shoulders above anyone else's, and so are the vegetables, even the root vegetables they serve in winter. The kitchen keeps a crate of lobster by the back door—you go and pick your own. It's on the menu until the middle of August, when it's at its best. They buy their crab, shrimps and scallops locally; they make their own multi-grain bread, their own partridge-berry pies and their own bake-apple cheesecake. But on the whole they're still at their best with fresh local seafood. Their wine-list offers such improbable things as Mission Hill sauvignon blanc and Peter Lehmann shiraz for only 45.00 a bottle, as well as some native berry wines.

Open daily noon to 9 pm from 25 May until 20 September. Licensed. Diners, Master Card, Visa. Book ahead if you can. &

L'ANSE-AUX-MEADOWS
See also CAPE ONION, ST.-LUNAIRE-GRIQUET.

L'ANSE-SAINT-JEAN, Quebec   MAP 7
AUBERGE DES CEVENNES   ☆
294 rue St.-Jean-Baptiste   **$110**
(877) 272-3180

L'Anse-Saint-Jean is one of the prettiest villages in the province and it's only four hours from Quebec City. The Auberge des Cevennes has a superb setting, just a few minutes from the starting point of Saguenay cruises. Enid Bertrand has energy, charm and a good command of English. She also likes to cook. Local people usually ask for one of the handful of dishes they've enjoyed for the last twenty years. Outsiders are apt to be more venturesome. Mme Bertrand has a big garden where she makes good use of the early springs and late winters in these parts. Her soups are full of garden-fresh vegetables, her cakes and pastries full of fresh raspberries and strawberries. Caribou have almost vanished from this area, but there are still roe deer that show up in her salads. There's usually quite a lot of seafood—salmon, scallops and lobster. She makes a beautiful white-mountain cake, which is a génoise filled with apples and maple syrup and served with fresh cream.

Open daily 6 pm to 9 pm from the beginning of June until the end of October, Saturday and Sunday 6 pm to 9 pm from the beginning of November until the end of May. Closed Monday to Friday in winter. Licensed. Master Card, Visa. You must book ahead. ♿

ANTIGONISH, N.S.   MAP 8
GABRIEAU'S BISTRO   ✩✩
350 Main Street   **$160**
(902) 863-1925

Gabrieau's has been completely redecorated inside and out, with cork-topped tables to keep the noise level down. The kitchen now offers sushi platters as well as the familiar Atlantic salmon with nasturtium pesto, local lamb, lobster-and-shrimp risotto and New York steak. The cooking has always been reliable and it still is; even the sushi is all it should be. The wine-list is, of course, extraordinary and it has few equals anywhere in the province. Unlike most wine-lists of its kind and quality, Gabrieau's offers remarkably low markups right across the board. For instance, there's an Antinori solaia for 239.95 and a Bolgheri sassicaia for 325.00, as well as a tignanello for less than 200.00. These prices may look pretty high, but the truth is they're all bargains. Most sensational of all is the petit mouton for 159.95, which is about half the cost of a regular Mouton-Rothschild— not that Gabrieau hasn't got a couple of those too.
Open Monday to Thursday 11 am to 9 pm, Friday 11 am to 9.30 pm, Saturday 4 pm to 9.30 pm. Closed on Sunday. Licensed. All cards. ♿

ATIKOKAN, Ontario   MAP 9
TOWN & COUNTRY
(807) 597-2533   **$95**

There may be days when Stephanie Torbiak gets tired of running this place, but she's not ready to give it up yet. Business has been slow in recent years, but Stephanie took the opportunity to install *en suite* bathrooms throughout the house. Recent work at the nearby generating station means business for the Town & Country, and so does the Ukrainian Christmas. But she knows her market. People want steak, baked beans and frozen seafood, period. All these are cooked to order and she makes all the soups and all the pasta. She makes a good quiche too and a very good salad, which comes with a poppyseed dressing. People like her cooking and that makes everything worthwhile for her.

Open Monday to Saturday 8 am to 9 pm (sometimes later). Closed on Sunday. Licensed. Master Card, Visa.

BANFF, Alberta   MAP 10

Banff has a number of surprisingly good inexpensive restaurants. Bumpers at 537 Banff Avenue (telephone (403) 762-2622) even encourages children. It's at the far end of town and doesn't look much from the outside. But inside it's a different story. They have swift, cheerful service and an all-you-can-eat salad bar. They specialize in well hung Alberta beef, and they sell a lot of triple-A prime rib. The Balkan at 120 Banff Avenue (telephone (403) 762-3454) was opened in 1982 by a Greek couple who had a lot of old family recipes. The cooking has always been completely authentic and the prices are as low as ever. The thing to have here is the so-called arni-psito, which is a version of lamb Greek-style, and it's a stunning dish. A few years ago, they decided to try something new, so they brought in a belly-dancer, and every Tuesday and Thursday invited customers to throw their plates on the floor. Some people love this sort of thing and the place is always crowded. The St. James Gate at 207 Wolf Street (telephone (403) 762-9355) is an Irish-style pub where they have 24 beers on tap and 30 single malts. Everybody admires the choice of beers and nearly everybody likes their barley soup, their meatloaf and their spicy shepherd's pie. The cooking is good, the helpings big and the prices fair. Finally, there's Nourish, a vegetarian bistro and tea-house located upstairs at 211 Bear Street (telephone (403) 760-3933). People seem to like almost everything on the menu, from the tapas and the daily specials to the sweets. There's plenty to drink—fully-blended teas, organic wines and real ale. The Balkan and the St. James are open all day every day, Bumpers every evening from 5 pm to 10 pm. Nourish is open on

*weeknights after 4.30 pm, on weekends from noon to 3 pm and
5 pm to 9 pm. They all have a licence and take most cards.*

BANFF   **MAP 10**
LE BEAUJOLAIS   ✩✩✩
212 Buffalo Street   **$250/$100**
(403) 762-2712

Albert Moser runs a lovely restaurant here on Buffalo
Street. The big, handsome, dining-room is quiet and
serene, the menu and the service civilized. Don't feel you
have to order the 95.00 *menu surprise,* because the regular
à la carte offers such things as Dover sole, elk osso buco
and filet mignon of Alberta beef. They're all beautifully
cooked and elegantly served. If you're lucky, you may be
able to start with a plate of raw chilled Malpèque oysters.
The wine-list is delightful. If you want to spend a lot of
money on a Pétrus or a Mouton-Rothschild, go ahead.
If you want a Canadian wine at a modest price, order it.
If you don't feel comfortable in such grand surroundings,
book a table in the adjacent Café de Paris (telephone (403)
762-5365), where everything is cheaper, though it's all
prepared in exactly the same kitchen.
*Open Monday to Friday 5.30 pm to 10.30 pm, Saturday and
Sunday 11.30 am to 2.30 pm, 5.30 pm to 10.30 pm from mid-
April until mid-October, Tuesday to Friday 5.30 pm to 10.30
pm, Saturday 11.30 am to 2.30 pm, 5.30 pm to 10.30 pm from
mid-October until mid-April. Closed on Sunday and Monday
in winter. Licensed. Master Card, Visa. Book ahead.*

BANFF   **MAP 10**
EDEN   ✩✩✩
Rimrock Resort Hotel   **$275**
300 Mountain Avenue
(888) 746-7625

The Rimrock is built right into the side of a mountain,
which gives it spectacular views in every direction. There
are people who complain about this or that at Eden, but
they all agree that the views are stunning. As for the

menu, it's wonderfully innovative. The tartar of Arctic char, for instance, tastes of lemon, bourbon, blue spruce and orange-blossom gelée. High-country bison is flavoured with elderflowers, juniper berries and saska-toons. Gilt-head sea-bream is grilled over Douglas fir and served with foie gras in vanilla consommé. Everything is beautifully presented and impeccably served. There are people who want more for their money. They should just settle for the multiple-course tasting menu at 124.00 a head, or go elsewhere. For those who don't want to do that, there's a seven-course tasting menu of foie gras. The wine-list is as extraordinary as everything else, and has 70,000 bottles from all over the world. Eden is the only triple-diamond restaurant, not just in Banff, but in the whole province of Alberta.

Open Tuesday to Sunday 6 pm to 9.30 pm from 1 June until mid-October, Wednesday to Sunday from mid-October until 31 May. Closed on Monday in summer, Monday and Tuesday in winter. Licensed. Amex, Master Card, Visa. Book ahead if you can. &

BARRIE, Ontario   **MAP 11**
THE CRAZY FOX
135 Bayfield Street   **$150**
(705) 737-5000

Coos Uylenbroek came here with his wife Lawna in 1986 and later moved up-market to the present location. His prices aren't low, but he cooks well and he has an impres-sive wine-list. The two-storey dining-room is dramatic and so is the kitchen, behind its wall of glass. The menu may not be particularly ambitious, but the ingredients are all the best that money can buy. The steaks, for in-stance are always tender, the vegetables (even the aspara-gus) correctly cooked and carefully seasoned. The wholewheat ravioli stuffed with spinach and butternut squash is a fine vegetarian dish. There are always some fresh berries at the end of the meal, and there's no sugar at all in the blood-orange sorbet. Lunch is a big, impor-tant meal and many of the evening dishes are also available at noon. Uylenbroek still does most of the cooking himself and it shows.

Open Tuesday to Thursday 11.30 am to 2.30 pm, 5 pm to 9.30 pm, Friday 11 am to 2.30 pm, 5 pm to 10 pm, Saturday 5 pm to 10.30 pm. Closed on Sunday and Monday. Licensed. Amex, Master Card, Visa. Free parking.

BAYFIELD, Ontario   MAP 12
THE BLACK DOG   ☆
5 Main Street N   **$160**
(519) 565-2326

For years the Little Inn and the Red Pump were thought to be the two best restaurants in Bayfield. You won't go wrong with either of them, but in our opinion the Black Dog now takes first place. Like the other two, it's in an historic building that was built in 1850 and is now the oldest commercial building on the street. It's always been known for its twenty draft beers and its many single-malt whiskies. But it's the kitchen we're interested in at the moment. They make a fine mushroom soup with fresh herbs and stilton cheese. They offer snails simmered in white wine with focaccia. Their chicken-liver pâté is big enough and good enough to share. They make their shepherd's pie with lamb and serve their Atlantic salmon with buttermilk mash, their black-angus beef with hand-cut fries.

Open Wednesday to Sunday 11.30 am to 5 pm (lunch), 5 pm to 9 pm (dinner). Closed on Monday and Tuesday. Licensed. Amex, Master Card, Visa. Book ahead if you can. &

BAY FORTUNE, P.E.I.   (MAP 39)
THE INN AT BAY FORTUNE
Highway 310   **$200 ($450)**
(902) 687-3745

The kitchen at the Inn at Bay Fortune is famous, if only as the first home of Michael Smith, who has become a star television chef. Several chefs have been in charge of the kitchen since Michael Smith left. Warren Barr was here for six years until he was forced to return to British Columbia last year. His place has been taken by Domenic Serio, who came with degrees in culinary and pastry arts from the Culinary Institute in Charlottetown. He has the resources of the Farmer's Market to draw on, as well as the Inn's own huge vegetable garden. Nearby suppliers bring him everything from local oysters and mussels to local beef and lamb. Serio is back and he'll be at Bay Fortune again this summer. David Wilmer believes in sticking with what he knows, and it's true, Serio is improving. His menu is still quite short, beginning with house-cured bresaola, pork terrine and mussels from St. Peters Bay and going on to salmon from New Brunswick, local pork and flank steak, now a rather fashionable dish. The specialty of the house is North Lake bluefin tuna, served both hot and cold, but since bluefin tuna is an endangered species we've always hesitated to mention it. This kitchen, however, is usually at its best with its sweets, the best of which (we think) is the chocolate pâté, beautifully served with house-made ice cream. The pâté goes particularly well with a glass of apple wine from Rossignol, which is the local winery.

Open daily 5.30 pm to 8.30 pm from 1 June until 30 September. Licensed. Amex, Master Card, Visa. Book ahead.

BEAMSVILLE, Ontario (MAP 167)
AUGUST
5204 King Street **$95**
(905) 563-0200

Both Ashton and Marc McKerracher, who opened August in Beamsville a couple of years ago, are serious about regional cuisine. They grow most of their own vegetables and forage locally for whatever they don't grow themselves. Their lunch menu is small and simple. There are always one or two soups, and they make all their own pasta—a different one every day of the week. They smoke their own fish and cure their own beef; they bake their own bread and make their own sweets. Outwardly, August is plain and straightforward, with hard hairs and bare tables. But in the evening they put on an ambitious menu at the same low prices: breast of chicken with curried pumpkinseed, gnocchi with parmesan cheese, seafood stew with sweet pepper and pork tenderloin dry-rubbed with molasses. Their wines are all raised on or near the Beamsville bench and several are sold by the glass. If you want a bottle, corkage is free on Fridays.

Open Tuesday to Saturday 11.30 am to 3 pm, Sunday 9 am to 3 pm (brunch). Closed on Monday. Licensed. Master Card, Visa. &

BEAVER CREEK, Yukon   MAP 15
BUCKSHOT BETTY'S
Highway 1   **$60**
(867) 862-7111

Betty is not the name of a person. The woman in charge is called Carmen Hinson, and she works much too hard. "People don't understand," she'll tell you, "that you can't just work an eight-hour day at this job." In winter, Carmen does sometimes take a couple of hours off to clean out a cabin or chop wood. She has five cabins (no view but no noise), three rooms in the main house, 40 seats in the dining-room and 40 more on the wrap-around deck. Beaver Creek is a good place to stop after the magnificent but scary drive from Whitehorse. It's 2500 feet above sea-level and quite close to the Alaska border. Carmen does all her own baking—the bread, the hamburger buns, the cookies, the brownies and whatever else she feels like baking. That might be carrot cake, apple strudel or lemon-meringue pie. She's good. Her sandwiches, for instance, are like no other.

Open daily 6.30 am to 10.30 pm (or later) from early April until mid-October, daily 8 am to 10 pm from mid-October until early April. Licensed. Master Card, Visa.

The price rating shown opposite the headline of each entry indicates the average cost of dinner for two with a modest wine, tax and tip. The cost of dinner, bed and breakfast (if available) is shown in parentheses.

BEDEQUE, P.E.I.   (MAP 39)

MAPLETHORPE CAFE   ☆
2123 Highway 112   **$65**
(866) 770-2909

Maplethorpe is hidden by a magnificent row of giant linden trees. The old blue farmhouse behind has a first-class cook, who happens to be a graduate of the Charlottetown Culinary Institute. She makes a fairly good lobster roll, but it's probably better to ask for a fishcake or the Acadian meat pie, which will remind you of the traditional rappie pie. She also has a first-class quiche and sometimes a lamb curry. If you're in a hurry, there are always plenty of sandwiches, all made with home-baked bread. The soups are great—just try the apricot soup with red lentils and fresh ginger. There are a number of beers from cottage breweries and a fine shiraz from Peller. But don't skip the caramelized bread pudding—it will amaze you. In the evening she offers a lovely seafood pie, served in puff pastry. Dinner costs only 24.95 for three courses, which is a great buy.

Open Tuesday to Thursday 11 am to 3 pm, Friday 11 am to 3 pm, 5 pm to 9 pm, Saturday 5 pm to 9 pm. Closed on Sunday and Monday. Licensed for beer and wine only. Master Card, Visa.

BELLEVILLE, Ontario   MAP 17

L'AUBERGE DE FRANCE
304 Front Street   **$90**
(613) 966-2433

Jean-Marc Salvagno made his name in Avignon before moving to Toronto and, more recently, to Belleville, where he opened his own bistro and bakery. If you come for lunch, you choose your soup, your quiche and your sandwich at the counter and it's brought to you in the small seating area at the rear. There are usually about half a dozen sandwiches on offer, all made with house-made bread. The sweets are all made on the premises, and our favourite is the lemon tart, though cheeses from Quebec are also available. Twice a month they offer what they call the chef's table, which has an innovative menu that costs only 35.00 a head.

Open Monday to Friday 10 am to 6 pm, Saturday 9 am to 6 pm. Closed on Sunday. Licensed. All cards. &

BELLEVILLE
See also BRIGHTON.

LE BIC, Quebec	**(MAP 162)**
CHEZ SAINT-PIERRE	☆☆
129 rue de Mont St.-Louis	**$215**
(418) 736-5051	

Colombe Saint-Pierre had a second child last year, but that hasn't kept her away from the kitchen that's become her passion. Le Bic is only ten miles west of Rimouski, but Chez Saint-Pierre isn't that easy to find. It's on a back street facing a car park and you'll probably have to ask your way. In these simple surroundings, Colombe is cooking as well as anyone in Quebec. Most of her ingredients come from neighbouring farms. She gets her pork from St.-Gabriel. She forages for mushrooms, for mountain spinach and salsify des prés. Sorrel grows wild on the shoulders of local roads. Colombe likes to begin her meals with something like ravioli of chanterelles or scallops marinated in Chinata paprika and finished with lemon and sundried tomatoes—a compelling and dramatic dish. She'll continue, perhaps, with fillet of bison or gravlax of Arctic char. She'll end with a chocolate financier, a biscuit bavarois or a plate of local cheeses. The choice of French and Italian wines matches the menu in quality and finesse. Chez Saint-Pierre is a restaurant you must discover for yourself. Be sure to book ahead.

Open Wednesday to Sunday 5 pm to 9.30 pm from 1 until 31 May, Tuesday to Sunday 1.30 am to 2 pm, 5 pm to 9.30 pm from 1 June until 31 August, Wednesday to Sunday 5 pm to 9.30 pm from 1 September until 30 April. Closed on Monday and Tuesday in the spring, fall and winter, on Monday in summer. Licensed. Master Card, Visa.

BLAIRMORE, Alberta
STONE'S THROW CAFE
13019 20 Avenue
(403) 562-2230

MAP 19

👉

$40

Steve and Jessica are starting their tenth year in this un-likely location, and so far they're making a success of it. They left Jasper because it had too many tourists; here they close at 5 o'clock because they want to have some time for their children. Everything in the place is cheap; nothing matches and everyone is Green. Steve and Jessica make most things themselves, and that means the bread, the scones, the wraps and the focaccia. Rhubarb squares are the best thing they do and they're worth the trip to Blairmore. But readers are pretty high also on their all-day breakfast. Right up to closing time, they'll make you an omelette or two eggs any style with bacon, potato pancakes and wholewheat toast. For lunch they have all the usual soups, salads and sandwiches, as well as several wraps and pitas. Blairmore is about twelve miles from the B.C. border on the way from the Crow's Nest Pass.
Open Monday to Saturday 7 am to 5 pm, Sunday 10 am to 4 pm. No liquor, no cards. &

BLOOMFIELD, Ontario
THE HUBB AT ANGELINE'S
433 Main Street
(613) 393-3301

(MAP 142)

☆

$135 ($235)

The Fidas still run the hotel and spa at Angeline's, and sometimes help out at the Hubb, which is run by Elliot Reynolds and his wife, Laura Borutski. They have a three-course table d'hôte, with three or four locally-sourced items in every course, all priced at 35.00. You start with something like duck tartar and go on to smoked pork shoulder, lamb shank with root vegetables or pumpkin ravioli. There are some good sweets, among them roasted bananas, chocolate ganache and chestnut mousse. Almost all of the wines come from Prince Ed-ward County and eight or nine are sold by the glass as

well as the bottle. They also have Waupoos cider and two or three local draft beers.
Open Thursday to Saturday 5 pm to 11 pm. Closed Sunday to Wednesday. Licensed. All cards. &

BLOOMFIELD (MAP 142)
THE CARRIAGE HOUSE ☆
260 Main Street **$150**
(613) 393-1087

The Carriage House was already in business long before Bloomfield became a destination for gourmets from Toronto. Nowadays it's as good as any restaurant in the area. It concentrates on local produce cooked in the Parisian style. Dinners usually begin with something like scallop-and-potato gnocchi or, perhaps, poached breast of pheasant served in a mushroom salad. That will be followed by wild salmon with creamed leeks or lamb-shank cannelloni with a ragoût of white beans. The sweet might be a triple-chocolate brownie or a selection of local cheeses. Lunch is a simpler meal and features soups, salads and quiches, as well as a variety of sandwiches. There's an extensive list of wines from Prince Edward County. Prices seem lower this year, so you should probably try a glass or two of sparking vidal, which is certainly more fun than a Duboeuf beaujolais.
Open daily 11.30 am to 2.30 pm, 5 pm to 9.30 pm from 1 July until 31 August. Licensed. All cards.

BOTWOOD, Newfoundland MAP 21
DOCKSIDE
243 Water Street **$130**
(709) 257-3179

Dockside is still open every day of the year and Jim Stuckless is still in the kitchen every second week. He taught himself to cook when he took over this old warehouse. He cooks the sort of plain food that he himself likes to eat, which means fresh local greens in summer and root vegetables in winter. The local greens are not just cabbage or Brussels sprouts. They might be something more like young spinach with Newfoundland strawberries. His beef is all triple-A from Alberta. His skin-on breast of chicken is stuffed with savoury and served with an orange and grand-marnier sauce. Mussels he sells by the boatload. His salmon is farmed and served three ways. Pan-fried cod and scrunchions cost just 13.99 for four ounces or 19.99 for eight ounces. Stuckless makes all his own sweets and that means Bavarian apple torte and partridge-berry kuchen. Every Sunday at noon he puts on a roast-beef or turkey dinner with carrots and turnips, and it costs only 15.00. Botwood is at the bottom of the Bay of Exploits. The landscape is stunning, and it's only twenty minutes by car from the Trans Canada by Highway 350.

Open daily noon to 2 pm, 4.30 pm to 8 pm. Licensed. All cards. &

BRACEBRIDGE, Ontario (MAP 78)

ONE FIFTY-FIVE
155 Manitoba Street **$140**
(705) 645-1935

One Fifty-Five is that rare thing in Muskoka—a restaurant that's calm, quiet and restful. Mike and Marlenne Rickard are both keen on local ingredients, though Mike likes to start with something like shrimp bisque, beef carpaccio or salmon gravlax. He makes all his own pasta (and all his own sweets), and has an excellent shrimp risotto. The rainbow trout with maple is always good, and so is the roast loin of pork with apple and apricot. The wine-list leans heavily (too heavily, we think) on wines from Chile and Argentina, and there are few wines by the glass and fewer still from Niagara or the Okanagan. The Cattail Creek merlot is a good buy at 56.00, though we miss the pinot noir, which used to sell for only 39.00 a bottle.

Open Tuesday to Sunday 11.30 am to 2.30 pm, 5 pm to 9.30 pm. Closed on Monday. Licensed. Amex, Master Card, Visa. Book ahead if you can. &

BRACEBRIDGE (MAP 78)
RIVERWALK
1 Manitoba Street **$150**
(705) 646-0711

Bracebridge now has at least two useful restaurants: One Fifty-Five and Riverwalk. Both are open year-round and both occupy heritage houses. One Fifty-Five is up the hill on Manitoba Street; Riverwalk overlooks the falls down at the foot of the street. Its menu is up-to-the-minute, starting with pan-seared foie gras with essence of truffle and charcuterie with sausage, cured meat and pickles and going on to diver scallops, roasted breast of duck, lamb shanks, Atlantic salmon and a couple of steaks. David Friesen makes a point of using ingredients grown in the Muskoka Region whenever he can. His wines, however, come from California, Australia, Italy and Chile as well as the Niagara Region.

Open Tuesday to Sunday 11.30 am to 2.30 pm, 5.30 pm to 8.30 pm (shorter hours in winter). Closed on Monday. Amex, Master Card, Visa. Book ahead if you can.

BRACKLEY BEACH, P.E.I. (MAP 39)
THE DUNES ☆
Highway 15 **$100**
(902) 672-1883

The Dunes has a spectacular garden, an art gallery and a café. The café offers first-class soup every day, an excellent lobster quiche, a pizza and a hot daily special. The special is sometimes good, sometimes not, and it's usually best to settle for the quiche. After that, go for the frozen maple mousse with crystallized sugar—it's lovely. The wine-list is small, but there's always something worth drinking: Wolf Blass eaglehawk chardonnay, perhaps, or the local chardonnay from Newman, or a glass of single malt from Glen Breton. Rossignol offers a number of interesting dessert wines—apple, wild blueberry and strawberry, all of which are available at the Dunes. *Note:* the bad news is that Emily Wells, who has been chef here for more than ten years, left last winter. It remains to be seen who can, or will, fill her shoes.

Open daily 11.30 am to 4 pm, 5.30 pm to 10 pm from 15 June until 30 September. Licensed. Amex, Master Card, Visa. Book ahead. &

BRANDON, Manitoba   **MAP 24**
BLUE HILLS BAKERY
1229 Richmond Avenue   **$40**
(204) 571-6762

Nothing ever changes at the Blue Hills, not even the frozen fruit pies. But Kelly and Becky, who run the place, have found a formula that works, no easy thing in a town like Brandon. They both come from a Hutterite background and both are passionate believers in fresh organic produce. They buy their vegetables and grains from nearby organic farms. They make their own granola and their own bread and serve them for breakfast until 11 o'clock on weekdays and 2 o'clock on Saturdays. At noon they offer old-fashioned soups—on Friday and Saturday it's always borscht. Every day there are sandwiches, salads and a special, which might be shepherd's pie or perhaps a quiche. After that there's a wide choice of cookies, muffins, squares and cinnamon buns. The pies are still frozen, but the coffee comes in fresh from Salt Spring Island.

Open Monday to Saturday 7 am to 5 pm. No liquor. Master Card, Visa. &

BRIER ISLAND, N.S.
See FREEPORT.

BRIGHTON, Ontario   **(MAP 17)**
THE GABLES   ☆
14 Division Street N   **$160**
(613) 475-5565

Dieter Ernst hasn't changed his menu in the last two

years. Why should he? Everyone thinks that every dish he serves is the best they've ever eaten. It's true, Dieter Ernst is a master chef. If you try his pastry you'll see what we mean. As for his meat and fish, they're all cooked perfectly *à point*. Notice that his whipping cream is the real thing, his snails are like no other and his wienerschnitzel is tender and full of flavour. His roasted duck with red cabbage and cherries, his Black Angus steak, his cod, salmon, scallops and rainbow trout all have their admirers. Dieter makes his own sweets and if the apple strudel is still on the menu you should ask for it. There are some surprising wines from Prince Edward County, as well as several single malts and a number of grappas. The dining-room is elegantly furnished and Kirsten Ernst is a charming and attentive hostess.

Open Tuesday to Friday 11.30 am to 2 pm, 5.30 pm to 9 pm, Saturday 5.30 pm to 9 pm. Closed on Sunday and Monday. Licensed. Master Card, Visa. Book ahead if you can. &

BRIGUS, Newfoundland   MAP 26
THE COUNTRY CORNER
14 Water Street   **$40**
(709) 528-1099

Brigus is a picturesque town on the shores of Conception Bay, built around a sheltered harbour and surrounded by hills. It's one of the few towns on the Avalon Peninsula that looks much as it did before Confederation. Actually, it's much older than that, having been established in 1612. The Country Corner has only twelve seats, but it has a covered patio and a gift shop. The menu is expanding, though the food is still pretty simple. They make a first-class split-pea soup from a ham bone, but the real specialty of the house is the cod chowder seasoned with savoury and served with a tea-biscuit. In season there's roast turkey (cheap unless you want nothing but white meat), pressure-cooked beef and fresh ham. The pick of the sweets is the wonderful blueberry crisp, made with fresh-picked blueberries and ice cream. At the counter they sell chocolate-chip cookies, ice-cream cones, sundaes

and milkshakes.
Open daily 8 am to 8 pm from Victoria Day until Thanksgiving.
No liquor. Master Card, Visa.

BURLINGTON, Ontario (MAP 83)
BLACKTREE ☆☆☆
Roseland Plaza **$165**
3029 New Street
(905) 681-2882

Matteo Paonessa has worked with some of the best chefs
in Canada, including Marc Thuet, Susur Lee and Michael
Stadtländer. He likes to begin his meals with an *amuse
bouche* of tuna with pickled vegetables or mushrooms
with sage and parmesan. Next comes a small loaf of
bread, sprinkled with sea-salt and still warm from the
oven. Appetizers include pan-seared foie gras with a
brown-sugar meringue and walnut brittle, a composed
salad of seared scallops and Asian pears and a white-grape
soup. Main courses always include some gnocchi, some
fish and some game. Once we had a partridge in a pear
tree (shredded partridge with pear jam and enoki mushrooms). On another occasion we had gnocchi with hon-
eyed goat-cheese, pesto and parmesan. After that, you
may be offered a roasted-pear turnover with dark-caramel
ice cream. Blacktree is by far the best restaurant in this
part of the country.
*Open Wednesday to Saturday 6 pm to 10 pm. Closed Sunday to
Tuesday. Licensed. Master Card, Visa. Book ahead if you can.*
&

BURLINGTON (MAP 83)
PANE FRESCO
414 Locust Street **$45**
(905) 333-3388

Pane Fresco is a bakery and café located close to the
lakeshore in downtown Burlington. They sell a lot of artisanal bread, which is handmade and contains no artificial preservatives. Apart from the bread, the menu has

always been very limited. In the last year or so, however, it's been much enlarged. They now always serve two soups, one of which is usually black bean. This year, the black-bean has been disappointing, and we now prefer something like roasted red pepper with crumbled goat-cheese. Some of the specials, like homemade meatballs in a fresh tomato sauce with provolone cheese, are available only on certain days of the week. Others are offered every day, and the best of these is probably the crab cakes with cabbage and mango relish in a lime-and-ginger vinaigrette. There used to be just two salads offered every day; now there are six. For dessert there are countless brownies, croissants, cannolis and handmade biscottis. In the summer they make some excellent ice creams as well. *Open Monday to Thursday 8 am to 6 pm, Friday and Saturday 8 am to 7 pm, Sunday 8 am to 4 pm. No liquor, no cards.* &

BURLINGTON (MAP 83)
SPENCER'S ☆
1340 Lakeshore Road **$115**
(905) 633-7494

Spencer's on the Waterfront is a little less formal than its sister restaurant, the old Mill in Ancaster. The appetizers here are usually the most exciting part of the meal. You can start with raw oysters, albacore tuna, calamari piri-piri, red-fife-and-ricotta gnocchi, charcuterie or foie gras—an unusual list of choices. Actually, there are more—we ourselves like to start with lobster dumplings in a bamboo steamer. The best of the main courses is probably the Alaska black cod, though there's also first-class Arctic char with chorizo, cauliflower and brown butter. This is almost as good as the Arctic char they served last year with quinoa and fresh lobster. There's also a nice rack of lamb with harissa and Jerusalem artichokes. At noon they have elk burgers with oyster mushrooms and blue cheese and beef burgers with black-truffle mayonnaise and brie. The sweet list has recently been done over and now features a chocolate-chestnut mousse-cake and a pear tart with ricotta and honey in an almond crust.

43

Open Monday to Saturday 11.30 am to 4.30 pm (lunch), 4.30 pm to 9.30 pm (dinner), Sunday 9.30 am to 3.30 pm (brunch), 5.15 pm to 9 pm. Licensed. Master Card, Visa. Free parking. &

CALGARY, Alberta MAP 28
BELVEDERE ☆☆
107 8 Avenue SW **$220**
(403) 265-9595

Belvedere is darkly handsome, well served and very expensive. They have, however, a great wine-list with many of the best pauillacs and super-Tuscans. The cooking is less inspired than it used to be, and the staples of the menu are still triple-A Alberta beef, rack of lamb, Pacific oysters and sturgeon caviar. A new chef took charge a couple of years ago, but so far he doesn't seem to have made many important changes.
Open Monday to Friday 11.30 am to 2 pm, 5 pm to 11 pm, Saturday 5 pm to 11 pm. Closed on Sunday. Licensed. Amex, Master Card, Visa. Book ahead. &

CALGARY MAP 28
BLINK ☆☆
111 8 Avenue SW **$190**
(403) 263-5330

Blink may have a ridiculous name, but it also has remarkable cooking. They keep a large menu, starting with beef tartar, chilled Pacific octopus, sea scallops and foie gras and going on to wild Pacific halibut, sablefish from Haida Gwaii, roasted steelhead trout and beef tenderloin. Everything is good, but the carpaccio of golden chiogga beets is brilliant, one of the most outstanding dishes we remember. The tart of wild foraged mushrooms comes on a bed of wonderfully tender pastry, but the beet carpaccio is something nobody should miss, whatever the reason. The wine-list is big and full of unusual drinking. The service is experienced and very well informed.
Open Monday to Friday 11 am to 2 pm, 5 pm to 10 pm, Satur-

day 5 pm to 11 pm. Closed on Sunday. Licensed. All cards. Book ahead if you can. ♿

CALGARY   MAP 28
BOXWOOD
340 13 Avenue SW   **$100**
(403) 265-4006

Boxwood was opened a couple of years ago by the River Café, which it closely resembles. It occupies the only building in a small grassy park between Twelfth and Thirteenth Avenues. They have a tiny menu and take no reservations. If you come for lunch there are no meats and only two fish dishes. The better of the two fish is the seared albacore tuna, which comes with sesame and an oriental green known as faro. Faro has an extraordinary texture and great flavour, and it makes the whole meal. Dinner is much the same, except that every night they offer four rotisseries, among them Bowden Farms chicken and Driview Farm lamb, which are among the best things they do. There's an open kitchen and friendly, efficient table service at both lunch and dinner. The two wines from Joie Farms are the best of the handful on the list. Prices are low for Calgary.
Open daily 11 am to 10 pm. Licensed. Amex, Master Card, Visa. No reservations.

CALGARY   MAP 28
BRAVA
723 17 Avenue SW   **$150**
(403) 228-1854

Brava is a friendly, unpretentious neighbourhood bistro conveniently located on 17 Avenue at 7 Street. As we've said before, people come here for the gingerbread soaked in whisky. It's a wonderful dish, but there are other good things on the menu too, notably the shrimp-and-avocado salad with beautiful ripe cherry tomatoes and the mussels with white wine and leeks. The salmon is usually over-cooked, but the Alberta beef tenderloin is a fine dish, with its boursin mash and garlic mushrooms. The wine-list features wines from California and Australia, but it's weak on wines from the Okanagan. However that may be, there aren't many restaurants in Calgary that we enjoy as much as Brava.

Open Monday to Wednesday 11.30 am to 3 pm, 5 pm to 10 pm, Thursday to Saturday 11.30 am to 3 pm, 5 pm to midnight, Sunday 5 pm to 10 pm. Licensed. All cards. Book ahead. ♿

CALGARY   MAP 28
DIVINO   ☆
113 8 Avenue SW   **$175**
(403) 410-5555

We used to write about Divino as if it served nothing but wine and cheese. And it's true, they maintain an excellent cheese card, listing nine or ten cheeses such as stilton, pecorino, gruyère, roquefort, brillat savarin and tête de moine. All but two of these are unpasteurized, but they're all kept and served in perfect condition. (Our favourite is the brillat savarin, which comes from Normandy. It's rich and buttery and has an inviting flavour.) The wine-list rises to a Lafite (for 1200.00) and a Mouton-Rothschild (for 585.00), but there are only a few Canadian wines, among them Blue Mountain, Laughing Stock and Painted Rock. In recent years, John Donovan has been developing the à la carte, which now runs to things like salt-cod brandade, bison tartar, foie gras ravioli and an interesting tempura of green beans with fireweed honey and hot mustard. There's also a sparkling list of sweets, the best of which, we think, is the lemon tartelette, served (in November) with beautifully ripe strawberries.

Open Monday to Friday 11 am to 4 pm, 5 pm to 10 pm, Saturday 5 pm to 11 pm. Closed on Sunday. Licensed. All cards. ♿

Where an entry is printed in italics this indicates that the restaurant has been listed only because it serves the best food in its area or because it hasn't yet been adequately tested.

CALGARY   **MAP 28**
MODEL MILK
308 17 Avenue SW   **$125**
(403) 265-7343

Model Milk occupies the old Model Milk Dairy factory,
which makes for an intriguing interior. The menu is unusual, but take care: some of the tapas dishes are better
than others. The foie gras parfait in a blackberry crust,
for instance, is delightful, the octopus with bone marrow
is merely tough; the medley of chanterelles is a charming
dish, the fricassee of squid with edamame dull, dull, dull.
But Model Milk is fun. The wine-list is quite small, but
it has some interesting drinking. The Joie Farm dry muscat, for example, is a surprising wine, as is the Angel's
Gate late-harvest riesling, which goes well with the trifle.
(They don't call it trifle, but that's what it is.)
*Open Monday to Saturday 5 pm to 1 am, Sunday 5 pm to 10
pm. Licensed. Amex, Master Card, Visa. Book ahead if you
can.* &

CALGARY   **MAP 28**
NOTABLE   ☆
4611 Bowness Road NW   **$150**
(403) 288-4372

Notable answers the telephone with the message,
"Happy chicken to go." Not a good sign, but let it go.
The place looks like a big, upscale burger joint, but it has
Michael Noble in the kitchen and that makes all the difference. First of all, the menu is large and quite unfamiliar, offering salmon with pickled daikon, saltspring
mussels, baked garganelle pasta, panko-crusted tuna and
Moroccan lamb sausages. The salmon with pickled
daikon is a wonderful dish and so is the panko-crusted
tuna. The St. Clair Pioneer Block sauvignon blanc from
Marlborough is a lovely drink and so, in a different way,
is the Spire cabernet sauvignon from Paso Robles. (Both
are available by the glass as well as the bottle.) They also

have bottles from Joie Farm, Cakebread and Laughing Stock, as well as Sarpa di Poli grappa by the glass. They don't have an espresso machine, but their filter coffee is very good indeed. The service is perfect.

Open Tuesday to Friday 11.30 am to 11 pm, Saturday 11 am to 11 pm, Sunday 11 am to 9 pm. Closed on Monday. Licensed. Amex, Master Card, Visa. Book ahead if you can. ♿

CALGARY　　　　　　　　　　　　　　　　**MAP 28**
OX & ANGELA　　　　　　　　　　　　　　　　☆
528 17 Avenue SW　　　　　　　　　　　**$130**
(403) 457-1432

Ox & Angela has a stylish interior and a central location in midtown Calgary. Ox is the chef; Angela is the hostess and she's the kind of person who puts on a winter coat and feeds your meter for you. Their menu features a variety of tapas dishes at prices that start at 5.00 for salt-cod with potato croquettes and rise to 27.00 for a charcuterie platter. They have a classic treatment of patatas bravas and it's worth its weight in gold. Their scallops come with peas and cherry tomatoes, their prawns with garlic, chilli and sherry, their serrano ham with harissa and mint. You can drink Canadian with a Quail's Gate dry riesling or a Dancing Coyote verdilho. Or you can drink Spanish with a rioja from Ramon Bilbao. We generally ask for the rioja.

Open daily 11.30 am to 11 pm (later on weekends). Licensed. Amex, Master Card, Visa. ♿

CALGARY　　　　　　　　　　　　　　　　**MAP 28**
RIVER CAFE　　　　　　　　　　　　　　☆☆
Prince's Island Park　　　　　　　　　**$175**
(403) 261-7670

The River Café, far away in Prince Island Park, has skilful cooking and the best local ingredients money can buy. They start at noon with raw oysters, Driview lamb and a quiche of chanterelles and corn. In the evening the menu is more expansive and features High Prairie bison, Haida

Gwaii halibut and, best of all, sturgeon from the Sunshine Coast. They also have a platter of bison bresaola, candied salmon, steelhead lox, wild-boar ciccioli and chicken-liver pâté, as well as a variety of lovely homemade pastries, muffins and jams. The wine-list has few equals anywhere in the city, offering some of the best wines from Pauillac and a number of good buys from the Okanagan. They also have seventeen bottled beers, including Big Rock from Calgary, Steamwhistle from Toronto and Cutthroat from Kelowna. The list of single malts includes a rare eighteen-year-old from Bunnahabhain. Park in the Eau Claire Market and cross the Bow River by the footbridge to the restaurant. It's a ten-minute walk and it's worth it, even in winter.

Open Monday to Friday 11.30 am to 2.30 pm, 5.30 pm to 10 pm, Saturday and Sunday 10 am to 3 pm (brunch), 5.30 pm to 10 pm. Licensed. Amex, Master Card, Visa. Book ahead if you can. &

CALGARY   MAP 28
RUSH   ☆
207 9 Avenue SW   **$160**
(403) 271-7874

Rush still has its stunning interior. It still has superb service. Trouble arrives with the suppliers. The kitchen used to be known for its beautiful regional produce. The lamb, once local, is now imported from New Zealand. The oysters come in from New Brunswick, though wonderful Kusshi oysters are close at hand. The sparkling water is no longer supplied by San Pellegrino. There are, of course, still good things to be had here, among them the minted pea soup, the cured salmon belly, the pork cooked *sous vide*, the dry-aged beef. As for the wine-list, it's big and handsome, though the choice of wines from the Okanagan, apart from the white wines from Joie Farm, is rather disappointing. Nothing, however, is ever overpriced.

Open Monday to Friday 11 am to 4 pm, 5 pm to 11 pm, Saturday 5 pm to 11 pm. Closed on Sunday. Licensed. All cards. Free valet parking after 6 pm. ♿

CALGARY   **MAP 28**
TEATRO   ☆☆
200 8 Avenue SE   **$235**
(403) 290-1012

Teatro occupies an old bank building on 8 Avenue SE. It's very well appointed, very well served and very expensive. You start with Pacific oysters on the half-shell or bison tartar. Follow that with seared scallops, which are usually better than the albacore tuna or the T-bone steak, which, it has to be admitted, is pretty rough. Teatro's place in the sun really depends on its marvellous wine-list, with its stupendous selection of pauillacs and super-Tuscans from Bolgheri. (They also offer a number of Niagara wines, an unusual amenity in the West.) Teatro is open late, which makes it the place to go after a play at the performing arts centre or a concert by the Calgary Philharmonic. Both are quite nearby.
Open Monday to Thursday 11.30 am to 2.30 pm, 5 pm to 11 pm, Friday 11.30 am to 2.30 pm, 5 pm to 11.30 pm, Saturday 5 pm to 11.30 pm, Sunday 5 pm to 10 pm. Licensed. All cards. Book ahead. ♿

CALGARY   **MAP 28**
VERO BISTRO MODERNE
209 10 Street NW   **$135**
(403) 283-8988

Vero is new to Calgary and the chef, Jenny Chan, is doing some rare and wonderful things. For example, she offers hand-rolled sweet-potato gnocchi to start with and serves her sablefish with miso, her bouillabaisse with tomato and saffron, her sea-bass with lemon risotto. There are, of course, more traditional dishes as well, dishes like herb-crusted Alberta lamb and Ahi tuna. And she likes to end most of her meals with a classic tiramisu for two. Her wine-list has a number of unfamiliar Italian wines on offer and we'd like to try more of them.

50

Open Tuesday to Friday 11 am to 2 pm, 5 pm to 10 pm, Saturday and Sunday 9.30 am to 2.30 pm (brunch), 5 pm to 10 pm. Closed on Monday. Licensed. Master Card, Visa. Book ahead if you can. &

CALGARY
See also CANMORE.

CAMBRIDGE, Ontario	**MAP 29**
LANGDON HALL	☆☆
1 Langdon Drive	**$275 ($510)**
(800) 268-1898	

Langdon Hall has been a member of the order of Relais & Châteaux for some years, but they don't wear their honours lightly. They ask guests to wear a dinner jacket in the evening, something few restaurants would presume to do. But if you have 275.00 in your pocket, they let you into the dining-room without. The Hall was built in 1898 in the Federal style and restored as a restaurant a century or so later. The chef is Jonathan Gushue. Last winter he disappeared for some weeks, but the kitchen staff carried on without him and not a single guest complained. He's back on the job now and his dinners usually begin with a lovely scallop soup. Medallions of lamb follow, though guests generally order the lobster, which is gorgeous. Most of the vegetables are organic. The pick of the sweets is the honey soufflé with crème anglaise. The cellar has a thousand labels on offer, but take note that there's nothing by the glass that costs less than 15.00. Every day they put on splendid afternoon teas at 2 and 4 o'clock at 64.00 for two. The service is impeccable, but all the prices surpass belief.
Open daily noon to 2.30 pm, 5.30 pm to 9.30 pm. Licensed. All cards. Book ahead.

If you wish to improve the guide send us information about restaurants we have missed. Our mailing address is Oberon Press, 145 Spruce Street: Suite 205, Ottawa, Ontario K1R 6P1.

CAMPOBELLO ISLAND, N.B. (MAP 76)

FAMILY FISHERIES
1977 County Road 774 **$55**
Wilson's Beach
(506) 752-2470

This is the only restaurant on Campobello Island. If you find it full, go to the carry-out window, where everything is the same as at the tables. The menu is surprisingly long, but the best thing on it is the whole lobster. The lobster stew is almost as good, and there are those who think the lobster sandwich is better than either. The haddock is good too—it's absolutely fresh and perfectly cooked. As for the scallops and shrimps, you won't get better anywhere on this shore. Start with smoked salmon and end with blueberry or raspberry pie. (They pick the raspberries in their own garden and serve them with real whipped cream.) Everything is cooked to order and the service is slow, but sitting back and slowing down, as somebody once said, is one of the things you come to the Maritimes for.

Open daily 11.30 am to 8.30 pm. No liquor. Master Card, Visa.

CANMORE, Alberta (MAP 28)

THE CRAZY WEED
1600 Railway Avenue **$150**
(403) 609-2530

The Crazy Weed is a successful upscale restaurant, but the truth is that it deteriorates with every year that passes. Meanwhile, prices have been rising. You now have to pay 38.00 for a rib-eye of beef and 10.00 for a butterscotch pudding. Prices are lower at noon, when they serve pork meatballs, confit of duck and jerk-pork flatbread for 10.00 or 15.00. The wine-list has expanded, though there are still only five Canadian whites and one Canadian red. The service can be hurried and it's hard to keep your table long enough to eat your meal in comfort.

Open Monday to Friday 11.30 am to 3 pm, 5.30 pm to 8.30 pm, Saturday and Sunday 5.30 pm to 8.30 pm. Licensed. Master Card, Visa. Book ahead if you can. &

CANMORE (MAP 28)
THE TROUGH ☆
725 9 Street **$200**
(403) 678-2820

Cheryl and Richard Fuller, mother and son, run the kitchen at the Trough; a daughter, Rebecca, runs the front of the house. They have only ten tables, but they always buy the best available produce, use nothing but Riedel glasses for their wine and employ experienced servers. Inevitably, the prices are high, but you can count on a menu that's full of new ideas and novel effects. For example, there's a bruschetta made with organic chèvre and a ceviche made with coconut milk, cilantro and crisp won-tons. Next, perhaps, an East Indian organic chicken with raita and red onions or jerk-spiced Alberta baby back ribs with a pineapple salsa. After that there's a date pudding with warm toffee and a wild-berry cobbler. There are no Canadian wines on the wine-list, but they do have some of the best grappas on the market today.
Open Tuesday to Sunday 5.30 pm to 10 pm. Closed on Monday. Licensed. Master Card, Visa.

CAP A L'AIGLE, Quebec (MAP 107)
AUBERGE DES PEUPLIERS ☆
381 rue St.-Raphael **$175 ($375)**
(888) 282-3743

Patrice Desrosiers is now in charge of the kitchen at the Auberge des Peupliers. Like his predecessor, he's passionate about local produce, especially his gravlax of salmon and his ravioli stuffed with salt-marsh lamb. He's still in his first year here, so it's hard to say how well he'll perform over the whole menu, which covers a lot of ground—from carpaccio and foie gras to cannelloni, fillet of veal and confit of duck. But we can say that dinner is a stylish meal and so is breakfast. The bedrooms up the hill are comfortable and well appointed. The wine-list is a little disappointing, but there's good drinking from Smoking Loon, which offers an attractive sauvignon blanc for 48.00 a bottle.

Open daily 7.30 am to 10.30 am, 6 pm to 9 pm. Licensed. All cards. Book ahead. &

CAPE ONION, Newfoundland (MAP 6)
TICKLE INN
Highway 437 **$90 ($165)**
(709) 452-4321

David and Barbara Adams and their cousin, Sophie Bessie, will again be in charge at the Tickle Inn this summer. Guests will again be seated around the big table in the kitchen, trading stories and listening to David talk about old Newfoundland. Cape Onion is at the far end of the Viking Trail, overlooking a bright blue sea studded with tiny islands, the surrounding hills thick with wildflowers. Captain William Adams settled here in this small frame house four generations ago. His descendants have since restored the house and turned it into a celebrated bed-and-breakfast. The owners have their own suppliers and their own pickers, because fresh produce isn't easy to get in these parts. Dinner starts with a soup, followed perhaps by a triple-fish casserole in puff pastry. Sundays are special. You can expect Arctic char or chicken wellington with screech. Upstairs there are several comfortable bedrooms. If you decide to spend a night or two, you'll find that there are good walking trails as well as the village of Anse-aux-Meadows, where you can visit the remains of the original Viking settlement, now almost a thousand years old.

Open daily at 7.30 pm by appointment only from 1 June until 30 September. Licensed. Master Card, Visa. You must book ahead. &

Our website is at www.oberonpress.ca. Readers wishing to use e-mail should address us at oberon@sympatico.ca.

CARAQUET, N.B.   MAP 34
HOTEL PAULIN
143 boulevard St.-Pierre o   **$160 ($315)**
(866) 727-9981

We stopped writing about the Hôtel Paulin, because it didn't seem serious about taking non-residents. We're recommending it again this year, because it's the best place to stay in town and a good place to eat. Three generations of the Paulin family have made this one of the oldest family-run hotels in the country. Built in 1891, it's a good example of turn-of-the-century Acadian architecture. It's been completely redecorated inside, with three luxurious suites on the third floor, each of which has a lovely view of the Baie des Chaleurs. After running the place alone for 30 years, Gérard Paulin married Karen Mersereau and found himself with a first-class chef. She changes her menu every day, always emphasizing regional produce. That of course means local seafood from the bay, local lamb and local cheeses, as well as hand-picked fiddleheads, chanterelles and strawberries. Everything is beautifully prepared. The service, however, is slow.

Open daily (if anyone is staying at the hotel) 7 pm to 8.30 pm. Licensed. Master Card, Visa. You must book ahead. &

CARAQUET   MAP 34
MITCHAN SUSHI   ☆☆
114 boulevard St.-Pierre o   **$95**
(506) 726-1103

You wouldn't expect to find a good Japanese restaurant in the heart of Acadian country, but there are those who think that Mitchan Sushi is the best restaurant of its kind in New Brunswick. Certainly, they have an enormous selection of sushi, sashimi, tempura and teriyaki. The dining-room is attractive and the plating will remind you of a bouquet of flowers. The prices are surprisingly low. We suggest the ramen noodles, the shrimp and pork dumplings, the seafood salad and the chicken kara aga. If you aren't happy with Japanese food, stroll along the street to Déja Bu at No. 47 boulevard St.-Pierre o (telephone (506) 727-7749). The motto at Déja Bu is FUN. Robert Noel has 250 wines, with seventeen by the glass as well as the bottle. He serves things like frites maison and a clam poutine. He inherited a recipe from his mother for a *chaudré avec fruits de mer*, a generous helping of which is yours for just 16.00.

Open daily noon to 3 pm, 6 pm to 11 pm from early May until late November, by appointment only Wednesday 5 pm to 9 pm, Thursday and Friday 11.30 am to 1.30 pm, 5 pm to 9 pm, Saturday and Sunday 5 pm to 9 pm from late November until early May. Licensed. Master Card, Visa. Closed on Monday and Tuesday in winter.

CARLETON-SUR-MER, Quebec   MAP 35
LE MARIN D'EAU DOUCE
215 route du Quai   **$130**
(418) 364-7602

We've been recommending this old house by the sea for years. The place was built in 1820 overlooking the beach. There's a jetty at the back and a bright, cheerful dining-room serving a variety of fish and shellfish. Mustapha Benhamidou is at his best with seafood, though some visitors prefer his lamb tagine, the only Moroccan dish on the menu. It's usually best to order the table d'hôte, which always has some fish on it. There are hardly any wines from either Niagara or Prince Edward County, but there are plenty from both France and Italy. The coffee is good, if not the local caviar. The cooking at the Gite Saint-Honoré, 527 boulevard Perron (telephone (418) 364-7618), is also reliable.

Open Monday to Saturday 5 pm to 9 pm . Closed on Sunday. Licensed. All cards.

If you wish to improve the guide send us information about restaurants we have missed. Our mailing address is Oberon Press, 145 Spruce Street: Suite 205, Ottawa, Ontario K1R 6P1.

CAYUGA, Ontario　　　　　　　　　　**MAP 36**
THE TWISTED LEMON　　　　　　　　　　☆
3 Norton Street W　　　　　　　　　　**$135**
(905) 772-6636

The Twisted Lemon opened in the summer of 2009, and already people are driving long distances for a meal here. Chef Dan Megna and his wife, Laurie Lilliman, have brought many years of experience to their dream. For instance, Megna learned a lot about good produce from Mark McEwan, and at the Twisted Lemon nearly everything they use grows right here in Haldimand County. We still admire the rack of lamb from Cumbrae; others prefer the duck. But for only 19.00 you can have gnocchi with sweet potatoes and for 23.00 there's great pappardelle made to an old family recipe. Every Thursday night there's a three-course *prix fixe* for 39.00 that ends with their wonderful chocolate pâté. The wine-list offers an ambitious selection of wines from the Old World and the New. There are also some very good ports.
Open Tuesday 5.30 pm to 9.30 pm, Wednesday to Friday 11.30 am to 2 pm, 5.30 pm to 9.30 pm, Saturday 5.30 pm to 9.30 pm. Closed on Sunday and Monday. Licensed. Master Card, Visa. Book ahead.

CEDAR, B.C.　　　　　　　　　　**(MAP 123)**
THE MAHLE HOUSE　　　　　　　　　☆☆
2104 Hemer Road　　　　　　　　　　**$145**
(250) 722-3621

The big news at the Mahle House is that Maureen Loucks and Delbert Horrocks have sold the place to Maureen's daughter, Tara Wilson, and her husband, Stephen. Naida Hobbs, who worked with Maureen for several years, will be in charge of the kitchen. Stephen Wilson will continue to sell his wines at rock-bottom prices, as Delbert Horrocks always did, to encourage customers to buy more and better wines. Lunch is being served for the first time this year and will feature a homemade soup and a mixed-green salad. Dinner will begin with tuna tataki, calamari dijonnaise or a caramelized onion tart, followed by steelhead trout in pesto and white wine or breast of chicken with spinach and goat-cheese. The meal will end with crème brûlée or homemade ice cream. The wine-list majors, as it always did, in the better wines from the Okanagan, California and Australia, and they've recently added an outstanding cabernet sauvignon from Burrowing Owl, priced at 80.00. You need a big appetite for all this, but you won't do better this side of Sidney.

Open Wednesday and Thursday 5 pm to 9 pm, Friday to Sunday 11.30 am to 2 pm, 5 pm to 9pm. Closed on Monday and Tuesday. Licensed. Amex, Master Card, Visa. Book ahead if you can. &

CHARLO, N.B.   MAP 38
LE MOULIN A CAFE   ★★
210 Chaleur Street   **$50**
(506) 684-9898

This tiny place (eight tables in summer, five in winter) has a huge reputation. The chef worked abroad for almost a quarter of a century before returning to the town where he started. He knows what the customers here want: soup (he makes five every day), pizza (he makes several), Acadian dishes and fresh local fish. There's always a daily special as well—flank steak, perhaps, marinated in red wine and served with onions and sweet potato. Andrea Boudreau, his partner, makes all the bread-rolls and the fabulous pies. The strawberry-rhubarb is the best of these, but don't overlook either the coconut or the pumpkin. They keep many teas and coffees on the list, and everything is very cheap.

Open Tuesday to Sunday 10 am to 8 pm. Closed on Monday. Bring your own bottle. Master Card, Visa. Book ahead if you can.

CHARLOTTETOWN, P.E.I.   MAP 39

We always urge visitors to the Island to go to the Farmer's Mar-

ket, which is held every Saturday morning. Most of the produce is organic, and you can snack on Kim Dormaar's smoked salmon or some of the best sausages you've ever tasted. Not far away, on a short stretch of University Avenue, there are three attractive restaurants. The newest, Leonhard's Café and Bakery at 42 University Avenue (telephone (902) 367-3621), has some of the best coffee in town. The young German owner also makes fine homemade bread and pastries, glorious Florentines, home-made stews and big, substantial sandwiches. This is a perfect place for lunch, but they aren't open for dinner and are closed on Sunday. Beanz at 38 University Avenue (telephone (902) 892-8797) is an espresso bar, but they also have soups, sandwiches and salads, and their squares, cookies and cheesecakes are all wonderful. They're open all day every day and take Master Card and Visa, but there's no liquor. Along the street from Beanz, at 44 University Avenue (telephone (902) 368-8886), is Shaddy's, a nice, comfortable Lebanese restaurant that has the only upright broiler in Charlottetown. The best thing they do is the shawarma with tabouleh. As for the falafel in a pita, one visitor thought it the best in the world. We ourselves admire the lamb kebabs and the kofta. The pastries all come from Montreal, where the chef spent ten years before coming here. Shaddy's is open all day Monday to Friday and all afternoon Saturday and Sunday, has a li-cence and takes Master Card and Visa. Off Broadway at 125 Sydney Street (telephone (902) 566-4620) has performed er-ratically for several years. This year it's become the Daniel Brenan Brickhouse. They've got rid of the old booths and developed a style of cooking that's sometimes excellent. The best things on the menu are the fishcakes and the lamb rogan gosht. The service may be slow, but the Brickhouse has great potential. They still have Off Broadway's awkward hours. They're open Monday to Thursday 11 am to 10 pm, Friday and Saturday 11 am to 11 pm, Sunday 11 am to 10 pm from Victoria Day until Thanksgiving, Monday to Thursday 11 am to 2 pm, 4.30 pm to 9 pm, Friday and Saturday 11 am to 2 pm, 4.30 pm to 10 pm, Sunday 5 pm to 9 pm from Thanksgiving until Victoria Day. They have a licence and take Amex, Master Card and Visa. The Pilot House at 70 Grafton Street (telephone (902) 894-4800) is a heritage prop-erty specializing in seafood, draft beer and scotch whisky. It's a great place for a quick lunch. They have a fine lobster sandwich *and perfect fish and chips. They're open all day every day but Sunday, have a licence and take all cards. Finally there's the Terre Rouge at 72 Queen Street (telephone (902) 892-4032). It opened in 2012 and quickly became the place to go in downtown Charlottetown. The cooking is good and everything is elegantly plated. Out in front there's a deli where you can get a pastry, local cheeses, prosciutto, homemade gelatos—or a whole barbecued chicken. Terre Rouge is open all day every day, has a license for beer and wine only and takes all cards.*

CHARLOTTETOWN   MAP 39
LOT 30   ☆
151 Kent Street   **$150**
(902) 629-3030

Governor Walter Patterson instructed Thomas Wright, his surveyor, to divide this area into five sets of a hundred lots. The land on which the restaurant stands was Lot 30 of the fourth hundred; hence the name. Gordon Bailey has an interesting menu that starts with Colville Bay oysters and goes on to steamed local blue mussels, seared sea scallops with carrot butter and curried pistachios, pan-seared Atlantic salmon with a butternut-squash purée, a seafood cioppino of oysters, salmon and mussels, caramelized scallops with Thai black rice, butter-poached lobster with blue cheese and prime rib-eye of beef. The cooking seems less inspired this year and the only really good thing about the wine-list—apart from the sauvignon blanc from Kim Crawford—is the chardonnay from a local vineyard known as Newman's. If you try it you'll be surprised.

Open Tuesday to Sunday 5 pm to 9 pm. Closed on Monday. Licensed. Master Card, Visa. ♿

CHARLOTTETOWN
See also BAY FORTUNE, BEDEQUE, BRACKLEY BEACH, GEORGETOWN, MONTAGUE, NORTH RUSTICO, ST. PETERS BAY, SOURIS, TYNE VALLEY, VICTORIA-BY-THE-SEA.

Nobody but nobody can buy his way into this guide.

CHATHAM, Ontario   MAP 40
CHURRASCARIA
525 *Grand Avenue E*   **$110**
(519) 355-1279

It's been a long time since we recommended a restaurant in Chatham, but the Churrascaria seems to be holding its own. It describes itself as the only steak house in the area, serving three meals a day in big portions at low prices. The breakfast menu is long, starting at bacon and eggs for 3.00 and rising to Portuguese pastries filled with custard for 5.95. For lunch and dinner the kitchen makes a specialty of fresh Atlantic sardines and Lake Erie pickerel. All the fish is cooked *à point;* the chickens are free-range; the soups are good and the salads are excellent. The wine-list features Portuguese wines, though there are a few local wines as well. But remember: dinner closes early. *Open Tuesday to Thursday 8 am to 8 pm, Friday and Saturday 8 am to 9 pm, Sunday 8 am to 8 pm. Closed on Monday. Licensed. Amex, Master Card, Visa.* ♿

CHELSEA, Quebec   (MAP 135)
L'OREE DU BOIS   ☆
15 *chemin Kingsmere*   **$135**
(819) 827-0332

The Orée du Bois has a pronounced *après-ski* feeling, though of course it's open also in summer. Dinner costs 38.00 a head, but for that you get several very good things—among them chilled green-pea soup, shrimps with tiny slices of tomato and fish soup with quenelles of pike and oil of tarragon. The kitchen is at its best with pastry and one of its finest dishes is the feuilleté of mushrooms from Le Coprin. But there are many other pleasures to be had here: white shrimps with local asparagus, breast of chicken from Saveurs des Monts, cervelle de veau with capers and green peppercorns and medallions of venison from Boileau with red-wine and black peppercorns. The thing to drink is the half-bottle of ornellaia (a rare find in Canada). As we went to press, they had only two left.

Open Tuesday to Saturday 5 pm to 10 pm. Closed on Sunday and Monday. Licensed. Amex, Master Card, Visa. Book ahead if you can.

CHEMAINUS, B.C. (MAP 58)
ODIKA ☆
2976 Mill Street **$125**
(250) 324-3303

Odika is the seed-kernel of the African wild mango, and when cooked and crushed it's used in soups and stews. The chef, Murray Kereliuk, likes to cook West African dishes, perhaps because his wife, Marina, comes from Ghana. He thickens his soups with odika; his gnocchi is made with baked polenta, stuffed with mozzarella and topped with wild mushrooms. His fish and chips are made with cod and crusted with a pakora batter that's a lot less greasy than the traditional English batter. His panaeng curries are all made with bok choy served on a bed of basmati rice; his lamb shanks come in a curry inspired by West African recipes. The best of the sweets, unless you like crème brûlée with grand marnier, is the mango sorbet. When the restaurant is busy, the service can seem hurried.

Open Sunday to Thursday 11 am to 9 pm, Friday and Saturday 11 am to 10 pm. Licensed. All cards. ♿

CHESTER, N.S. (MAP 82)
CHESTER GOLF CLUB
227 Golf Course Road **$85**
(902) 275-4543

The Chester Golf Club has breathtaking views of the open sea and the islands that lie offshore. The building used to be a traditional farmhouse; today the plain white-frame structure is surrounded by an open deck where you can take your meal if you like. The menu is large and full of seafood. Don't bother with the salads or perhaps even the lobster sandwich. Ask instead for one of the so-called club favourites (scallops with fries and fish and chips). The pastries and breads all come from the kitchen, and though they're proud of their carrot cake, you'll probably do even better with the chocolate-lava cake or one of the fruit crisps.

Open daily 11 am to 7 pm from 1 May until 15 October. Licensed. All cards. ♿

CHESTER (MAP 82)
NICKI'S
28 Pleasant Street **$100**
(902) 275-4342

Nicki's is an attractive place, with floor-to-ceiling windows and an abundance of fresh flowers. The menu is seasonal, but the Sunday-night carvery has become a local institution. There's roast beef, lamb, pork and chicken, with Yorkshire pudding and roasted vegetables, all served from 5 o'clock until 8.30. On weeknights they offer a variety of small plates. There may be Village Bay oysters, beet salad with greens and a goat-cheese fritter. They also have some larger plates: steak-and-kidney pie with mashed potatoes, planked salmon and lamb shanks braised in red wine. Every night there are several lavish (and very filling) sweets. They have an impressive wine-list and very good coffee, which is served by the carafe.

Open Wednesday to Sunday 5 pm to 8 pm from 1 May until 15 October, Thursday to Sunday from 16 October until 30 April. Closed on Monday and Tuesday in summer, Monday to Wednesday in winter. Licensed. All cards. Book ahead if you can.

CHICOUTIMI, Quebec MAP 44
LA VOIE MALTEE ☞▯
777 boulevard Talbot **$75**
(418) 549-4144

Saguenay cruises start at L'Anse-Saint-Jean and the Auberge des Cevennes (see above). La Voie Maltée is light-years away from both. The Cevennes is an exercise in nostalgia, the Voie Maltée is very much now—the cur rent rage among young local people, crowded and very noisy. A second Voie Maltée has been opened in Jonquière at 2509 rue St,-Dominique (telephone (418) 542-4373) and a third is planned for Quebec City. They all offer ten micro-brews, ranging from a dark stout to a blond pilsner, made on site from local ingredients. There are also a number of dishes based on beer. The food is good and very cheap. Start with a plate of spiced northern shrimps and go on to a salmon salad, followed by fish and chips, a pork chop or a steak. After that everyone seems to like the biramisu, which is a tiramisu made with beer.

Open Monday to Friday 11.30 am to 3 am, Saturday and Sunday noon to 3 am. Licensed. All cards. No reservations.

CHURCHILL, Manitoba   MAP 45
GYPSY'S
253 Kelsey Boulevard   **$115**
(204) 675-2322

People still come to Churchill to see polar bears and beluga whales. The bears have to wait until the end of November before the sea-ice gets thick enough to support their weight. Visitors who want to keep warm usually go to Gypsy's for a meal. The place seats a hundred, but it's often full. It's a good idea to book ahead, because the food is good and the wine-list excellent. Tony De Silva likes to close up at the beginning of December, because he wants to keep warm too. He came to Churchill from Montreal almost 30 years ago and for a time he kept Gypsy's open all year. He's an expert on French pastry and Portuguese wine and his kitchen has always been known for the consistency of its cooking. They usually have Arctic char, Manitoba pickerel and local caribou, but if you want to have caribou you should let them know the day before. The menu never changes. If you can't get what you want this year, try again next year.

Open Monday to Saturday 7 am to 9 pm from 1 March until 30 November. Closed on Sunday. Licensed. All cards.

CLARK'S HARBOUR, N.S. (MAP 185)
WEST HEAD TAKEOUT
81 Boundry Street   **$40**
(902) 745-1322

About 800 people live in Clark's Harbour, which is the only settlement on Cape Sable Island. Everybody enjoys the drive in and everybody admires the white-sand beaches, but you may have to ask your way to the West Head Takeout. It's a tiny building at the end of the town wharf, with a fish-processing plant on either side. The place looks like nothing from the outside and there's little to indicate what goes on inside. Still, the Takeout is busy from morning till night. It used to be called the Seaview, but if the name has changed the menu hasn't. Nor has the fish. It's easy to recommend the lobster roll, which is as good as any we've tasted. They also have a scallop burger for 4.25 and very fresh fish and chips for 8.95. Anyone who finds himself within 25 miles of this place and doesn't come in for a meal is making a big mistake.
Open daily 10.30 am to 8 pm from late March until late September. No liquor, no cards. &

COBBLE HILL, B.C. (MAP 58)
BISTRO AT MERRIDALE   ☆
1230 Merridale Road   **$75**
(250) 743-4293

This place used to be called La Pommeraie and, like La Pommeraie, it's located right in the middle of a working apple farm producing organic cider. The restaurant offers cider pairings with many of its dishes, which are inspired by produce raised in nearby Cowichan Valley farms. In fair weather meals are served outside on a covered patio overlooking the apple orchards. Kim and Ian Blom, both of whom have had experience with Georg Szasz at Stage in Victoria, now do most of the cooking. Start with a brick-oven pizza prepared by Alain Boisseau, go on to parsnip apple or a lamb tagine with figs and apricots and finish with a piece of apple pie, made with apples raised

65

right here on the farm.
Open Monday to Thursday noon to 3 pm, Friday and Saturday noon to 3 pm, 5 pm to 9 pm, Sunday 10.30 am to 3 pm (brunch). Licensed. Master Card, Visa. &

COBOURG, Ontario   **MAP 48**
FRENCHIE'S   ☆
246 Division Street   **$70**
(905) 372-7200

The ebullient owner of Frenchie's suffered a serious concussion early in 2012 and had to cut down on her hours for a year. Come summer, however, she'll be running full steam again. Her menu is seasonal and everything is made on the premises—the bread, the pastries, the chutneys and the mayonnaise. Everybody likes her smoked-meat sandwich. It's piled high with smoked meat cut straight from the brisket and served with homemade coleslaw and dill pickles. Of course, there are other good things too. There are ham crêpes, seafood crêpes and a tourtière. With Steam Whistle beer on tap, you've got yourself a meal. There's a different sweet every day and right now she's planning an amaretto-espresso mousse. Not that she's resting on her laurels. She's bought three of the adjoining stores and before long there'll be a sweet shop, a deli and a bistro with a small bar. We plan to come back soon for an old-fashioned milkshake or perhaps a soda.
Open Monday to Wednesday 10.30 am to 5 pm, Thursday and Friday 10.30 am to 8 pm, Saturday 8.30 am to 8 pm. Closed on Sunday. Licensed. Master Card, Visa. Book ahead if you can.

COBOURG   **MAP 48**
WOODLAWN INN   ☆
420 Division Street   **$125 ($295)**
(905) 372-2235

The Woodlawn Inn is a good place for a special occasion or for a weekend break. Cobourg itself is a fine old town, with a magnificent cold-water beach and splendid views of Lake Ontario. The Della Casa family bought the Inn in 1988 and have since restored the whole place, which now has comfortable beds, excellent service and a competent dining-room. Stephen Della Casa is a professional *sommelier*, with more than 300 wines in his cellar and a bar with two dozen single malts The menu offers fresh pan-seared Chilean sea-bass with roasted tomatoes, smoked breast of Brome Lake duck with cranberries, sea scallops wrapped in prosciutto and Australian lamb with figs and whisky. The cooking is straightforward and correct. The kitchen buys fresh and local, and the presentation is always attractive. Sunday brunch costs only 17.95 (7.95 for children under six) and there's an omelette station where omelettes are made to order and beef and turkey are carved on demand.

Open Monday to Saturday 11.30 am to 2 pm, 5.30 pm to 9 pm, Sunday 11 am to 2 pm (brunch), 5.30 pm to 8 pm. Licensed. All cards. ⅃

COLLINGWOOD, Ontario   MAP 49
CHARTREUSE
70 Hurontario Street   **$85**
(705) 444-0099

Most readers find Chartreuse one of the best buys in town. It's a relaxed and informal place, with a big sofa filled with children's toys. You order your meal at the counter and it comes to your table in a moment. Patrick Bourachot, the chef, trained in France and worked at Montebello before settling down in Collingwood with his wife, Ruth, who manages the restaurant. Others do much of the cooking nowadays, especially Zacharie, the pastry chef, whose creations, among them a double-chocolate mousse-cake with fresh strawberries, are fabulous. At lunchtime there are several imaginative soups (often potato-and-leek), several interesting salads (apple and beets in a raspberry vinaigrette) and three or four sandwiches. The service is friendly and helpful.

Open Monday and Wednesday to Saturday 2 pm to 5 pm, Sunday 11.30 am to 4 pm. Closed on Tuesday. Licensed. Master Card, Visa. ⅃

COLLINGWOOD

DUNCAN'S
60 Hurontario Street
(705) 444-5749

MAP 49

$110

Duncan was a cat that had nothing whatever to do with the restaurant of today. The menu is enormous and never changes. Popular dishes, like the potato soup with leeks and stilton cheese, remain on the list for years. The salad-dressings are all made in the kitchen and the mango salad with jerk chicken is a knockout. People come here for the chicken club sandwich, the quesadillas, the baked brie in phyllo and the wild-mushroom ravioli. Prices are higher in the evening, when you can have a fine 10-ounce striploin with blue cheese or a fillet of Atlantic salmon in puff pastry. (The chicken stuffed with goat-cheese is big enough to keep two people full for a week.) The kitchen isn't much interested in sweets, but there's a big wine-list. *Open Monday to Thursday 9 am to 8 pm, Friday and Saturday 9 am to 10 pm, Sunday 9 am to 4 pm. Licensed. Master Card, Visa.* &

COLLINGWOOD   MAP 49

HURON CLUB
94 Pine Street
(705) 293-6677

$140

The menu here seldom ventures far from such things as shepherd's pie, Atlantic cod, roast beef and yam fries. But everything is perfectly fresh and most of the recipes have a bit of a kick. You may be up to your ears in butternut-squash soup, but you'll like this one. The kitchen is always at its best with seafood—cod, halibut, squid and fish tacos. The tacos are always good and they have a nice choice of local cheeses. The restaurant occupies a fine old heritage house and it's run by a family that always welcomes other families, even if they bring their children. In the evening they make much of live music, and every Sunday there's a jazz-and-blues brunch. (They have a big dance floor and not one but two bars.) Some diners leave

68

when the music starts; others like it that way. There's no membership fee, and if you wish you can have your dinner outside on the patio.

Open daily 11 am to 4 pm (lunch), 4 pm to midnight (dinner). Licensed. Master Card, Visa. &

COLLINGWOOD   MAP 49
SANTINI
166 Hurontario Street   **$60**
(705) 994-4200

Santini is still pretty new, but so far it seems more genuinely Italian than the competition. Everything here is fresh, while the others seem to keep the same old things forever. The young couple who run the place are having a lot of fun, and they seem to have plenty of money. They specialize in thin-crust pizzas, but they have a fine mushroom tortellini, several paninis and several soups; the caprese salad comes with fior de latte mozzarella. Some time this year a full-service restaurant of the same name will open at 66 Hurontario Street (telephone (705) 443-8383). It'll be open every day but Wednesday from 11 am to 9.30 pm. It'll have a licence and will take most cards. Meanwhile, the café at No. 166 is open Monday to Friday 8 am to 3 pm. Closed on Saturday and Sunday. Licensed. Master Card, Visa. &

COLLINGWOOD   MAP 49
THE SIAMESE GECKO
14 Balsam Street   **$50**
(705) 446-2167

The Siamese Gecko has moved back to Balsam Street, where they started out. Their smart new quarters on the main street have gone, but the menu hasn't changed. Narry Dopp comes from Bangkok, and her recipes are all completely authentic. She starts her meals with Tom Yum soup, which is a mixture of mushrooms, lime and lemon grass with chicken, beef, shrimps or tofu. Curries come next—red, yellow, orange and green. People who should know really admire her pad ho ra pa, with its hot chillies and Thai basil. We ourselves prefer the pad kee mow, with lime and lemon grass. If you insist on meat, ask for the gang panaeng, a red curry with beef, lamb or chicken and no vegetables at all. They have Thai beer to drink and several wines, but we usually go for a pot of jasmine tea.

Open Monday 5 pm to 9 pm, Tuesday to Saturday 11.30 am to 3 pm, 5 pm to 9 pm. Closed on Sunday. Licensed. Master Card, Visa. &

COLLINGWOOD   **MAP 49**
THE STUFFED PEASANT   ☆☆
206 Hurontario Street   **$125**
(705) 445-6957

Scott Carter believes in service. He has an attentive staff and a chef who takes the time to chat with the customers. He has a three-course *prix-fixe* menu—three courses for 33.00. Some things never leave it, things like the mushroom pâté, the provimi liver, the cassoulet of lamb. Last Christmas he tried sweetbreads, sautéed in a reduction of port with spinach and potatoes. He also got in two cases of Alberta lamb. Both sold well. Nearby there's an organic fish hatchery, the only one in Canada. They supply him with rainbow trout and speckled trout, and he grills them and serves them with chopped chives. The steaks are always first-rate and so is the duck with pomegranates. The best of the sweets is usually the sticky-toffee pudding. The wine-list is small but useful.

Open Tuesday to Saturday 5 pm to 10 pm. Closed on Sunday and Monday. Licensed. Amex, Master Card, Visa.

COLLINGWOOD
See also THORNBURY.

COOMBS, B.C.   **(MAP 157)**
THE CUCKOO
2310 Alberni Highway   **$125**
(250) 248-6280

The Cuckoo is conveniently located for anyone on their

way to Tofino or Ucluelet. They're open in the afternoon until 3 and again in the evening until 10, which makes it ideal for lunch on the way to the Coast and for dinner on the way back. Readers will certainly be happy with one of their wood-fired pizzas at noon, one of which is topped with grilled breast of chicken, roasted red peppers and mozzarella. The salmon is another good choice; it's topped with lox, goat cheese, tomatoes and spinach. (For children they offer a great take on Mac and cheese.) The best of their dinner dishes is the gnocchi in pesto with grilled tomatoes and fresh asparagus, though the Piemontese (with chanterelles and porcini mushrooms) is almost as good. The lemon torte is the best of the sweets. If you get a chance, book one of the tables on the outside patio; they're lovely in summer.

Open daily 11.30 am to 3 pm, 5.30 pm to 10 pm. Licensed. All cards. &

COWICHAN BAY, B.C. (MAP 58)
THE MASTHEAD ☆
1705 Cowichan Bay Road **$125**
(250) 748-3714

This seaside hotel, built in the style of the eighteensixties, is a charming place. Charm aside, it offers some of the best in fresh local seafood and some of the best in local fruits and vegetables. They have oysters on the halfshell, steamed mussels and clams from Cortez Island and a lovely chowder full of local shellfish. The salads are all great, especially the so-called simple salad, which features smoked sockeye salmon, goat cheese and an apple-cider vinaigrette. They have a reputation for steaks, but if you try the Ahi tuna crusted with black sesame, or even the halibut crusted with hazelnuts, you'll be surprised. Everything is served with *pot-au-feu* vegetables and potatoes cooked in duck fat. The banana fritters are wonderful, though there's also a first-class pavlova served with warm raspberry liqueur.

Open daily 5 pm to 10 pm. Licensed. All cards. Book ahead if you can. &

71

COWICHAN LAKE, B.C.   (MAP 58)

STONE SOUP INN   ☆☆
6755 Cowichan Lake Road   **$215**
(250) 749-3848

The Stone Soup Inn is a charming bed-and-breakfast nestled in the heart of the Cowichan Valley. Brock Windsor, the chef, spent some time at the Sooke Harbour House and the Bearfoot Bistro before opening his own restaurant. The Stone Soup is open only three nights a week, but everything is made from scratch and served with the best local wines. He has a small farm where he raises pigs. He forages for wild mushrooms and is famous for his local chanterelles. At Stone Soup there's no written menu. Instead, Windsor offers a five-course tasting menu for 65.00. It usually starts with stinging-nettle soup or marinated black cod with warm cucumber and celery-root slaw and goes on to side-striped shrimps or house-smoked picnic ham braised with fresh oregano. The sweets are all inviting, especially the rhubarb soufflé with sour cream ice cream. If you stay the night, the breakfast will usually feature house-smoked bacon and farm-fresh eggs.

Open Thursday to Saturday 5 pm to 10 pm. Closed Sunday to Wednesday. Licensed. Master Card, Visa.

CRESTON, B.C.   MAP 53

REAL FOOD CAFE   ☆☆
223 10 Avenue N   **$125**
(250) 428-8882

Two readers who crossed the country last year thought this was the best of the many restaurants they'd tried. Look for Creston at the foot of Kootenay Lake, just north of the border on Highway 7. At the Real Food Café everybody is fiercely loyal to the Creston Valley and its produce, from their fruit and greens to their Nestralia cheese, from their black-cherry juice (a pound of cherries in every bottle) to most of the wines on their wine-list. They're also loyal to the British connection. For instance, you can get fish and chips with mushy peas (served in a newspaper if you like), sticky-toffee cake (with white chocolate) and bread-and-butter pudding. You can also get what they call Britain's favourite dish, which is tikka masala. Vegetarian and gluten-free items appear right on the regular menu. All the prices are reasonable. Inside there's a lot of local art and outside there's a big open-air patio.

Open Monday to Friday 11 am to 2 pm, 4.30 pm to 8 pm, Saturday 4.30 pm to 8 pm. Closed on Sunday. Licensed. Master Card, Visa. Book ahead if you can. &

DAWSON CITY, *Yukon*   MAP 54

Everybody wants to go north these days, but the trouble is that the north is more about scenery than good food. Whenever we find a useful restaurant it's gone before the next edition appears. At the moment the best place to eat in Dawson City is Cheechako's Bakeshop on Front Street (telephone (867) 993-5303). It opens early and closes when everything is sold. There aren't many tables, but chances are you can get some ice cream and good coffee, as well as some intriguing pastries and made-to-order sandwiches. If you want dinner, try the Drunken Goat Taverna at 950 2nd Avenue (telephone (867) 993-5868). It looks better inside than out, and they do give you big helpings of Greek food. Some people even admire the steaks. The Drunken Goat is open all day Monday to Saturday and takes Master Card and Visa, but it has no liquor and takes no reservations.

DIGBY, N.S.   MAP 55
BOARDWALK CAFE
40 Water Street   **$85**
(902) 245-5497

Esther Dunn will be back in the kitchen full-time this summer. We may think her split-pea soup is too thick, but there's certainly nothing wrong with her shrimp-and-avocado salad. Come to that, she makes everything herself: the quiches and the lasagne, of course, but also the bread and the salad-dressings. The pies are all brilliant—try the apple-lattice and see for yourself. In the evening you can expect fresh haddock, halibut, scallops (from Digby Bay), lobster and salmon. The Boardwalk doesn't have any bottled wines, just one or two house wines served by the glass. Inside, the restaurant is pretty plain, but the big windows look out on the harbour and the scallop fleet. The servers are all friendly and everyone has a good time here, especially if they have one of Esther's pies.

Open Monday to Friday 11 am to 2 pm from the beginning of March until late June, Monday to Saturday 11 am to 2 pm, 5 pm to 8 pm from late June until the end of September, Monday to Friday 11 am to 2 pm from 1 October until 20 December. Closed on Saturday and Sunday in the spring and fall, on Sunday in the summer. Licensed. All cards. &

DILDO, Newfoundland	**MAP 56**
INN BY THE BAY	☆☆
80 Front Road	**$215**
(709) 582-3170	

When they started, Todd Warren and Dale Cameron were both in love with the idea of becoming innkeepers and self-taught cooks with all the right ideas. But by the spring of 2013, they were ready to sell. They chose a local businessman called Nolan Hall, who installed a new chef, Christopher Gillard. He's an experienced cook and so far everyone seems to be happy with his work. He has only seven tables, so you have to book ahead. His food is all fresh and organic and most of it is grown nearby. He gets fresh cod from the bay. He buys local lamb and his pasta is all made in house. He has a steamed blueberry pudding for sweet that comes with a brown-sugar sauce and real whipped cream. His three-course table d'hôte dinner costs 57.00 plus wine—the wines are well chosen, but they're not cheap. Look for Dildo on the south arm of Trinity Bay, about an hour's drive from St. John's. It's well worth the trip.

Open five days a week 5 pm to 10 pm from early June until late September. Licensed. All cards. Book ahead.

DORCHESTER, N.B.   MAP 57
THE BELL INN
3515 Cape Road   **$55**
(506) 379-2580

David McAllister and Wayne Jones are soldiering on here after almost 30 years on the job. The Bell Inn is said to be the oldest stone building in New Brunswick. It was once a stop-over for stage-coaches, but in time it fell into disrepair. Eventually it was restored as a restaurant and filled with comfortable Victoriana. True, Jones and McAllister serve frozen lobster and sole as a matter of course, but that hardly seems to matter. They have a first-class homemade soup every day. They have fresh greens in their garden salad. They make fine sandwiches (turkey, tuna, egg-salad and cheese). There are also three or four hot dishes—scrambled eggs or an omelette, lasagne or liver and onions. They make all their own sweets, the best of which is probably the apple crisp. There's no liquor, not even a glass of Moosehead. Fortunately, they make very good coffee.

Open Wednesday to Sunday 11 am to 7 pm from 1 April until 15 November. Closed on Monday and Tuesday. No liquor. All cards. Free parking.

DUNCAN, B.C.   MAP 58
BISTRO 161
161 Kenneth Street   **$95**
(250) 746-6466

Fatima da Silva, who is running both Bistro 161 and Vinoteca (see below), was born and grew up in Mozam-bique. Her background has Portuguese, Indian, Arabic, Spanish and Chinese elements, all of which show up in her cooking. Chris Szilagyi, the chef de cuisine, also has a multicultural background, stemming from Chinese, African, Portuguese and Irish ancestors. We like almost everything they do: the yam-and-ginger soup with gar-lic, the penne with sundried tomatoes and artichokes, the mussels steamed in wine with chorizo, the ceviche of scallops with orange and star anise, the duck biryani and even the pork and beans with its ten secret spices. The service, however, is uneven at best, poor at worst.

Open Monday to Saturday 11 am to 3 pm, 5 pm to 10 pm. Closed on Sunday. Licensed. Amex, Master Card, Visa. &

DUNCAN   MAP 58
CRAIG STREET BREW PUB
25 Craig Street   **$95**
(250) 737-2337

Craig Street offers hand-crafted beer and home-style cooking in a brick-and-timber post-and-beam setting in front of a beautiful open fireplace. Our favourite drink here is the Shawinigan Irish ale, but others admire the Arbutus pale ale, both made right here on the premises. At noon you can sample their poutine or (even better) their rock crab with sundried tomatoes and roasted garlic. They do good pizzas too, the best of which is the Sicilian, topped with black olives, spinach, red onion, feta and mozzarella cheese. In the evening they add steaks, blackened red snapper and maple-glazed wild salmon with great sweet-potato fries. There's triple-chocolate cheesecake to follow, as well as several other cheesecakes and pies.

Open Monday to Wednesday 11 am to 11 pm, Thursday to Saturday 11 am to midnight, Sunday 11 am to 10 pm. Licensed. Master Card, Visa. &

DUNCAN   MAP 58
HUDSON'S ON FIRST .   ☆☆
163 First Street   **$125**
(250) 597-0066

Hudson's on First is a comfortable place. It's situated just a block from downtown Duncan in an impeccably restored century-old building. It has two Edwardian dining-rooms and a bar with a hammered-tin ceiling. Their cooking has been praised by all the critics. Lunch is certainly an impressive meal, featuring a salad made with Dragonfly Farm greens, Daniel Hudson's own apples, spiced hazelnuts and goat-cheese. The carpaccio of rabbit and the dungeness crab with an organic-potato terrine are their most interesting appetizers. In the evening there's Arctic char and pan-seared scallops in a delicate lemon purée. The waiters are sensitive to every detail of setting and presentation.

Open Tuesday to Friday 11 am to 2.30 pm, 5 pm to 8.30 pm, Saturday and Sunday 11 am to 2.30 pm (brunch), 5 pm to 8.30 pm. Closed on Monday. Licensed. Amex, Master Card, Visa. Book ahead.

DUNCAN   MAP 58
RIVERWALK
200 Cowichan Way   **$90**
(250) 746-4370

Beverly Antoine has left Riverwalk, which, however, still makes it its business to marry First Nations traditions with West Coast styles of cooking. If you want to sample a recent menu, ask for the pulled bison slow-roasted in a fireweed-peppercorn sauce, topped with sautéed peppers and onions. That or the farmed venison with fresh tomatoes, aged cheddar cheese, sour cream and avocado. There's also a Salish seafood platter that features wild Pacific salmon, cod and prawns garnished with sea asparagus.

Open Monday to Saturday 11 am to 4 pm from 15 June until 15 September. Closed on Sunday. Licensed. Master Card, Visa. Book ahead if you can. &

DUNCAN   MAP 58
VINOTECA
Zanatta Winery   **$100**
5039 Marshall Road
(250) 709-2279

Vinoteca is located in an old farmhouse near the Zanatta winery. It was recommended in *Where to Eat in Canada* from 2000 until 2005, when it was run by Fatima da

Silva. When she left, the restaurant ran quickly downhill and was taken out of the guide. All that has changed now that Fatima is once again in charge. She has created a new menu based on produce grown on or close to the Zanatta farm. Further reports needed.

Open Wednesday to Sunday 11.30 am to 2.30 pm from mid-May until mid-October. Closed on Monday and Tuesday. Licensed. Master Card, Visa.

DUNCAN
See also CHEMAINUS, COBBLE HILL, COWICHAN BAY, COWICHAN LAKE, MAPLE BAY, MILL BAY.

DUNDAS, Ontario	**(MAP 83)**
QUATREFOIL	☆
16 Sydenham Street	**$120**
(905) 628-7800	

Quatrefoil is a fairly new restaurant. It's run by Fraser Macfarlane and Georgina Mitropoulos, who met when they were both working at Scaramouche in Toronto. The cooking is a mixture of classic and modern French, and the chef has a vigorous interest in fresh, organic local produce. He starts with sea scallops in a clementine vinaigrette, white asparagus with the yolk of an egg, tagliatelle of braised rabbit and textbook-perfect smoked salmon with red-onion pickles. The best of the main courses is the beef tenderloin from Cumbrae, served with a purée of smoked potatoes and cheek cromesquis, a dish so good that it reminded one diner of one of his mother's Easter dinners. The vanilla crème brûlée delighted the same diner, when he broke the crust and smelled the hot vanilla inside.

Open Tuesday to Saturday noon to 2.30 pm, 5 pm to 9.30 pm. Closed on Sunday and Monday. Licensed. Amex, Master Card, Visa.

The map number assigned to each city, town or village gives the location of the centre on one or more of the maps at the start of the book.

EDMONTON, Alberta MAP 60
CORSO 32 ☆☆
10345 Jasper Avenue **$120**
(780) 421-4622

Corso 32 is a newcomer to Edmonton. It's an Italian restaurant but it has no fish, no veal and no liver, most of which other Italian restaurants have in spades. What it does have is noise, deafening noise. Apart from noise, Corso 32 is all about local ingredients—milkfed veal, for instance, is almost unknown in Alberta and so it doesn't appear on the menu. Daniel Costa starts his list of antipasto with pear carpaccio and ends it with house-made goat ricotta. His pork-cheeks terrine isn't a terrine at all, not at least as we think of it. Terrine or not, it's a wonderful dish. If they don't have any, ask for the gnocchi of wild boar, which is out of the class of most other gnocchis on the market. Cornish game hen is rarely offered in Tuscany, or in Puglia for that matter, but this one is charming. The chocolate cake is made with salted hazelnuts in the modern fashion, and it's good. They have a Batasiolo barolo by the glass and it's about as good as any we've had. The same is true of the macchiato.
Open Wednesday to Saturday 5 pm to midnight. Closed Sunday to Tuesday. Licensed. Amex, Master Card, Visa. You must book ahead. ♿

EDMONTON MAP 60
MARC
9940 106 Street **$150**
(780) 429-2828

Marc occupies the ground floor of a modern office block near the high-level bridge. Inside it's all white, with wide steel-and-glass windows. Scott Ards is no longer in charge of the kitchen, having been replaced by Bryan Cruz. At noon, Cruz serves salmon tartar, smoked breast of duck, fresh trout, braised open-faced lamb sandwiches and steak with (far too many) fried potatoes. In the evening he adds scallops, char and charcuterie. The wine-list offers a little of everything, from California to Portugal, all at reasonable prices. Marc may not be exciting, but it's a useful, convenient restaurant with capable cooking and first-rate service.

Open Monday to Friday 11.30 am to 2 pm, 5.30 pm to 9 pm, Saturday 5.30 pm to 9 pm. Closed on Sunday. Licensed. Amex, Master Card, Visa. Book ahead. &

EDMONTON   **MAP 60**
NINETEEN   ★★
5940 Mullen Way NW   **$215**
(780) 395-1119

This is a new restaurant. Look for it beyond Whitemud Drive on the way to the Nisku airport. It's an inconvenient location, but it's a sumptuous place with elegant service, a stunning wine-list and an enterprising menu. The kitchen has no hesitation about serving bone marrow, raw tuna, pork belly and foie gras. Loin of Alberta lamb comes with dijon mustard, chicken linguine with truffles. There are beef short-ribs, lamb shanks, chinook salmon and beef tenderloin. The cooking is poised and prices are modest. The selection of open wines is amazing. There's a sauvignon blanc from Katherine Hall, a pinot gris from Burrowing Owl, a chardonnay from Cakebread and cabernet sauvignons from Two Hands and Sexy Beast. There's nothing else like this in Edmonton.

Open Tuesday to Sunday 5 pm to 10 pm. Closed on Monday. Licensed. All cards. Book ahead. &

EDMONTON   **MAP 60**
NUMCHOK WILAI   🍴
10623 124 Street   **$75**
(780) 483-7897

This is one of the best Thai restaurants in Edmonton and one of the cheapest. They have a liquor licence and offer Singha beer, which is the thing to drink. Lunch costs just

10.95, for which you get a small bowl of lemon-grass soup and red and green curries of beef and chicken, as well as panaeng chicken and beef, pad Thai and a variety of vegetarian dishes. In the evening they add several scallop, squid and mussel curries for only a few dollars more. Numchok Wilai is a streetfront restaurant with a comfortable arrangement of tables and chairs inside. The service is competent but rather impersonal.

Open daily 11.30 am to 2.30 pm, 4.30 pm to 9 pm (later on weekends). Licensed. Master Card, Visa.

EDMONTON   MAP 60
THE RED OX INN
9420 91 Street   **$175**
(780) 465-5727

The Red Ox Inn is bare inside and out, but it's a sensible place with a short, straightforward menu and good cooking. The pork belly with sweet-and-sour marmalade is a good way to start—that or the beef tartar. Both are much better than the house-smoked salmon, which with its plain slice of corn bread is dry and rather tasteless. When it comes to the main course, the kitchen is at its best with its halibut with quinoa and scallions and its breast of duck, which is tender and quite piquant. Berkshire pork appears again as a main course and for only 38.00 you can have a good, substantial rack of lamb. Most of the real excitement, however, takes place on the wine-list. For almost nothing there's a good Amity pinot blanc and a Columbia Crest grand-estates merlot—two of the best and most important wines from Oregon. If you prefer to drink Canadian, there's a first-rate cabernet sauvignon from Poplar Grove for 49.00. The cabernet from Rodney Strong costs a bit more, as it should. The service is attentive and personal. They care.

Open Tuesday to Sunday 5 pm to 9 pm. Closed on Monday. Licensed. Amex, Master Card, Visa. &

If you use an out-of-date edition and find it inaccurate, don't blame us. Buy a new edition.

EDMONTON　　　　　　　　　　　　　　　**MAP 60**
TAVERN 1903
Alberta Hotel　　　　　　　　　　　　　　　　**$135**
9802 Jasper Avenue
(780) 424-0152

The Alberta Hotel is a new venture by the owners of the Hardware Grill, which in its great days was in *Where to Eat in Canada* for many years. The old hotel has been lovingly restored and a sparkling new tavern and restaurant installed, named 1903, which was the year the Alberta Hotel was built. The appointments are luxurious, the service stylish and the menu interesting. They start with black-bean soup and continue with goat-cheese fritters, braised short-ribs, lamb burgers and lovely potato-crusted salmon. In the evening they add pork belly, smoked ribs, charcuterie and a variety of fresh pasta. They offer several wines by the glass, among them Stump Jump shiraz from Australia, Marquéz de Riscal rioja from Spain and Stag's Leap from Napa. 1903 is a good place to know about, because it's open for lunch, dinner and late-night supper six days a week.

Open Monday to Thursday 11 am to 2 pm (lunch), 2 pm to 5 pm (dinner), 5 pm to midnight (supper), Friday and Saturday 11 am to 2 pm, 2 pm to 5 pm, 5 pm to 1 am. Closed on Sunday. Licensed. Amex, Master Card, Visa. &

EDMONTON　　　　　　　　　　　　　　　**MAP 60**
THREE BOARS　　　　　　　　　　　　　　　☆
8424 109 Street　　　　　　　　　　　　　　　**$75**
(780) 757-2600

This place is tiny and holds about twenty people at a sitting. But right now it's the hottest place in town. There's a bar downstairs and many people come here just for the beer. They have almost 50 beers and a good choice of cocktails. Upstairs there's a big menu, which is full of exciting, creative dishes. Everything comes one at a time and everything is meant to be shared. The wild-boar terrine is perhaps the most interesting dish, that or the sangudo beef, but the duck rillette is something of a specialty and so is the steelhead trout. The dining area is rather plain and uncomfortable. There's a big blackboard along one wall and a narrow, precipitous stairwell. But after all, you come here to eat, not to admire the architecture.

Open Monday to Thursday 4 pm to 10 pm, Friday and Saturday 4 pm to midnight, Sunday 4 pm to 10 pm. Licensed. Master Card, Visa.

EDMONTON   **MAP 60**
THE UNHEARDOF   ☆☆
9602 82 Avenue   **$210**
(780) 432-0480

The Unheardof is expensive, but Lynn Heard is an accomplished cook who does some wonderful things. She's still making her celebrated tomato soup with gin, but nowadays you may do better with her golden-beet salad or her seared tuna with chilli. Next, we like the bison with chanterelles, but others prefer her halibut with wasabi or even her loin of lamb with pomegranates, which admittedly are two very splendid dishes. As for her *amuse bouche* of broccoli soup with cheddar cheese, it's pretty hard to beat. The list of bottled wines is impressive, and the list of wines by the glass is equally remarkable. There's a wonderful sauvignon blanc from Katherine Hall in the Napa Valley and a lovely Little Demon shiraz from McLaren Vale. The Okanagan vintners will have to look sharp if they want to compete with these two.

Open Tuesday to Saturday 5.30 pm to 8.30 pm, Sunday 5.30 pm to 8 pm. Closed on Monday. Licensed. Amex, Master Card, Visa. Book ahead. ♿

This is a guide to Canadian restaurants from coast to coast—the first ever published and the only one of its kind on the market today. We accept no advertisements. Nobody can buy his way into this guide and nobody can buy his way out.

EDMUNDSTON, N.S.   MAP 61
LOTUS BLEU
52 chemin Canada   **$55**
(506) 739-8259

This bright and colourful little café is the best place to eat
in town, which of course isn't saying much. But it's saying something. They offer a different hot dish every day
of the week. We ourselves have had a first-class Indian-
style vegetable stew and a lovely dal. Sometimes there's
a quiche and there are always several good salads. The
vegetables are all organically grown and the bread comes
from Première Moisson in Montreal. The sweets are
made in-house and they have leaf teas of every sort. The
Lotus Bleu has been in business for seven years now and
every year has been a struggle. It deserves better.
*Open Monday to Wednesday 7.30 am to 6 pm, Thursday and
Friday 7.30 am to 7 pm, Saturday 9.30 am to 5 pm. Closed on
Sunday. No liquor. Master Card, Visa.* &

ENGLISHTOWN, N.S.   MAP 62
THE CLUCKING HEN
45073 Cabot Trail   **$40**
(902) 929-2501

Look for the Clucking Hen ten miles north of the Eng-
lishtown ferry. Melody Dauphney offers plain, simple
home-cooking seven days a week in season. You line up
to place your order and pay the bill, then carry your tray
to a table. She makes a good soup (turkey or fish chowder) and a number of sandwiches, as well as lobster stew,
which everyone seems to like. There's a lot of baking here
too and there are always cinnamon rolls and butter tarts
as well as oat-cakes, which are a specialty of the house.
The Clucking Hen is a good place to stop for breakfast,
lunch or dinner before you set out on the Cabot Trail.
*Open daily 7 am to 8 pm from 1 July until 31 August (shorter
hours in the spring and fall). Licensed for beer and wine only.
Master Card, Visa.* &

FERRYLAND, Newfoundland

MAP 63

LIGHTHOUSE PICNICS
Highway 10
(709) 363-7456

$55

The lighthouse was built in 1869 and there isn't much left of it now. The waves break on the rocks, whales surface and blow and the nearest road is a 30-minute walk, after an hour's drive from St. John's. Call before you set out—the picnics are in great demand. Jill Curran and her staff of thirteen make everything on the spot, even the bread. The picnics cost between 20.00 and 25.00 and consist of a salad—our favourite is the orzo and fresh mint—a sandwich, lemonade and a sweet. The chutney-glazed ham-and brie is the most popular sandwich, but we also like the seafood club and the curried chicken with mango. After that, most people order gingerbread with warm custard, but we think you should try the peach short-cake or one of the bake-apple tarts. For the fresh lemonade they squeeze more than 6000 lemons every year. You can have tea instead if you like, with homemade scones and fresh berry jam.

Open Wednesday to Sunday 11.30 am to 4.30 pm from 1 June until 30 September. Closed on Monday and Tuesday. No liquor. Master Card, Visa.

FIELD, B.C.

(MAP 98)

TRUFFLE PIGS
Kicking Horse Lodge
100 Centre Street
(250) 343-6303

☆

$140

There's something about Field that attracts travellers. It's what people from the East think of when they think of Western Canada—a small town with a general store and a lodge that Truffle Pigs bought a few years ago with he help of some local people. They have ten tables and a modern kitchen. They have all the best Okanagan wines on their wine-list. They have the best triple-A beef on their menu. They offer a variety of fruit pies, all made

with local fruit. Breakfast means eggs benedict with Hutterite smoked sausages; lunch means bul-go-gi of pork
belly or short-rib nachos. At night the longtime favourite
is beef bourguignon, but they also offer green-salt Brome
Lake confit of duck. The service is very concerned and
very friendly.

*Open daily 11 am to 3 pm, 5 pm to 9 pm from late May until
the end of September (shorter hours in winter). Licensed. Amex,
Master Card, Visa. No reservations.* &

FLORENCEVILLE, N.B.   MAP 65
FRESH   ☆☆
9189 Main Street   **$180**
(506) 392-6000

The restored railcar that houses Fresh is the first of three
old C.P.R. cars parked on the track next to the Shogo-
moc railway station in the former village of Bristol. Sara
Caines opened the place a few years ago with the idea of
selling fresh food cooked from scratch. The menu contains all the usual things, plus a few surprises. Actually,
you can have pretty well anything you like, despite the
fact that James Freeman (the current chef) works in a tiny
space with four burners and a small oven. The dining-
room has only 26 seats, so you should book ahead. You
can start with veal saltimbocca or shrimps with fresh
pears and sweet peppers in a sweet-and-sour vinaigrette.
The best seller is still the triple-A beef tenderloin with a
dry brown-sugar rub and chipotle-pepper sauce. The
vegetables and greens all come from local suppliers and
fresh fish is nearly always available. The sweets change
every day, but keep an eye out for the chocolate mousse.
The wine-list is ambitious but fairly priced. The Wolf
Blass Red Label cabernet merlot, for instance, sells for
just 42.00.

*Open Monday to Saturday 5.30 pm to 10 pm. Closed on Sun-
day. Licensed. Amex, Master Card, Visa. Book ahead.*

Our website is at www.oberonpress.ca. Readers wishing
to use e-mail should address us at oberon@sympatico.ca.

FOGO ISLAND, Newfoundland

MAP 66

☆

NICOLE'S

Joe Batt's Arm

$125

Highway 334

(705) 658-3663

It's possible to get to Fogo Island, spend a few hours there and get back to Twillingate the same day, but that would be a pity. Fogo Island deserves a longer visit. It's just off the northeast shore of Newfoundland. It's windswept and wet and very beautiful. Caribou graze on the uplands in summer, humpback whales migrate past its shores in winter. Zita Cobb, a woman of enormous energy and substantial means, is determined to preserve the island through tourism. Early in 2013, a multi-million-dollar hotel, the Fogo Island Inn, opened on Joe Batt's Arm. It has only 29 rooms and each costs a thousand dollars a day, all of which will go back to the community. Not five minutes away, Nicole has opened a café right on the edge of the sea. The kitchen is manned by local people and so far we've received no complaints. Every day they have a cod chowder with shrimps as well as a crab panini with green-onion mayonnaise. They get their cod from cod-pots. The cod are caught in pots instead of nets, and they're kept alive until they're ready to be used. The vegetables are all organic and grown on nearby farms. For sweet there's a bake-apple crème brûlée, partridge-berry jam-and-molasses tarts and sorbets made from ice chipped off ancient icebergs. Nicole hopes to stay open all year now that the Fogo Island Inn is up and running. *Open Monday to Saturday 10 am to 2 pm, 5 pm to 8.30 pm. Closed on Sunday. Licensed. All cards.* ♿

FORT MACLEOD, Alberta

MAP 67

RAHN'S

☞

228 24 Street

$40

(403) 553-3200

If you're anywhere near, Rahn's is a nice place for a quick lunch. It's part bakery, part café. The soups are so so, but the sandwiches are quite good. The pastries, however, are the real thing. They're all fresh and they're all first-rate. They also sell homemade ice cream. Rahn's is open for breakfast and lunch every day of the week. No liquor, no cards. &

FREDERICTON, N.B.   MAP 68
THE PALATE
462 Queen Street   **$100**
(506) 450-7911

The Palate is large, well served and remarkably cheap. They're at their best with their soups. Just try the cream-of-zucchini or the seafood chowder. There's a long list of pizzas, paninis, quesadillas and stir-fries. They make a very good club sandwich too and the molten-lava cake is known all over town. (Frankly, we prefer the sticky-toffee pudding.) There are precious few wines—six reds and six whites—but the house wines are from Banrock Station and they're both pretty good.
Open Monday 11 am to 3 pm, Tuesday to Friday 11 am to 3 pm, 5 pm to 9 pm, Saturday 10 am to 3 pm (brunch), 5 pm to 9 pm. Closed on Sunday. Licensed. All cards. Book ahead.

FREDERICTON   MAP 68
WOLASTOQ WHARF   ☆
527 Union Street   **$125**
(506) 449-0100

The St. Mary's First Nation has had several commercial successes. Now they're trying a restaurant, and Wolastoq Wharf has already established itself as one of the best places to eat in town. They major in seafood, which means oysters from the North Shore, shrimp spring-rolls, fish chowder and seafood risotto. Our favourite dish is the salmon three ways, maple smoked and tequila-cured. If you like, you can have lobster, tuna, scallops, whole clams, pan-fried haddock and even beef short-ribs. The service is prompt and very friendly.
Open Monday and Tuesday 11 am to 4 pm (lunch), 4 pm to 8 pm (dinner), Wednesday to Friday 11 am to 4 pm (lunch), 4 pm

to 10 pm (dinner), Saturday 9.30 am to 2 pm, 4 pm to 10 pm, Sunday 9.30 am to 2 pm, 4 pm to 8 pm. Licensed. All cards.

FREEPORT, N.S.   MAP 69
LAVENA'S CATCH   ☆
15 Highway 217 W   **$70**
Long Island
(902) 839-2517

If you want to take a whale-and-seabird tour, you'll have an arduous journey from Digby to Long Island, which is the last stop before Brier Island. Freeport is a five-minute ferry trip from the tip of Digby Neck. It was settled by Loyalists in 1784 and many of the original buildings are still standing. St. Mary's Bay and its warm waters are on your left; Fundy's cold, rocky coast is on your right. Overhead, in the spring and fall, migrating birds travel the Atlantic Flyway in their thousands. On the Fundy side you may see, if you're lucky, minke or humpback whales. You can buy tour tickets at Lavena's Catch, which is run by the captain's sister and is the best place to eat anywhere near. Lavena makes everything from scratch. The service may be slow but the meal, when it comes, will be full of fresh seafood, served with mashed potatoes and a Caesar salad. The greens and the vegetables come straight from the garden. Don't overlook the chowder either, or the peanut-butter pie. The coffee is organic and it's very good.

Open Friday and Saturday 4 pm to 9 pm from 1 April until 31 May, daily 11.30 am to 8 pm from 1 June until 15 October, Friday and Saturday 4 pm to 9 pm from 16 October until 30 November. Closed Sunday to Thursday in the spring and fall. Licensed. All cards.

FROBISHER BAY, Nunavut
See IQALUIT.

GANDER, Newfoundland
See BOTWOOD.

GASPE, Quebec

MAP 70

LA BRULERIE
101 rue de la Reine
(418) 368-3366

$70

It's always a treat to stop here. The place was built by the C.N.R. as a telegraph office. Later it was used as the city hall. It now makes a cozy restaurant that's open all year, with a chef who has the same menu and enough English for any anglophone. The fresh shrimps from Rivière-au-Renard appear in both the salads and the sandwiches. Home-smoked salmon comes by the plateful. They make their own sausages, their own pizzas and their own pasta. The helpings are generous, the prices low. They roast their own coffee right here and offer everyone endless refills. We couldn't find the Belgian-chocolate truffle-cake this year, but we certainly liked the caramel mousse. *Open Monday to Friday 7 am to 10.30 pm, Saturday and Sunday 8 am to 10.30 pm. Licensed. Master Card, Visa.*

GEORGETOWN, P.E.I.

(MAP 39)

CLAMDIGGERS
7 West Street
(902) 652-2466

$110

This former railway station has a splendid location right on the shore of Cardigan Bay. It also has a big deck where you can dine al fresco in summer. They buy all their fish daily and fillet it by hand in the kitchen. The clams are served whole, battered and deep-fried only when you order them that way. Both steamer clams and regular clams are treated as an appetizer, much like mussels. The scallops, however, are deep-fried unless you ask for them with the Caesar salad, when they come to the table just lightly pan-fried. The fish chowder and the fish and chips are both outstanding, but that's not all. They also have lobster, crab, halibut, salmon and even a first-class steak. There's a nice salad of baby greens and the vegetables are all fresh, but the sweets are disappointing. Georgetown has one of the country's oldest live theatres, a three-acre memorial garden and a golf-course.

Open daily 11 am to 8.30 pm. Licensed. Amex, Master Card, Visa. &

GIBSONS, B.C. (MAP 207)
BONNIEBROOK LODGE ☆☆
1532 Ocean Beach Esplanade **$130**
Sunshine Coast
(604) 886-8956

A couple from Moose Jaw write to say that the Bonniebrook Lodge was everything they had hoped for on the Sunshine Coast: good food, perfect service and magnificent sunsets. On the menu they say that two can dine for 69.00. If you take them up on that, you'll find that dinners begin with a red-pepper tapenade on warm bread, followed by breast of duck with fresh raspberries, Lois Lake steelhead trout or pork tenderloin with apple, apricots and cider. They have a very good cellar and offer a useful wine pairing for just 29.00 a head.

Open Tuesday to Sunday 5 pm to 9 pm. Closed on Monday. Licensed. Master Card, Visa.

GLENVILLE, N.S. (MAP 151)
GLENORA DISTILLERY ☆
Highway 19 **$145 ($350)**
Cape Breton
(800) 839-0491

The dining-room is right next door to the distillery. There's a ceilidh every evening and that's the main reason for stopping here—that and the single-malt whisky. (There are several vintages, the best of which is aged for seventeen years.) There's also a big menu that offers such things as scallops with (too little) whisky, lobster salad with grapefruit (an interesting idea), pork tenderloin, breast of chicken and rack of lamb with dark gravy. The cooking is no longer what it used to be, but the ceilidhs are and so are the bread pudding and the sticky-toffee pudding. The wines are almost all from Jost. There are also one or two from Gaspereau and they're the things to ask for.

Open daily noon to 3 pm (in the pub), 5 pm to 9 pm from mid-May until mid-October. Licensed. Amex, Master Card, Visa. &

GODERICH, Ontario MAP 74
THYME ON 21 ☆
80 Hamilton Street **$115**
(519) 524-4171

Peter and Catherine King and their chef, Terry Kennedy, have stuck together for years, ever since this old Victorian house was turned into a restaurant. Kennedy comes from Toronto, but he has cultivated relationships with most of the local suppliers and he has the gift of cooking the simplest dish as if it were foie gras. His grilled provimi liver is the sort of dish that'll melt your heart. You can order fresh pickerel and know that it'll be correctly cooked. The pork tenderloin comes from Metzger and is beautifully served in an orange sauce with cranberries. The beef comes from Huron County and is always cooked *à point*. If you start with panko-crusted crab-cakes, you can if you like go on to fresh Atlantic salmon with lemon-dill butter. But you won't see Kennedy at his best unless you order his vegetable soufflé with goat-cheese and sundried tomatoes. It's surely a mistake, however, to offer (for a price) to add three garlic shrimps or a four-ounce lobster tail to your dish—any dish. How absurd!

Open Tuesday 5 pm to 8 pm, Wednesday to Sunday 11.30 am to 2 pm, 5 pm to 8 pm (later on weekends) from early May until late September, Tuesday to Friday 11.30 am to 2 pm, 5 pm to 8 pm, Saturday 5 pm to 8 pm, Sunday 11.30 am to 2 pm, 5 pm to 8 pm from early October until late April. Closed on Monday. Licensed. All cards.

Every restaurant in this guide has been personally tested. Our reporters are not allowed to identify themselves or to accept free meals.

GOLDEN, B.C.   MAP 75
THE CEDAR HOUSE   ☆
735 Hefti Road   **$175**
(250) 290-0001

Darrin de Rosa and Tracy Amies are doing a very good job at the Cedar House. Their chef may occasionally cut corners to save money, but everyone seems to like the place and many find the food amazing. The beef is triple-A from Alberta, and they still have a big vegetable garden. In the winter they do remarkable things with root vegetables and they keep fresh bison on the menu all year. The wine-list is small, but they usually have several wines from Burrowing Owl in the cellar. What more can one ask? The setting, which overlooks the Rocky Mountains, is magnificent.
Open Tuesday to Sunday 5 pm to 10 pm from 1 June until 30 September and from 1 December until 15 April. Closed on Monday. Licensed. Amex, Master Card, Visa. &

GOLDEN   MAP 75
ELEVEN 22   ☆
1122 10 Avenue S   **$110**
(250) 344-2443

Kenan Wah calls this place a restaurant, a grill and liquids. The wine-list, to be sure, is very large and very cheap. So is the menu, which changes all the time. They don't make their own cannelloni any more, but what they do serve is so good that few people seem to have noticed. Their Asian dishes (nasi goreng and pad Thai) are attractive takes on familiar dishes. There's always some fresh fish, but the chef isn't as good with fish as with meat. He's at his best with veal bratwurst, Kassler pork chops and, of course, Black Angus beef with stilton and roasted garlic or smoked paprika butter. Sweets are one of the specialties of the house, and the chocolate truffles are very good too.
Open daily 5 pm to 10 pm from mid-May until mid-October and from mid-November until mid-April. Licensed. Master Card, Visa. &

GRAND MANAN, N.B.
MAP 76

THE INN AT WHALE COVE ☆☆
26 Whale Cottage Road **$150 ($300)**
North Head
(506) 662-3181

Last year *Forbes* magazine named the Inn at Whale Cove one of its five top world destinations. Actually, you don't have to be rich to stay here. Dinner for two costs only about 150.00. Now that fast car ferries make six round trips a day, you should come to North Head before it goes the way of so many precious places. Just remember to book early—visitors have been coming here for more than a century. The main house was built in 1816 and Willa Cather once owned one of the cottages. The interior has been renovated and filled with old Shaker furniture and lots and lots of books. You can often see whales, porpoises and seals from the front verandah. The ground fish that used to be the backbone of the menu are gradually disappearing. The scallop season lasted only a week this year, but lobster is still plentiful and you can still get salmon and halibut. There's still local lamb, beef and pork, usually served with rhubarb or sour cherries. Blueberries and strawberries are plentiful, but there aren't many wines to be found in the local liquor store.

Open Saturday and Sunday 6 pm to 8 pm from Mother's Day until late June, daily 6 pm to 8 pm from late June until mid-October. Closed Monday to Friday in the spring. Licensed. Master Card, Visa. Book ahead.

GRAND MANAN
See also CAMPOBELLO ISLAND.

GRAND PRE, N.S.
(MAP 220)

LE CAVEAU ☆
Highway 1 **$150**
(902) 542-7177

Le Caveau is designed to show off the best Acadie wines, including the award-winning Tidal Bay. They also have a longish list of imported wines, many of them from Australia. But, unless you want to drink Tidal Bay, it's best to ask for a bottle of Vero from Benjamin Bridge. Nova 7 is a sparkling wine that sells for the same price, but most drinkers will feel safer with the Vero. The brilliant timbale of Arctic char with avocado and sticky rice is (we think) the best thing on the menu, though the tasting pâtés run it a close second. The main courses are rather less interesting. Sea bream is aptly served with wilted greens and quince and there's lobster risotto for 30.00 and Moroccan chicken for 26.00. Le Caveau is a little hard to find; look for it opposite the Evangeline (see below), two ore three miles east of Wolfville.

Open Tuesday to Saturday 5 pm to 9 pm from early April until mid-May, 11.30 am to 2 pm, 5 pm to 9 pm from mid-May until late October, 5 pm to 9 pm from late October until the end of December. Closed on Sunday and Monday. Licensed. Amex, Master Card, Visa.

GRAND PRE (MAP 220)
EVANGELINE
Highway 1 **$30**
(888) 542-2703

Marjorie Stirling ran the Evangeline, then called the Evangeline Snack Bar, for almost 50 years until her death in 1996. She left the place to her nephew, Ralph Stirling, who sold it to his daughter, Sheila Carey, four years later. Since then, the place has been completely redecorated inside and out and the lawns filled with flowers. Everything, one is tempted to think, is better than it used to be. Not so. Everything has improved except the food. The fish chowder, once a delight, now comes with overcooked fish. The pies, which Robert Stanfield used to call the best in the world, now lack flavour. The apple is still good, but the blueberry is a lot like the commercial product. The famous cherry tastes of gelatin. The lemon hasn't got enough lemon. Perhaps this is all because Sheila's sister, who used to make most of the pies, left recently to take charge of a Stirling fruit market. The Evan geline is still good, but it's certainly no longer the best in the world.

Open Monday to Saturday 8 am to 7 pm, Sunday 9 am to 7 pm from early May until late October. No liquor. Amex, Master Card, Visa. &

GRAVENHURST, Ontario   MAP 78
BLUE WILLOW
900 Bay Street   **$90**
(705) 687-2597

This is by far the best place for lunch in Gravenhurst. You can have a wedge of quiche Lorraine if you like, but if you want to save money ask for the mini-quiche, which comes with a green salad or a Caesar salad (take the Caesar) and a bowl of homemade soup. There's often a tourtière or meat-loaf as well, plus a number of sandwiches (take the grilled cheese). There's good gingerbread to follow and homemade pies in season. They have a short wine-list and good coffee. High tea is served every day between 2 and 5 pm.

Open Monday, Tuesday, Thursday and Sunday 11 am to 5 pm, Wednesday, Friday and Saturday 11 am to 8 pm from 1 July until 31 August, Tuesday, Thursday and Sunday 11 am to 5 pm, Wednesday, Friday and Saturday 11 am to 8 pm from 1 September until 30 June. Closed on Monday in winter. Licensed. Amex, Master Card, Visa. Book ahead if you can. &

GRAVENHURST   MAP 78
TABOO   ☆☆
Muskoka Beach Road   **$345**
(705) 687-2233

The Culinary Theatre, as the top restaurant at Taboo is called, continues to thrive. The chefs change every year. No-one knows who will be in charge this summer, but if there are no important changes there'll be an eight-course dinner from Tuesday to Sunday. There's just one sitting (at 7 o'clock) and it costs about 100.00 a head, 150.00 a head if you order the wine service as well (which

you should). The menu changes frequently, but the meal usually starts with something like raw char with water-melon, followed by sea scallops in a coulis of lettuce and passion fruit. Next may come tomato and asparagus in white foam, then a ceviche of sea-bass with tender, young bok choy, then a fruit sorbet in chopped ice, then a morsel of filet mignon with parsnip and ginger. Then there might be a cheval steak with barley, chopped onions and beetroot, after which the meal will end with a choco-late confection of one sort or another. The Culinary Theatre is not a comfortable place to have dinner and most meals lack any genuine continuity. But there's a lot of excitement here and a lot of remarkable cooking.
Open Tuesday to Sunday at 7 pm by appointment only. Closed on Monday. Licensed. Amex, Master Card, Visa. You must book ahead.

GRAVENHURST
See also BRACEBRIDGE.

GUELPH, Ontario   **MAP 79**
ARTISANALE CAFE
214 Woolwich Street   **$115**
(519) 821-3359

The Artisanale has recently moved to a new location in downtown Guelph. Here they have a century-old stone building with white walls and linen table-cloths. The menu is quite small, but it changes with the seasons. Typ-ically, they have a couple of appetizers and a couple of main courses. They also have a *prix-fixe* menu—four courses for the extraordinary price of 25.00. In January beef bourguignon comes, as it should, with carrots and basmati rice. Roasted chicken comes with root vegetables like turnips, carrots and sweet potatoes. There may also be rabbit on the menu and there's usually a steak. They have a big wine-list and a large number of wines from Niagara.
Open Tuesday to Saturday 11 am to 3 pm, 5 pm to 9 pm. Closed on Sunday and Monday. Licensed. Master Card, Visa. Book ahead if you can. &

GUELPH
See also MORRISTON.

GUYSBOROUGH, N.S.
DESBARRES MANOR
90 Church Street
(902) 533-2099

MAP 80

$175 ($400)

Guysborough is in a patch of unspoilt country a few miles along Highway 16 from the Trans Canada. DesBarres is an old house that will remind you of Lunenburg, with its brightly painted houses and trim green lawns. The DesBarres Manor was built in 1837 for W.F. DesBarres, who was a justice of the supreme court. It's been a restaurant for some years, serving a menu *surprise* by appointment only. There are two handsome bedrooms upstairs, and it's a good idea to ask for one when you book a table because Antigonish is 50 miles away by Highway 16 and 104. It isn't easy to say what the cooking will be like this summer and further reports are needed.

Open daily 6 pm to 7 pm by appointment only. Licensed. Master Card, Visa. You must book ahead.

HAIDA GWAII, B.C.

MAP 81

Queen Charlotte City (it's really just a village) is a mile or so east of the ferry terminal on Graham Island. There are two good places to eat there. One is the Purple Onion at 3207 Wharf Street (telephone (250) 559-4119). Leanne Vugstad says she's been making bread since she was in kindergarten, which may be why everyone seems to like it. The Purple Onion has a drab exterior, but inside it's quite artsy, with a pretty view of the harbour and very good service. It's really a deli, but it has a few tables and offers soups, salads, sandwiches and sweets. Leanne's carrot cake wins prizes and her sandwiches are all noteworthy—the turkey, the brie with raspberry, the corned beef with avocado, even the fried egg with bacon. They're open on weekdays from 8 am to 5 pm, Saturday from 9 am to 5 pm and Sunday from 9 am to 4 pm. They have no liquor but take Master Card and Visa. The Queen B at 3208 Wharf Street (telephone (250) 559-4463) is a funky place that caters to vegans and vegetarians. The menu offers such things as fish and vegetables, but little shellfish, because it's too expensive. Dana Adams changes her menu every day and makes everything in her own kitchen. She's good with such things as soups, quiches and pasta and in season she has blackberries, salmon-berries and huckleberries. Wild raspberries grow right next door. They're open Monday to Saturday from 9 am to 5 pm and take all cards. No liquor.

HAIDA GWAII   MAP 81
BRADY'S BISTRO   🖎
Sandspit Airport   **$35**
Moresby Island
(250) 637-2455

People come to Haida Gwaii to get to know the people who live there. Brady is one of them and you'll find her—she's not a man—right by the airport. She grinds her own coffee and sells it for 2.00 a cup (or two cups). She opens earlier these days (at 8 o'clock in the morning), because she finds that people don't want to wait for their coffee, or for some good company either. She makes everything herself, even the fish chowder. She makes a lot of sandwiches and does a lot of baking—bread, muffins, brownies and cinnamon buns. People speak of her coffee and muffins as the best breakfast in the world—and probably one of the cheapest.
Open daily 8 am to 2 pm. No liquor. Master Card, Visa. ♿

HAIDA GWAII   MAP 81
CHARTERS   ☆☆
1650 Delkatla   **$85**
Masset
(250) 626-3377

Mike Picher and Kaylene MacGregor resurrected the Trout House a few years ago, then moved on, as people so often do in this part of the world. But Mike is a superlative chef, so it was good to hear that he had reappeared at Charters. His menu changes often, depending

99

on what's fresh on the local market. Mike used to be at his best with meats such as lamb and duck, but at Charters he's developing a new interest in fresh seafood. He never overcooks either his halibut or his salmon, and his seafood chowder is always a delight. Diners also speak highly of his Caesar salad, which is more of a novelty in Haida Gwaii than in Toronto. The same is true of his chocolate mousse. Everything is beautifully presented and there are wines from all over the world on his short wine-list. There aren't many tables, so you should call ahead to get one.

Open Wednesday to Sunday 5 pm to 9 pm. Closed on Monday and Tuesday. Licensed. Master Card, Visa. Book ahead. &

HAIDA GWAII   MAP 81
HAIDA HOUSE
2087 Beitush Road
Tlell
(250) 557-4600

Tlell is about 30 minutes from Queen Charlotte City. Look for it half a mile along the road that turns right just before you come to the bridge across the river. (Or book a trip with B.C. Ferries and let them get you there.) The Haida House is a new 34-room lodge on seven acres of land—a beautiful building in a beautiful setting. It's the best place to stay anywhere on the islands, which are about the closest thing this country has to the Galapagos. Recently, the Gwaii Haanas National Park was named the best nature park in North America. Certainly the bird life is spectacular. The chefs prepare aboriginal dishes as well as regular Canadian fare. As for breakfast, it's a feast, offering such things as smoked-salmon omelettes, homemade jam and excellent coffee. Everything is made from scratch and the ingredients are all the real thing.

Open daily 5 pm to 7.30 pm from the beginning of May until the end of September. Licensed. Master Card, Visa. &

Nobody can buy his way into this guide and nobody can buy his way out.

HALIFAX, N.S.   **MAP 82**
BISTRO LE COQ   ☆
1584 Argyle Street   **$150**
(902) 407-4564

This is an authentic Parisian bistro. It's right across the
street from the Neptune Theatre, which makes it an ideal
place for a pre-theatre dinner. They make boudin blanc,
steak tartar, pot au feu (with an amazing broth), poulet
chasseur and french-fried potatoes fried in duck fat. This
is one of the few restaurants we know of that serves champagne by the glass. Not that you have to drink champagne—there's an expansive list of French wines that many
think the best in the city. Their crème brûlée is outstanding
and their grand-marnier soufflé is amazing.
Open Monday to Thursday noon to 10 pm, Friday noon to 1
am, Saturday 11.30 am to 1 am, Sunday 11.30 am to 10 pm.
Licensed. All cards. Book ahead if you can. ठ

HALIFAX   **MAP 82**
CHEELIN   ☆
Brewery Market   **$95**
1496 Lower Water Street
(902) 422-2252

If you're looking for Chinese Canadian food, go some-
where else. What they serve here is real Chinese food
with a bias toward the Szechuan style. The best things
on the menu are probably the twice-cooked pork, the
eggplant stuffed with ground pork, shrimps, ginger and
garlic, the tofu with garlic greens and the chilli chicken,
made with dried chicken, chilli paste, five-spice powder,
ginger and soy sauce. The last two are fairly new; the
others have been on the menu for years. But Fanny Chen
will make anything you want and make it better than almost any one else. Just ask.
Open Monday 11.30 am to 2.30 pm, Tuesday to Saturday
11.30 am to 2.30 pm, 5.30 pm to 10 pm, Sunday 5.30 pm to
10 pm. Licensed. All cards. ठ

HALIFAX

MAP 82

CHEESE CURDS GOURMET BURGERS
380 Pleasant Street   **$25**
Dartmouth
(902) 444-3446

This place is located in a small strip mall a couple of blocks from the Woodside ferry terminal. Bill Pratt is a retired Navy chef. He opened Cheese Curds early in 2012 and it was an immediate success. The concept is simple. You order a burger and then choose as many toppings from the list of 50 or more that are on offer. These include sliced tomatoes, pickles, red onions, guacamole, cilantro, banana peppers and lemon hummus. There are long lineups at the door and Pratt plans to open a second location in the Burnside Industrial Park before the end of the year.

Open Monday to Saturday 11 am to 10 pm, Sunday 11 am to 9 pm. No liquor. All cards. No reservations. &

HALIFAX

MAP 82

CHIVES   ☆☆
1537 Barrington Street   **$150**
(902) 420-9626

Craig Flinn continues to lead the eat-local movement in Halifax—along with Dennis Johnston, once of Fid. His menu is constantly changing, though several dishes carry forward from one season to the next. Dinner starts quite brilliantly with a double-baked goat-cheese soufflé, served with pickled beets, spiced walnuts, apple and buttermilk. Instead of the too-familiar smoked salmon, they offer salmon cured with spiced molasses and served with cucumber, red onions and a free-range hard-boiled egg. In season there's lobster gnocchi, which is an incredible dish. Of the main courses, the braised lamb shanks are as good as any in town, as are the sesame-crusted tuna and the sea trout with a potato cake, wilted greens and pickled beets. Finish up with the sugar-moon crème brûlée, sweet-mango chutney. In the evening there's an excellent rack of lamb and roasted duck with honey and coriander. For brunch, keep an eye out for the French toast stuffed with banana and strawberries.

Open Tuesday to Friday 11.30 am to 3 pm, 5 pm to 8 pm, Saturday 10.30 am to 2.30 pm, 5 pm to 9 pm, Sunday 10.30 am to 2.30 pm, 5 pm to 8 pm. Closed on Monday. Licensed. All cards. &

HALIFAX   MAP 82
DA MAURIZIO   ☆
Brewery Market   **$185**
1496 Lower Water Street
(902) 423-0859

Last year we talked about the service at Da Maurizio. This year we want to talk about the food. At its best, the cooking is brilliant. The squid, for instance, are spiked with garlic and tomatoes, and the result is amazing. There are other good things too, of course, like the zucchini stuffed with ricotta, lemon and basil, the carpaccio of lamb, the mussels sautéed with onions, garlic and white wine and, of course, the foie gras with honey, peaches and ginger. There's a nice scallop of veal to follow, as well as tenderloin of pork, pan-seared Atlantic halibut and, best of all, rack of lamb, tender and lean and naked on the plate. The sweets are indifferent, but the wine-list has improved. For the very rich there's now a sassicaia, a solaia and a tignanello, all of them well into three figures. For the rest of us, there's a very good chianti riserva from Grignano for 50.00.

Open Monday to Saturday 5.30 pm to 10 pm. Closed on Sunday. Licensed. All cards. Book ahead if you can. &

HALIFAX   MAP 82
MODA   ☆
1518 Dresden Row   **$170**
(902) 405-3480

Matthew Pridham is in charge here and he says his plan

is to use local suppliers to make global cuisine. We think this means that he aims to use local produce to prepare dishes from all over, but we can't be sure. If you come here, it's probably a good idea to order the four-course tasting menu for 60.00. If, however, you prefer to order à la carte, there's usually a variety of local seafood (lobster, scallops and salmon), snails from France, risottos and pastas from Italy and curries from India. The kitchen does a surprisingly good job with this rather implausible menu. Their fishcakes and their beef tenderloin are equally accomplished. Lunch, of course, is a different story. The noon-hour menu features burgers and risottos (mushrooms stuffed with asiago cheese). Diners tell us that they can't recommend Moda highly enough.

Open Monday to Friday 11.30 am to 2.30 pm, 5 pm to 10 pm (later on Friday), Saturday 5 pm to 11 pm. Closed on Sunday. Licensed. All cards.

HALIFAX　　　　　　　　　　　　　　**MAP 82**
MORRIS EAST　　　　　　　　　　　　　　☆
5212 Morris Street　　　　　　　　　　　**$80**
(902) 444-7663

Jennie Dobbs is still making her wonderful wood-fired pizzas. Her oven was made in Naples and is fueled by applewood from the Annapolis Valley. The best of the pizzas, we think, are the lamb with apricots and the salmon with peaches. You can also have a wood-fired sandwich or even a charcuterie board. Korean tacos come with crisp pork belly, pickled garlic and kimchee. If you bring your own bottle the corkage is only 10.00.

Open Tuesday to Friday 11.30 am to 2.30 pm, 5 pm to 10 pm, Saturday 10 am to 2.30 pm (brunch), 5 pm to 9 pm, Sunday 10 am to 2.30 pm (brunch). Closed on Monday. Licensed. All cards. No reservations. &

If you wish to improve the guide send us information about restaurants we have missed. Our mailing address is Oberon Press, 145 Spruce Street: Suite 205, Ottawa, Ontario K1R 6P1.

HALIFAX

STORIES
The Halliburton Hotel
5184 Morris Street
(902) 444-4400

MAP 82

☆☆

$150

Stories is as good as anything in Halifax, maybe better. Inside, it's small and elegant. The menu is distinguished, offering such things as house-made charcuterie, sea scallops wrapped in rice paper, carpaccio of bison (a magnificent dish), crab-cakes made with Queen crab, big-eye tuna and salmon from the Faroe Islands. The cooking is accomplished, but you don't need to bother looking through the wine-list, because they offer the wonderful Nova 7 from Benjamin Bridge, by far the best wine ever raised in Nova Scotia and still something of a rarity in restaurants. A bottle of Benjamin Bridge—it costs only 51.00—makes any meal a memorable occasion and is a must-buy.

Open daily in summer 5 pm to 9 pm. Closed on Monday in winter. Licensed. Amex, Master Card, Visa. Book ahead if you can.

HALIFAX

TAREK'S
3045 Robie Street
(902) 454-8723

MAP 82

☞

$75

A local newspaper says that Tarek has the best Middle Eastern cooking in Halifax. We agree. It's hard to believe that healthy food can taste this good. The prices have risen a little over the years, but Tarek's is still a great bargain. It's in an out-of-the-way location in the North End and they take no reservations—everyone just lines up at the door. Tarek himself is a Syrian who came to Canada as a sailor when he was nineteen years old. He learned to cook in various hotel kitchens in Vancouver and Toronto before settling in Halifax, where he opened Tarek's in 2000. He's succeeded because he always uses the best of fresh local produce. This is a great place for vegetarians. Tarek's falafel is usually thought to be the best in the city.

His squid are all marinated and barbecued, never deep fried. He cooks chicken Mediterranean-style or with ochre, tomato sauce and coriander, and he has some fine Middle Eastern salads. His juice-bar serves a variety of freshly-squeezed juices, among them grapefruit, orange, tomato, apple and carrot.

Open Monday to Saturday 11.30 am to 7.30 pm. Closed on Sunday. No liquor, no cards. No reservations. &

HALIFAX   MAP 82
2 DOORS DOWN
1533 Barrington Street   **$95**
(902) 422-4224

Craig Flynn has opened a new restaurant and already it's become very fashionable. Since it's two doors down the street from Chives, he's named it 2 Doors Down. It's broadly similar to Chives, but it's more casual (and a lot noisier). Meals start well with a barbecued pork-belly slider on a brioche or a chicken poutine with sweet peas and sage, but if you don't want a slider or a poutine, ask for tacos with panko-crusted line-caught halibut. Kung fu chicken is served as a main course with sweet and sour kimchi, bok choy and soba noodles, and we like it better than the smoked pork chop with macaroni and cheese and pumpkin chutney. Our favourite sweet is Flynn's mother's recipe for cheesecake in a Mason Jar. Others may prefer the warm gingerbread with English toffee and chantilly cream.

Open Monday to Friday 11 am to 10 pm, Saturday and Sunday 10 am to 2 pm (brunch), 5 pm to 10 pm. Licensed. All cards. No reservations. Book ahead if you can.

HALIFAX
See also CHESTER, TANTALLON.

Where an entry is printed in italics this indicates that the restaurant has been listed only because it serves the best food in its area or because it hasn't yet been adequately tested.

HAMILTON, Ontario   **MAP 83**
LA CANTINA
60 Walnut Street S   **$125/$75**
(905) 521-8989

The cooking at Vicolo 54, the formal dining-room at La Cantina, has improved this year. The best dish on the menu is, however, still the risotto of porcini and crimini mushrooms. This is a rich but wonderful dish and it's full of flavour. They also have an excellent chicken saltimbocca stuffed with goat-cheese and spinach, as well as a couple of other memorable dishes. One is the grilled French-cut veal chop with caramelized onions, the other the ostrich drizzled with raspberry vincotto. Everybody likes the focaccia and with good reason. La Spiga has a wood-burning pizza oven, but there have been changes in personnel lately that make the pizzas less consistent than they used to be. They still offer nineteen varieties, some with too much oil, some with too little. The margherita pizza, however, is always good, and that's the thing to order. There's a well stocked wine-cellar and several wines by the glass.
Open Tuesday to Thursday 11.30 am to 2.30 pm, 4 pm to 10 pm, Friday 11.30 am to 2.30 pm, 4 pm to 11 pm, Saturday 4 pm to 11 pm. Closed on Sunday and Monday. Licensed. Amex, Master Card, Visa.

HAMILTON   **MAP 83**
EARTH-TO-TABLE BREAD BAR
258 Locke Street S   **$85**
(905) 522-2999

The Bread Bar has developed quite a following in Hamilton. It's an artisanal bakery by day and a restaurant for lunch and dinner. They have some interesting salads as well as fried bread with burrata cheese, olive tapenade and sundried tomatoes. Then there are beef burgers with mushrooms and umami sauce or with quinoa and guacamole. The big attraction, however, is the pizzas. There are a dozen of them and they're all good. The best, we think, is the Popeye, which comes with spinach, ricotta cheese and lemon zest. The lemon zest and ricotta combine to send this one over the top. Our favourite sweet is the milk-chocolate profiterole with salted caramel and dark chocolate. The spiked milkshakes are a pleasant surprise. Try the Creamsicle with triple-sec.

Open Monday to Friday 11.30 am to 4.30 pm, 5 pm to 10 pm, Saturday and Sunday 8 am to 4.30 pm, 5 pm to 10 pm. Licensed. Master Card, Visa. &

HAMILTON
See also ANCASTER, BURLINGTON, DUNDAS.

HEDLEY, B.C. (MAP 161)
THE HITCHING POST
916 Scott Avenue **$60**
(250) 292-8413

Hedley is long past its glory days. The Hitching Post was built in 1903, at a time when Hedley was expected to become the centre of the Simulkameen, then one of the richest mining centres in the province. The building ran downhill for most of the century until 1995, when a businessman and his wife (an artist) decided to restore it. A few years later, in 2004, a local chef, Wilson Wiley, bought it and created a modestly-priced menu of homemade dishes to be sold at attractive prices. In the years since then, the Hitching Post has become one of the few useful stops on the Crow's Nest Highway. It has friendly service and excellent coffee. Their eight-ounce New York steak is topped with a homemade peppercorn-and-brandy sauce and it's beautifully tender. The meal starts well with a Caesar salad, grilled calamari or mussels from Prince Edward Island. (If you choose the soup instead, it'll cost you all of 2.95.) Most of the wines are local and they're all priced to sell.

Open daily 11 am to 8 pm from early June until late October, Wednesday to Sunday 11 am to 8 pm from late October until early June. Closed on Monday and Tuesday in winter. Licensed. Master Card, Visa.

HOPE, B.C.   MAP 85
OWL STREET CAFE   ☞
19855 Owl Street   **$55**
(604) 869-3181

The Owl Street Cafe has a big street number, but in fact it's no distance at all from Exit 168 on the Trans Canada Highway. Look for an A-frame built of pine that came from trees killed by pine beetles in Manning Park. (The tables inside are made of hunks of other dead pine trees.) Graeme and Sonia Blair are a friendly couple who cook everything from scratch, making full use of fresh local produce. There's an all-day breakfast for you to eat while you wait for your laundry to get washed in one of the coin-operated washing-machines. That means bacon and eggs, a good omelette or organic oatmeal porridge with fresh fruit on top. Lunch means one of several soups and a string of sandwiches and chillies. There's a good chicken club, but the smoked-meat sandwich is even better.
Open Tuesday to Saturday 8.30 pm to 4 pm. Closed on Sunday and Monday. Licensed. Master Card, Visa. ♿

ILE D'ORLEANS, Quebec   (MAP 158)
LE CANARD HUPPE   ☆
2198 chemin Royal   **$175**
Saint-Laurent
(418) 828-2292

It's easy to forget that the Ile d'Orléans is only twenty minutes from the heart of Quebec City—it feels a world away. This is a small *hôtel champètre*, run by Philip Rae. He has a regional menu that every year makes more of duck and foie gras. On the table d'hôte, for instance, the meal starts with foie gras with apple or smoked breast of duck en croûte. Then come breast of duck with orange and curried chutney or confit of duck with tarragon in a strawberry vinaigrette. The wine-list is long and ambitious, but offers nothing from either the Niagara Region or Prince Edward County in Ontario.
Open daily 6 pm to 10 pm from late May until the middle of

October. Licensed. Master Card, Visa.

ILE D'ORLEANS (MAP 158)
FERME AU GOUT D'AUTREFOIS ☆☆
4311 chemin Royal **$100**
Sainte-Famille
(418) 829-9888

Jacques Legros, who with his partner, Lise Marcotte, runs
this place, was once a candidate for the Green Party, and
he and Lise spent years developing their organic garden
and poultry farm, where they produce foie gras without
force-feeding their ducks and geese. They grow greens
and vegetables of all sorts and maintain breeding quarters
where ducks, geese and wild turkeys are raised in the
open air on an all-natural diet. They cook well too and
everything is full of flavour. Dinner costs 35.00 for three
courses, 45.00 for four and 125.00 for twelve. All their
dinners feature rillettes of duck and goose, breast of
pheasant, guinea-fowl and wild turkey.
*Open daily by appointment only. Bring your own bottle. Master
Card, Visa. You must book ahead.*

ILES DE LA MADELEINE, Quebec
See MAGDALEN ISLANDS.

INVERMERE, B.C. MAP 87
BIRCHWOOD
722 13 Street **$150**
(250) 342-0606

Marc LeBlanc made his name at the Earl Grey Lodge in
Panorama and later at the Eagle Ranch at Saliken on the
outskirts of Invermere. Now he's moved downtown,
where he's cooking as well as ever, if not better. There's
marinated squid to start with and ravioli with figs. Main
dishes (except the candied salmon) are on the whole less
successful, but there's usually Alaska black cod with a
crust of pumpkinseeds and pork chops with sour cherries
Beef tenderloin is always on the menu. The vegetables

are all organic and the ice-cream sandwiches make an exciting finish. The à la carte is quite expensive, but early in the week there's an attractive table d'hôte at a reasonable price. There aren't many wines by the glass and the large list of bottled wines is quite expensive.

Open Monday to Saturday 5 pm to 10 pm. Closed on Sunday. Licensed. Amex, Master Card, Visa. Book ahead.

INVERMERE
See also RADIUM HOT SPRINGS.

IQALUIT, Nunavut	**MAP 88**
THE GALLERY	
Frobisher Inn	**$190**
(867) 979-2222	

The Gallery remains the best place to eat in Iqaluit, in spite of the departure of Rick Cole. It gets its name from the wall of prints in the dining-room, which come from the Pangnirtung Print Collection. Prices are pretty high, though that's probably true of almost everything in Iqaluit. But you can count on fresh beef and lamb and fresh greens and vegetables whatever the weather is like outside, because Iqaluit is on the great circle route between Europe and the West Coast. Arctic char, here called maple char, is one of their best dishes. There's always a lot of game. Elk osso buco is served with elderberry juice; musk-ox comes in from Cambridge Bay and appears with caribou, duck confit and game sausage in a dish they call Arctic cassoulet. If you can't afford 50.00 for your main course alone, ask for the pizza menu. There's a good wine-list and it's less expensive than you'd expect. The service is sometimes good, sometimes not.

Open daily 11 am to 2 pm, 5 pm to 9 pm. Licensed. All cards. Book ahead. &

The price rating shown opposite the headline of each entry indicates the average cost of dinner for two with a modest wine, tax and tip. The cost of dinner, bed and breakfast (if available) is shown in parentheses.

111

IVY LEA, Ontario (MAP 93)
THE IVY
61 Shipman's Lane **$160**
Lansdowne
(613) 659-2486

The Ivy used to be known as the Captain's Table, and before that the Ivy Lea Inn, but patrons from those days will
find the place much changed. The upstairs dining-room
is large and airy and has a fine view of the river. Robert
Gobbo is still the chef, but nowadays he's catering to a
more sophisticated (and wealthier) clientele. Gobbo likes
to call his menu locally-inspired world cuisine. Dinner
might start with lobster salad or shrimp and grits with
brandy and cream. The main dishes are more traditional
than they used to be, and you're now quite likely to be
offered something like seared scallops with twice-baked
potatoes, veal chops with chimichurri, pan-seared rainbow trout or oven-roasted breast of chicken. Sticky-
toffee pudding is the best of the sweets. The wine-list is
expensive and wines by the glass start at 9.00. Better to
ask for a pint of draft. Downstairs there's an informal
bistro offering pizzas and sandwiches. They have a good
lobster roll, served with homemade Yukon Gold fries.
Open daily 5.30 pm to 9 pm from Victoria Day until Labour
Day, Friday and Saturday 5.30 pm to 9 pm from Labour Day
until Victoria Day. Closed Sunday to Thursday in winter. Li-
censed. All cards.

JASPER, Alberta MAP 90
KIMCHI
407 Patricia Street **$75**
(780) 852-5022

Monica An has what they used to call a lot of personality,
and her employees are just as friendly and personable as
she is. That seems to be enough for most visitors. Some
people (most of them new to this part of the world) find
the prices high, but they're not—see above. Monica An

is proud of her seafood, especially her sautéed squid. Travellers will tell you not to miss the beef short-ribs on a sizzling plate or the deep-fried dumplings. The kimchi (Korean pickles) are certainly a treat. The food here is lighter than in most Korean restaurants, which may be why some people find the helpings small. To us they seem large, especially if you drink Korean beer with your meal.

Open daily 11 am to 10 pm. Licensed. Master Card, Visa. &

JASPER **MAP 90**
TEKARRA ☆☆
Highway 93 S **$190**
(780) 852-4624

Tekarra opened in 1952, a mile south of central Jasper, on what is now called Hazel Avenue. It's a beautiful setting and you should climb the cliff for the view before you leave. But people became aware of the kitchen only after the arrival of David George Husereau. Husereau had put in 25 years elsewhere before he returned to Jasper, and he still travels the world in search of new recipes. Everything he serves is made in the kitchen—the smoking, the curing, the baking. We have particularly liked the spiny-lobster roll, the venison *sous-vide* that comes with a parsnip purée and Alberta rosehip jus, the macadamia-crusted lamb and the crisp confit of duck. Their most popular sweet is now probably the molten-chocolate cake. The wines are all cheap, even the Mission Hill reserve chardonnay and the J. Lohr Seven Oaks cabernet sauvignon. Tekarra doesn't offer lunch, but their breakfast buffet is famous.

Open daily 8 am to 11 am, 5.30 pm to 10 pm from 9 May until 5 October. Licensed. All cards. &

This is a guide to Canadian restaurants from coast to coast—the first ever published and the only one of its kind on the market today. We accept no advertisements. Nobody can buy his way into this guide and nobody can buy his way out.

KAMLOOPS, B.C.

ACCOLADES
Thompson Rivers University
900 McGill Road
(250) 828-5354

MAP 91
☆☆
$135

Accolades offers a five-course tasting menu four nights a week for 45.00. This is a very good buy, considering that the cooking here is about the best in Kamloops. The first course is an Italian chutney seldom seen in Canada. It's made of candied fruit with hot mustard. Soup follows, or pork belly with fennel and apple chutney. Next come Pacific spot prawns topped with saffron foam, or perhaps Qualicum Bay scallops on a bed of lentils in a horseradish vinaigrette. The best main course is the venison from Sidney Island with port, blueberries and caraway. It's cooked *sous-vide* and then lightly pan-seared. Sometimes there's also farm-raised lamb from Diamond Creek and breast of duck from the Fraser Valley. The sweets are served from a cart and they're all made in house, even the lemon tart and the chocolate ganache.

Open Tuesday and Wednesday 6 pm to 7.30 pm, Thursday and Friday 11.30 am to 12.45 pm, 6 pm to 7.30 pm. Closed Saturday to Monday. Licensed. Master Card, Visa. You must book ahead.

KELOWNA, B.C.

OLD VINES
Quail's Gate Winery
3303 Boucherie Road
(800) 420-9463

MAP 92
☆☆
$160

Roger Sleiman and Andrea Callan create seasonal menus based on local produce supplied by neighbouring farmers. Their noon-hour menu is surprisingly elaborate, featuring such things as albacore tuna with radicchio, celeriac and cilantro and duck confit with quinoa, cabbage and mirin. In the evening they do a surprisingly good job with line-caught sablefish and a vegetarian treatment of goat-cheese soufflé. For sweet they offer a sticky-toffee pudding in a brown-butter purée, as well as some marvellous artisanal cheeses, each paired with a wine from the Quail's Gate vineyard. Their Optima icewine makes a perfect companion for any of them.

Open Monday to Saturday 11.30 am to 2.30 pm, 5 pm to 9 pm, Sunday 10.30 am to 2.30 pm (brunch), 5 pm to 9 pm. Licensed. Amex, Master Card, Visa. &

KELOWNA   MAP 92
RAUDZ   ☆
1560 Water Street   **$145**
(250) 868-8805

Rodney Butters came here from the Wickaninnish Inn in Tofino, where he first made his name as a chef. His restaurant in Kelowna is less formal, but equally good, except that they take no reservations. (Travellers have been known to wait for three hours in season.) The menu is fairly priced, but the wine-list is certainly not. Dinner begins with squid stuffed with tapenade and goes on to braised and pan-seared lamb, served with smoked lentils and house-made gnocchi—though you'll do equally well with the oat-crusted Arctic char or the scaloppine of wild boar with a potato-and-apple torte. There's comfort food too, including, meat-loaf, fish and chips and steak. At Raudz they're all bakers and their flourless-chocolate cake is out of this world. But there are no really good buys on the wine-list.

Open daily 5 pm to 10 pm (later on weekends). Licensed. Amex, Master Card, Visa. No reservations. &

KELOWNA   MAP 92
THE TERRACE   ☆☆
Mission Hill Winery   **$160**
1730 Mission Hill Road
(250) 768-6467

Matt Batey makes sure that the food here at the Terrace is every bit as good as the view. The ingredients are mostly local, though some come from as far away as Salt

Spring Island or Vancouver Island. Visitors find themselves starting lunch with a tart of duck prosciutto or perhaps with a simple green salad made with heritage tomatoes and artisanal cheese. They may then move on to braised venison with figs or pan-seared sablefish. Or they may choose to sample dishes from Batey's *cuisine de terroir*. In the evening the meal starts with a torchon of foie gras with Martin's Lane pears, Sloping Hills pork belly or smoked Pacific tuna with preserved apple and a shiso lemon confit. The best of the main courses, we think, is the bison tenderloin with creamed cabbage and cranberry buckwheat. After that we usually ask for the glazed lemon tart.

Open daily 11 am to 3 pm, 5.30 pm to 8.45 pm from mid-May until mid-September. Licensed. Amex, Master Card, Visa. &

KELOWNA   **MAP 92**
THE WATERFRONT   ☆
1180 Sunset Drive   **$145**
(250) 979-1222

The Waterfront in Kelowna is one of our favourite restaurants. Small, chic and very well served, it has four stainless-steel half-round tables facing an open kitchen. There's a big wine-list and a number of good open wines, among them the Noble Blend from Joie Farm and the syrah from Church and State. The wonderful braised-beef short-ribs are still off the menu, so ask instead for the Quadra Island scallops or the milkfed veal cheeks. It's best to start with the masala squid and end with a cup or two of the wonderful espresso.

Open daily 5 pm to 10 pm (later on weekends). Licensed. Amex, Master Card, Visa. Book ahead. &

KELOWNA
See also OKANAGAN CENTRE, OLIVER.

KINGSTON. Ontario   *MAP 93*

There are several restaurants in Kingston, in addition to those

116

listed in full below, that you should know about. *Woodenheads* at 192 Ontario Street (telephone (613) 549-1812) is busy and noisy, but it serves the best thin-crust pizzas in town. You have the run of about three dozen different varieties, or you can make up your own from a big list of ingredients. They also serve tapas and paninis and such main dishes as breast of chicken and sockeye salmon. There's a big wine-list with more than twenty wines by the glass and four draft beers. A couple of blocks away at 369 King Street E (telephone (613) 767-2558) is the *Red House*, which stands out among the city's pub-style restaurants for its dedication to doing things right. They start butchering their own meat every morning at 7, and everything on the small menu is made from scratch, whether it's polenta with gorgonzola, crispy gnocchi with house fennel sausage, or cumin pork tacos with smoked corn salsa. The most interesting dish is often the blackboard special, which if you're lucky may be something like lemon-pepper chicken with apple squash spring rolls, brown sugar and chili. *Windmills* at 184 Princess Street (telephone (613) 544-3948) offers an eclectic menu that includes Thai and Cajun dishes as well as a number of burgers and stir-fries. Windmills is a good place for breakfast or a weekend brunch, when you can have an omelette with Monterey Jack cheese. At lunch there are salads and sandwiches; in the evening they add lamb osso buco with hoisin sauce and Louisiana gumbo with chorizo and shrimps. All the sweets are made in house and there's a wide array of cakes and cheesecakes. *Tango Nuevo* at 331 King Street E (telephone (613) 548-3778), having appeared in this guide for many years, closed last year. Later in the year it was bought by a former employee, who has put together a similar menu, featuring tapas, salads, sandwiches and sweets, plus a couple of dozen open wines and a large number of craft beers. All four restaurants are open all day every day, have a licence and take most cards.

KINGSTON   **MAP 93**
AQUATERRA BY CLARK   ☆
Delta Kingston Hotel   **$135**
1 Johnson Street
(613) 549-6243

Clark Day has been a major figure on the restaurant scene

in Kingston for a long time. When he was retained to design a restaurant in the Radisson Hotel, he transformed both the space he was given and the menu. Most people thought he would eventually move on to other interests, but he's chosen to stay here on Johnson Street and AquaTerra is still about as good as it gets in Kingston. Day is interested in both fish and meat—hence the same of his restaurant. So you get to choose between terrine de foie gras and a fricassee of snails, between rack of lamb (or lamb shanks) and a seafood risotto. There's also a *prix-fixe* menu offered at the remarkable price of 30.00 a head. There are four appetizers and four main dishes—rabbit terrine, perhaps, and pork belly (or pork tenderloin), followed by a spicy fruit tart. Lunch is, of course, a simpler meal. There's a three-course *prix-fixe* at noon that costs just 17.00. Clark is passionate about wine and his wine-list, which is the best in Kingston, is well chosen and well-priced. Wines by the glass start at 3.35 for three ounces; bottles start at 28.00.

Open Monday to Saturday 11 am to 11 pm, Sunday 11 am to 10 pm. Licensed. All cards. &

KINGSTON   **MAP 93**
CASA DOMENICO
35 Brock Street   **$150**
(613) 542-0870

If you want something more than a pizza, try the Casa Domenico. But don't come here looking for new ideas. The cuisine here is traditional Italian. You can begin with a salad, say, or with seared scallops with sweet potato, pine-nuts, currants and arugula—or perhaps with shrimps with garlic and capers. The main courses are more conventional—steak, lamb chops or breast of chicken with sautéed spinach and caramelized potatoes and onions. Sweets are familiar too, but the coccinella (hazelnut brownie with caramel ice cream) is well worth the money. There's a useful list of Italian wines, most of them modestly priced. The service is warm and friendly.

Open Monday to Thursday 11 am to 10.30 pm, Friday 11.30

am to 11.30 pm, Saturday noon to 11.30 pm, Sunday noon to 10 pm. Licensed. All cards.

KINGSTON   MAP 93
CHEZ PIGGY   ☆
68 (rear) Princess Street   **$135**
(613) 549-7673

Chez Piggy has been loved by Kingston people for nearly 40 years. It was renovated this year, but it still has the same owners and many of the same staff. The cooking is basically French with a noticeable Italian accent, as well as a few Asian words. Old favourites reappear year after year. We like to start our meal with a stilton pâté or perhaps with shrimps brought to the table in the pan with garlic and spices. Our favourite main dishes are the breast of chicken stuffed with truffles, the confit of duck with white beans and roasted vegetables and the lamb shank with orange gremolata. There's also a three-course table d'hôte for only 35.00. They have some good beers on tap and a well-chosen list of wines.

Open Monday to Saturday 11.30 am to midnight, Sunday 10 am to midnight. Licensed. All cards. ♿

KINGSTON   MAP 93
CHIEN NOIR
69 Brock Street   **$140**
(613) 549-5635

Chien Noir looks and feels like a Parisian bistro. In the evening you start with a small plate of fried smelts, perhaps, or smoked ribs of bison with green cabbage. Next comes coq au vin, mussels with fries and duck confit with lentils. Sweets are all made in-house, but they're not very exciting. Lunch offers all the same dishes, as well as omelettes and sandwiches. Most of the wines come from France, though there are a few from Prince Edward County as well. They also have ten beers on draft, two of them brewed in Quebec and sold only in this restaurant.

Open Monday to Friday 11.30 am to 2.30 pm, 5 pm to 11 pm,
Saturday and Sunday 11 am to 2.30 pm (brunch), 5 pm to 11
pm. Licensed. All cards. Book ahead if you can.

KINGSTON   **MAP 93**
THE CURRY ORIGINAL   🖎▯
253A Ontario Street   **$70**
(613) 531-9376

The Curry Original is still about the best Indian (or
Bangladeshi) restaurant in Kingston, or so we think. The
place was opened by Ali and Weais Afzal more than
twenty years ago and they're still in charge of the front
of the house. They have all the traditional dishes—curries, kormas, vindaloos, dhansaks, saags, bhoonas and
tandooris. Everything is fresh and carefully prepared, but,
sad to say, the menu almost never changes. It's best to
start with an onion bhaji, a samosa or daal, then go on to
tandoori chicken (cooked in a traditional clay oven),
chicken tikka, a korma, a vindaloo or dhansak, a bhoona
or a biryani. They also offer a number of special dishes
like kashmiri chicken, with peanuts, sultanas, coconut
and homemade yogurt. Then try the barfi, which is
homemade cottage cheese with coconut and pistachio
nuts. On weekdays they offer a string of lunch dishes, all
priced at less than 10.00. The wine-list majors in wines
from Prince Edward County and draft beers from India.
Open Tuesday to Saturday 11.30 am to 2 pm, 5 pm to 9.30 pm,
Sunday 5 pm to 9.30 pm. Closed on Monday. Licensed. All
cards. ♿

KINGSTON   **MAP 93**
DAYS ON FRONT
730 Front Road   **$135**
(613) 766-9000

Matthew Day is the son of the well-known restaurateur,
Clark Day. They ran AquaTerra together for several
years, but this year Matthew has opened his own restaurant. Despite the location, close to the airport and a cou-

ple of miles from downtown Kingston, business is booming. The dinner menu starts with what they call fried items (duck wings and shrimp tempura), followed by small plates (pork-belly nachos and seared scallops in a purée of leeks) and large plates. There are ten of these—pan-seared halibut, lamb-shank stew and steak frites. There's only one sweet of interest and that's the bread pudding with bananas. Lunch features some small plates from the evening menu, as well as a variety of sandwiches. The wine-list is large and varied, and you can bring your own bottle if you pay a corkage fee of 15.00. *Open Monday to Thursday 11.30 am to 10 pm, Friday and Saturday 11.30 am to midnight. Closed on Sunday. Licensed. All cards.* ♿

KINGSTON   **MAP 93**
PAN CHANCHO
44 Princess Street   **$95**
(613) 544-7790

Zal Yanovsky opened Pan Chancho to supply Chez Piggy (see above) with bread and pastries when there was nothing else of comparable quality in town. Nowadays it's really an upscale bakery and deli with a café at the rear. The café is open every day for breakfast and lunch, but not, except on special occasions, for dinner. Croissants and cakes, soups, charcuterie and cheeses are always available in the deli. In the café at breakfast there's a variety of dishes, some traditional, some not. We particularly like the sweet-potato hash, which comes with mushrooms, spinach and poached eggs. The lunch menu changes often, but there are always a couple of first-class soups, a lamb pita spiced with cumin, a venison burger with bacon, dried cherries, red cabbage and parsnip chips and a poutine with pork perky and crisp corn fritters. The meal ends with cheese or one of the sweets from the deli. Pan Chancho has a licence and maintains a useful wine-list and several draft beers.
Open daily 7 am to 4 pm. Licensed. All cards. ♿

KINGSTON
See also IVY LEA.

KINGSVILLE, Ontario *(MAP 218)*
MATTAWAS STATION
169 Lansdowne Avenue **$110**
(519) 733-2459

If you're looking for the Jack Miner bird sanctuary or Point Pelee National Park, you'll be happy to find this place, which is in an old railway station. The cooking is Italian and it's pretty good, though admittedly not fancy. They're at their best with pasta. Last year was a good year for tomatoes, and their tomato dishes were all outstanding. Diners have spoken highly also of the chicken al parmigiano and the veal marsala. They're open Tuesday to Saturday from 11 am to 9 pm and closed on Sunday and Monday. They have a licence and take all cards.

KIPLING, Saskatchewan **MAP 95**
PAPERCLIP COTTAGE
503 Main Street **$40**
(306) 736-2182

Kyle MacDonald of Montreal traded one big red paperclip for this house and then turned it into a delicatessen and bakery. All the meats are cooked on site, the cheesecakes are made from scratch and so are the cinnamon buns. There are fresh-fruit pies and home-style sandwiches on home-baked bread. On Thursday and Friday you can have supper between 5 o'clock and 7.30. You pay only about 15.00 for a soup or a salad, roast beef and Yorkshire pudding, roast pork, turkey or poached haddock, sweet and coffee. There's always a hot dish at noon and on Sunday they do a real brunch. You'll find Kipling about 90 minutes from Regina on Highway 48.
Open Monday to Wednesday 5.30 am to 4 pm, Thursday and Friday 5.30 am to 4 pm, 5 pm to 7.30 pm, Sunday 9 am to 2 pm. Closed on Saturday. No liquor. Master Card, Visa.

Nobody but nobody can buy his way into this guide.

KITCHENER, Ontario   **MAP 96**
MARISOL   ☆☆
30 Ontario Street S   **$160**
(519) 954-5336

Marisol is new to Kitchener, and it's not easy to find. Look for a corrugated-iron façade, behind which the chef, Jeff Ward, prepares seafood better than anyone else in town. Notice the understated sweetness that contrasts with the rich, romantic Moroccan spices of the potato tagine. Sea-bream is sometimes offered as a daily special, stuffed with lemon and green herbs and served whole, bone in, skin on, head in place. Pasta usually comes with the fish and it's always cooked *al dente*. We generally ask for the seafood, but they also have an excellent rack of lamb that comes with red pepper and ricotta cheese. They have a fine wine-list and a number of craft beers.
Open Monday to Wednesday 5 pm to 9 pm, Thursday and Friday 11.30 am to 11 pm, Saturday 5 pm to 11 pm. Closed on Sunday. Licensed. All cards.

KITCHENER   **MAP 96**
VERSES   ☆☆
182 Victoria Street N   **$185**
(519) 744-0144

Verses opened about a dozen years ago in an abandoned church. You have dinner in the nave or, if you prefer, in the sanctuary. Nobody tucking into their rack of lamb seems to feel uncomfortable with this arrangement, but, uncomfortable or not, the food isn't quite what it used to be. Not that the cooking has no virtues. The foie gras with pickled rhubarb is a lively dish and so are the seared scallops with fennel and anise. The beef tenderloin is well served with wasabi and Yukon Gold potatoes; the pork tenderloin from Willow Grove is dry-rubbed and comes with an apple salad, which is a nice touch. The cannelloni is made from elk and the fish of the day may be something like tooth-fish. The lamb is imported from Alberta and the last bottle of Organized Crime recently sold for more than 90.00. But the kitchen is relying more and more on the singularity of its menu and less and less on the quality of its cooking. Prices are as high as ever, but the chardonnays and traminers are less expensive than the pinot noirs and cabernet sauvignons. Keep an eye out for the Gemtree Moonstone traminer, which cost only 55.00 a bottle last winter.

Open Tuesday to Friday 11.30 am to 2.30 pm, 5 pm to 9.30 pm, Saturday 5 pm to 9.30 pm. Closed on Sunday and Monday. Licensed. All cards. No smoking. Free parking.

KITCHENER
See also WATERLOO.

LA HAVE, N.S. (MAP 104)
LA HAVE BAKERY
3421 Highway 331 **$25**
(902) 688-2908

The La Have Bakery exudes character and charm. It operates in a ship's outfitters building and they bake and sell the best oatcakes in the province, as well as traditional date squares, Nanaimo bars and Queen Elizabeth cakes. They also sell several kinds of bread, among them potato bread Irish-style and milk-and-honey bread. This year they have a new cappuccino machine that makes nothing but double shots of cappuccino at a time. At noon they serve paninis, pulled-pork sandwiches, falafel burgers, smoked-salmon bagels, lobster rolls and a variety of pizzas. They have a wonderful brunch on Sunday and during the off-season serve themed dinners every-second Thursday evening.

Open daily 8.30 am to 6.30 pm (shorter hours in winter). No liquor. Master Card, Visa.

This is a guide to Canadian restaurants from coast to coast—the first ever published and the only one of its kind on the market today. Every restaurant in the guide has been personally tested. Our reporters are not allowed to identify themselves or to accept free meals.

LAKE LOUISE, Alberta   MAP 98
THE POST HOTEL   ☆☆☆
200 Pipestone Road   **$300 ($650)**
(800) 661-1586

If you come here for the view of Lake Louise, take a room at the Fairmont, but make sure to eat at the Post on Pipestone Road. The Post was one of the first Relais & Chateaux in Canada and it's one of the very few remaining mountain lodges built of the original rough-hewn logs, complete with a wood-burning fireplace in every room. The wine-cellar has 25,000 bottles, and the Post Hotel is the winner of one of the *Wine Spectator's* grand awards, only four of which have ever been won in Canada. George and André Schwartz bought the place in 1978, when it was little more than a ruin. Over the years the dining-room has been restored, the wine-cellar re-stocked and a fabulous new menu created. There's now a six-course table d'hôte for 105.00 a head, but if you prefer you can order from the à la carte, where they have such delicacies as carpaccio of caribou with lime mayonnaise, duck consommé with foie gras dumplings, grilled fillet of wild red spring salmon on a bed of asparagus and morels and a fillet of ranch-fed bison with herb butter. They have the largest collection of burgundies in the country and a selection of old barolos and super-Tuscans that beggars belief.
Open daily 11.30 am to 2 pm, 5 pm to 9.30 pm. Licensed. All cards. Book ahead. ♿

LAKE LOUISE
See also FIELD.

LANIGAN, Saskatchewan   MAP 99
JAN'S STEAK HOUSE   ☜🗏
17 Hoover Street   **$75**
(306) 365-4366

Jan still misses her career on Broadway, but she came back to Lanigan because she missed her family more. Her father died recently at 101. Her mother is 93 and worked in the restaurant well into her eighties. Jan still does all the baking herself, and makes 60 different kinds of highball. Her salad bar is as good as any on the Prairies. Her beef is all custom cut. She sells a lot of Black Forest ham with black currants and a lot of roast pork with orange sauce. In October she celebrates Oktoberfest with a set dinner of smoked chops with bratwurst, warm German-style potato salad, red cabbage with apples, pumpernickel bread and chocolate cake. St. Patrick's Day in March brings Irish soda bread and corned beef with cabbage. Since a flood seeped into her basement she's no longer putting on Scandinavian weekends, though if you can get together a party of six she'll make you a Scandinavian dinner. But the fact is, she doesn't charge enough for anything on her menu to make a profit.

Open daily 5 pm to 10.30 pm. Licensed. Master Card, Visa. &

LETHBRIDGE, Alberta   MAP 100
MIRO
212 5 Street S   **$120**
(403) 394-1961

Miro Kyjak trained in Europe and ran a successful restaurant in Calgary before he moved to Lethbridge. He makes everything from scratch, and that means the bread, the soups and the sweets. Pheasant ravioli is his specialty, but diners all seem to like his poached salmon, his beef bourguignon, his lamb ragoût and his penne with goat-cheese. He makes a first-class pavlova, but if you're looking for something new, you aren't likely to find it here. Recently he's expanded his wine-list, and he now has a strong list of French and Australian wines and an excellent selection of beers.

Open Tuesday to Friday 11 am to 2 pm, 5 pm to 10 pm, Saturday 5 pm to 10 pm. Closed on Sunday and Monday. Licensed. All cards. &

Nobody but nobody can buy his way into this guide.

LETHBRIDGE
ROUND STREET CAFE
427 5 Street S
(403) 381-8605

MAP 100

$50

Everybody likes the Round Street Café. Bonny Green-shields genuinely cares for people and often employs Special Needs personnel in her restaurant. Travellers come away from the Café saying that they have never encountered such warmth and friendliness. Bonny taught for ten years before realizing an old dream of owning her own place. She and her husband bought the old Wallace Block in 2004 and moved in upstairs. They make everything on the premises, often to old family recipes, several of which are pretty wild. They have some very good sandwiches, all made on multi-grain bread. Bonny does a lot of baking and if you think you're tired of carrot cake, just try hers. *Open Monday to Friday 7 am to 5 pm, Saturday 9 am to 5 pm. Closed on Sunday. No liquor. Master Card, Visa.* ♿

LONDON, Ontario
THE ONLY ON KING
172 King Street
(519) 936-2064

MAP 101

☆☆

$150

The Only on King is now the only restaurant we recommend in London. Paul Harding is a wonderful chef, and everything he cooks tastes as if it had been made half a minute before. The restaurant is a stone's throw from the Covent Garden Market and his four-course *prix-fixe* is built around what they can supply. It may be sea-bass with lemon and pistachio nuts; it may be pickerel or pork. Harding is good with pork and serves it with braised red cabbage, homemade spaetzle and grainy mustard. The soups and salads are all good, especially the winter-vegetable with fine Tuscan olive-oil. All the bread and all the sweets, including the chocolate cake, are made on the premises. The wine-list may not be up to the cooking, but there's a useful selection of wines by the glass.

Open Tuesday to Saturday 5.30 pm to 10 pm, Sunday 11 am to 2 pm (brunch). Closed on Monday. Licensed. Master Card, Visa.

LORNEVILLE, N.S.   MAP 102
AMHERST SHORE COUNTRY INN   ☆
5091 Highway 366   **$160 ($260)**
(800) 661-2724

The Amherst Shore is run by a charming young couple, Rob Laceby and his wife, Mary. They have a huge garden where they grow most of their vegetables and all of their herbs. They also have three or four attractive chalets where you can spend the night (if you book ahead). Dinner is served in a handsome dining-room that faces Northumberland Strait. Laceby usually starts his meals with a soup made with seasonal vegetables (broccoli, say, in late summer), followed by a mixed green salad. After that there'll be something like chicken or scallops. The pavlova is still the best of the sweets, just as it used to be in Rob's mother's day. The wine-list is small but serviceable, and you won't go wrong if you order a bottle of sauvignon blanc from Oyster Bay.

Open daily at 7.30 pm by appointment only from early May until late October, Friday and Saturday at 7.30 pm by appointment only from late October until early May. Closed Sunday to Thursday in winter. Licensed. Master Card, Visa. ♿

LOUGHEED, Alberta   *MAP 103*
HAUS FALKENSTEIN   🍽
Lougheed Hotel   **$65**
4917 51 Avenue
(780) 386-2434

Lougheed is in the middle of nowhere, according to the owner of the Lougheed Hotel himself. It's about 50 miles east of Camrose on Highway 13, and some 250 people live there. The Haus Falkenstein carries more varieties of pan-fried schnitzel than anywhere else in Canada. There are at least 40 of them. Visitors report that the quality of the schnitzels is high and the service always obliging. The Haus Falkenstein is open Tuesday to Friday for lunch and dinner, Saturday for dinner only. They have a licence (and a beer garden) and take Master Card and Visa.

LUNENBURG, N.S.   MAP 104
FLEUR DE SEL   ☆☆
53 Montague Street   **$200**
(902) 640-2121

This exquisite restaurant is often compared with the best restaurants in Halifax, and rightly so. Martin Ruiz Salvador regularly wins gold in cooking competitions (most recently in Halifax), and here in his own restaurant every detail speaks of perfection. Martin's wife, Sylvie, runs the front of the house with grace and style. Prices have risen in the last few years, but if you want a memorable meal this is it. The menu changes with the seasons according to what's available on the market. But normally, dinner begins with oysters on the half-shell and goes on to a charcuterie board of summer sausage, beef tongue, pig's ears and pickled garlic scapes. It costs only 18.00, which is considerably less than foie gras at 25.00. The tomato salad is typical of the restaurant at it best, with its yellow, beefsteak, cherry and grape tomatoes and stuffed zucchini blossoms in a gazpacho vinaigrette. The best of the main dishes is probably the butter-poached lobster with potato salad, bok choy and lobster-roe mayonnaise. The duck with mung beans and miso is cheaper, and so are the lamb, the beef tenderloin with hand-cut fries and even the halibut cheeks and the sweetbreads. All the sweets are made in house as a matter of course, but we usually ask for the superb cheese plate. Benjamin Bridge used to be the feature of the wine-list. If the 2010 vintage is still available, be sure to ask for a bottle.

Open Wednesday to Sunday 5 pm to 9 pm from mid–April until late October. Closed on Monday and Tuesday. Licensed. Amex, Master Card, Visa. Book ahead. ♿

If you use an out-of-date edition and find it inaccurate, don't blame us. Buy a new edition.

LUNENBURG

MAP 104

MAGNOLIA'S
128 *Montague Street*   **$95**
(902) 634-3287

Magnolia's is a Lunenburg institution. It's been on this site for more than twenty years, and now has a patio at the back from which you can watch the boats in the harbour below. The menu never changes, except for the daily specials. There's always a seafood chowder, as well as peanut soup and French-onion soup. There's always haddock, pan-fried scallops and Alma's vegetarian stew. The meal always ends with key-lime pie. The wine-list is small, perhaps too small. The service is hurried, but friendly, even when the restaurant is packed.

Open Monday to Saturday 11.30 am to 9 pm from 1 April until 31 October. Closed on Sunday. Licensed. Amex, Master Card, Visa. Book ahead if you can. &

LUNENBURG   MAP 104

SALT-SHAKER DELI
124 *Montague Street*   **$95**
(902) 640-3434

This popular deli has expanded its menu in the last few years and now offers an adventurous Sunday brunch (capicola and spinach Benedict), a wider variety of pizzas (spiced shrimps with basil pesto), more sandwiches and a number of specials (Korean barbecued burrito). They also serve Indian Point mussels with either garlic or sausage Portuguese-style. They have the nicest patio in town, so you can watch the shipping in the harbour while you eat. The service is friendly and knowledgeable and, best of all, they're open year-round.

Open daily 11 am to 9 pm (shorter hours in winter). Licensed. Amex, Master Card, Visa. &

Our website is at www.oberonpress.ca. Readers wishing to use e-mail should address us at oberon@sympatico.ca.

LUNENBURG
See also LA HAVE, MAHONE BAY, MARTIN'S BROOK.

MAGDALEN ISLANDS, Quebec   MAP 105

There are sixteen islands in the 60-mile arc of the Magdalens. All but Entry Island are linked by sand dunes, and route 199 runs the whole length of the archipelago. More than half of the total population live on Ile Cap-aux-Meules. The next largest is Ile Havre-Aubert, which is at the southern end of the chain. Everywhere there's fine hiking, swimming and sailboarding. The Madelon Bakery at 355 chemin Petitpas on Cap-aux-Meules (telephone (418) 986-3409) has a wealth of baked goods, cheeses and made-to-order sandwiches, and it's a good place to go if you want a packed lunch. The Islands are known for their soft raw-milk cheese, which resembles reblochon and is produced by the indigenous breed of cow, known as Canadienne. You can get it at the Fromagerie Pied-de-Vent on Havre-aux-Maisons (telephone (418) 969-9292). The ferry from Souris, P.E.I. takes five hours, but you can also get here by plane. Few travellers come to the Magdalens, which is a pity because there are so many pleasures to be had here, including some very good cooking.

MAGDALEN ISLANDS   MAP 105
CAFE DE LA GRAVE
969 route 199, La Grave   **$85**
Ile Havre-Aubert
Saint-Laurent
(418) 937-5765

On the west side of Ile Havre-Aubert there's a village called La Grave, where a number of old fishing boats have been turned into boutiques and restaurants. One of these is the Café de la Grave, which is right next to the theatre. For years we've recommended it for its sandwiches and its wonderful custard cakes. But the fact is, the place does more good things than that. For one thing, it's filled with music all day long, because Sonia Painchaud, the daughter of the house, is a talented musician. Sometimes she plays the accordion alone; sometimes she plays old folk

131

tunes with a three-piece band. The music is magic—nobody criticizes anything they cook, not the bouillabaisse or the boar stew or the mussels or the fries with curried mayonnaise. The dining-room may be small, but it's comfortable and very well appointed. And the music is lovely.
Open Monday to Saturday 9 am to 11 pm, Sunday 10 am to 10 pm from 1 May until 15 October. Licensed. Master Card, Visa.

MAGDALEN ISLANDS MAP 105
CAPITAINE GEDEON
1301 chemin de la Vernière **$240**
Etang du Nord
(418) 986-5341

Next year Takanori Serikawa will convert this bed-and-breakfast into a full-service restaurant, serving meals by appointment only. Dinner will be at 7 o'clock and there'll be no printed menu. For nine courses of the chef's choosing you will pay 90.00 plus tip and taxes. Remember to bring your own bottle, as wine is not included. The chef is Japanese and most of the dishes will be Japanese or Japanese-French fusion. This is a superb kitchen and that's why we've included it in the guide this year. The Capitaine Gedeon is only five minutes from the ferry to Souris and it's open all year except in high summer, when it's closed on Sunday and Monday. It will have a licence and take most cards. You must book ahead.

MAGDALEN ISLANDS MAP 105
LA REFECTOIRE ☆☆
Hôtel Vieux Couvent **$135**
292 route 199
Ile Havre-aux-Maisons
(418) 969-2233

The old convent has long been one of the most attractive places to stay in the Magdalens. Now Réginald Gaudet's wife, Evangeline, is running one of the best kitchens on the Islands right here in the convent. The Réfectoire is a gay and lively place with a big menu. Mussels are cultivated in a nearby lagoon and prepared either as an appetizer or as a main course. Evangeline also has cod, halibut, scallops, clams, herring, mackerel, shrimps and lobster. A lot of the fish goes into her bouillabaisse, which is rightly celebrated, but readers speak also of halibut with a barley risotto, squid with parmesan cheese and salmon crusted with sesame. If you've had enough seafood for a while, ask for the local veal or the home-bred boar. There's also a four-course *prix-fixe* for just 16.00, plus the cost of your main course. There are some good local cheeses and a variety of fruits and berries. They have only a dozen wines, all sold by the glass and the bottle, and they're all private imports.

Open daily 6 pm to 9 pm from 1 May until 15 June, daily 5 pm to 10 pm from 16 June until 15 September, daily 6 pm to 9 pm from 16 September until 5 October. Licensed. Master Card, Visa. Book ahead.

MAGDALEN ISLANDS MAP 105
LA TABLE DES ROYS ★★★
1188 route 199 **$250**
Etang du Nord
(418) 986-3004

After being on her own for 25 years, Joanne Vigneault has found a partner. He's not only passionate about her restaurant, but he's also the love of her life. His name is Paul Lemoine and he's responsible for the greenhouse, where he grows such things as Jerusalem artichokes, herbs and greens of all sorts and a variety of edible flowers. The wine-list has been expanded and there are now about 200 labels, many of them organic. La Table des Roys isn't cheap, but an astonishing amount of thought goes into everything they offer. Joanne is one of the best chefs in Quebec, but as she gets older she forgets more and more of her English, so when choosing their meal visitors are more or less on their own. Look for the fresh local seafood. In spring it'll usually be lobster—a whole half-lobster goes into the bouillabaisse, which you'll always find on the menu. Scallops are prepared in five different ways and served as an appetizer, along with mussels, which are always readily available. Lamb was on the menu last year; this year it's more often veal. At the end of the meal there's an exquisite maple soufflé that Joanne has been offering for many years. There's a store on site where you can buy several take-away dishes as well as balsamic vinegar and extra-virgin olive-oil.

Open Tuesday to Saturday at 8 pm by appointment only from 1 June until 30 September. Closed on Sunday and Monday. Licensed. Amex, Master Card, Visa. Book ahead.

MAHONE BAY, N.S. (MAP 104)
MATEUS ☆
533 Main Street **$150**
(902) 531-3711

Mateus is attractive and well served—and relatively inexpensive. They have sandwiches and burgers, of course, but they also serve such substantial dishes as mussels from nearby Indian Point, rack of lamb, panko-crusted haddock and grilled steelhead trout. People from away will be excited by such unfamiliar wines as Luckett's (ask for the Ortega) and Petite Rivière (ask for the Risser's Breeze). Both are well known locally, but are seldom seen elsewhere in the country. Likewise, few of us have ever tasted halibut with Lunenburg chow, which is made with onions soaked in brine. The brine is left to stand overnight and then served with tomatoes and purslane. Matthew Krizan learned his trade at the Cordon Bleu schools in Ottawa and London, England and settled in Mahone Bay two or three years ago. He's good.

Open Monday to Friday 11.30 am to 9 pm, Saturday and Sunday 10.30 am to 9 pm. Licensed. Master Card, Visa. &

MAHONE BAY (MAP 104)
VALENTINO'S ☆☆
525 Main Street **$140**
(902) 531-3666

Valentino's has an unassuming façade, but once inside you're in another world. Valentino is the chef and his wife, Joanne, is in charge of the front of the house. Service is leisurely, but one feels that that's part of the atmosphere. Everything is made from scratch and the vegetables and the herbs all come from the garden. Everyone is happy to start with the frutti de mer or the stracciatella. The pasta that follows is the best we've had since we were last in Italy. The leg of lamb and the salt cod are both excellent, though the Italian dishes usually show the restaurant at its best. Valentino is very strong on sweets and his chocolate cheesecake with raspberries is as good as any we've ever had.

Open daily 5 pm to 9 pm. Licensed. All cards. Book ahead.

LA MALBAIE, Quebec   MAP 107
CHEZ TRUCHON
1065 rue Richelieu   **$140 ($275)**
Pointe-au-Pic
(888) 662-4622

Dominique Truchon spent many years at the Auberge des Peupliers in Cap à l'Aigle (see above), and that's where he made a name for himself. A couple of years ago, he opened his own restaurant in a handsome old house on rue Richelieu in Pointe-au-Pic. Here he has a darkly formal dining-room and several comfortable bedrooms. His menu makes much of such regional dishes as smoked-salmon pie, emu pâté, halibut with red peppers and roast beef with potatoes fried in duck fat. With the sweet, he splurges on panna cotta, flavoured with basil. His prices are modest—a four-course table d'hôte sells for just 25.00.
Open daily 5.30 pm to 9 pm. Licensed. Amex, Master Card, Visa. Book ahead if you can.

LA MALBAIE   MAP 107
LE PATRIARCHE   ☆
30 rue du Quai   **$160**
Pointe-au-Pic
(418) 665-9692

The Patriarche occupies an old house that faces the

parking-lot of the Café Gare. It's hard to find. Turn south on the chemin du Havre by the museum, then sharply right again on the rue du Quai. Michel Dussuart, thin and very young, hardly looks the part of a *québécois* chef, but he cooks well and his menu of meat and fish, all prepared country-style, gives him plenty of opportunities. He prepares so many shrimps that the restaurant actually smells of shrimp.

Open Tuesday to Sunday 5.30 pm to 8.30 pm. Closed on Monday. Licensed. All cards. Book ahead and be on time. &

LA MALBAIE
See also CAP A L'AIGLE.

MANITOULIN ISLAND, Ontario   MAP 108
GARDEN'S GATE   ☆
Highway 542 $90
Tehkummah
(705) 859-2088

People today are just as enthusiastic about the Garden's Gate as they were the day John and Rosemary Diebold opened the restaurant. If you turn west off Highway 6 in Tehkummah, you'll be at the Garden's Gate in two minutes. The gate opens into a pretty garden, beyond which stands the restaurant, with an old barn and a split-rail fence in the middle distance. Here Rosemary works as her grandmother would have worked, making all her own bread-rolls, her own salad-dressings, even her own hamburger buns. She grows all the fresh vegetables she can and buys her blueberries, organic strawberries and organic raspberries from long-time suppliers. Each year she and John search the vineyards of Niagara for new and exciting wines. They track down local craft beers with the same passion. This year travellers are singing the praises of their Manitoulin lamb with apricots and Moroccan spices. Every evening there are at least ten different sweets, and the Dutch apple pie is known all over the Island. With the sweets they serve fair-trade coffee and loose teas.

Open Tuesday to Sunday 11 am to 8 pm from 1 April until 30 June, daily 11 am to 10 pm from 1 July until 31 August, Tuesday to Sunday 11 am to 8 pm from 1 September until 31 October. Closed on Monday in the spring and fall. Licensed. Master Card, Visa. Book ahead if you can. &

MANITOULIN ISLAND   MAP 108
THE SCHOOL HOUSE   ☆
46 McNevin Street   **$115**
Providence Bay
(705) 377-4055

Greg Niven remembers a time when 60 percent of his customers were American. The Americans have gone and people from southern Ontario are gradually moving in, some from the Georgian Bay, some from Muskoka, where property values have become unreal. Niven has sold the fish-and-chips parlour down the road, and is now giving his whole mind to the School House. He gets his vegetables from a neighbour, who has a vegetable garden as big as a tennis-court. A local abattoir opened, then closed again. A new, state-of-the art supplier will open this summer, so Niven will be able once again to get well-hung fresh meat. Most of his customers, however, ask for fresh Lake Huron whitefish, and Niven does what he can with this rather tasteless fish. He also has beef wellington and ravioli stuffed with smoked trout. He trained in France and he knows just how to make a first-class risotto. He's also pretty good with French chocolate. Most of his wines come from the Niagara Region and Niven always goes for the best he can get.

Open daily 5 pm to 9 pm from mid-May until mid-October. Licensed. Master Card, Visa. &

MAPLE BAY, B.C.   *(MAP 58)*
BAD HABITS
6701 Beaumont Avenue
(250) 597-8089

Bad Habits is right on the water and offers breakfast and lunch

all day every day but Monday and dinner on Friday and Satur-
day. The decor is edgy but comfortable. They serve soup and sand-
wiches at noon; the dinner menu is more elaborate. They have a
licence and the cooking is good. Further reports needed.

MARTINS BROOK, N.S. (MAP 104)
OLD BLACK FOREST CAFE 🖙
Highway 3 **$80**
(902) 634-3600

The Black Forest Café is popular both with local people
and with tourists, who crowd the place every summer.
Look for it about halfway between Lunenburg and Mahone Bay. It has wonderfully fresh seafood, as well as a
number of German specialties like goulash and sauerkraut. The Black Forest cake is baked on the premises,
and there's a beer soup on rye bread for just 4.50.
The sauerbraten costs 18.00, the schnitzelburger 10.00,
the schnitzel sandwich 13.00. We usually order the
maultaschen with onions, which is house-made ravioli in
a beautiful light gravy. In summer you can eat outside on
the deck. Service is friendly and efficient.
Open Tuesday to Sunday 11.30 am to 9 pm from mid–April
until mid–December. Closed on Monday. Licensed. Master
Card, Visa. Book ahead if you can.

MASSEY, Ontario MAP 111
DRAGONFLY 🖙
205 Imperial Street **$65**
(705) 865-3456

This stretch of Highway 17 has scenery and a few gas-
stations, but very little for anyone looking for good food.
Dragonfly has a big (too big) menu of international
dishes, with all the comfort foods and quite good cooking. The dining-room is often packed, but the service is
always patient and friendly. Burgers are the big seller, but
we still prefer the stir-fries. First-class chicken soup costs
all of 3.00 and the crab-cakes cost only a bit more.
They're all bargains—everything is a bargain. As for the

deep-fried cheesecake, it's worth all the calories, and it has a lot of those.

Open Tuesday to Sunday noon to 9 pm. Closed on Monday. No liquor. Master Card, Visa. Book ahead if you can. &

MATTAWA, Ontario   MAP 112
MOOSEHEAD ESTATE   ☆
655 Moosehead Road   **$125 ($275)**
(705) 744-0322

Melanie Viau and Marc Bouthillier spent almost two years restoring this century-old lodge on Lake Champlain before opening it as a bed-and-breakfast. If you want a meal at the Moosehead Estate you have to book the day before—they are open by appointment only. There's no real menu. Melanie will decide what to give you. She does all her shopping at the local store, because there are no farmers or fisherman anywhere near. Sometimes the store gets in some salmon, and they always have plenty of fresh vegetables. In winter they have butternut squash and she uses that to make some first-class soups. One day she found a bin of limes, so she started making chocolate-and-lime mousse. Lamb might be local, but usually it's just what's on the meat counter. She makes all her own bread and serves it with every meal. She works alone, with one helper, her son, Max. Max is eleven.
Open daily by appointment only. Bring your own bottle. No cards. You must book ahead.

MATTAWA   MAP 112
MYRTS   👉🍽
610 McConnell Street   **$40**
(705) 744-2274

Mattawa is a friendly place and even in a dine-and-dash place like Myrt's the waiters quickly make you feel like a local. Scott Edworth serves comfort food and serves it fast all day long. He never lets you down; in fact, you'd have to go a long way to find a better cheeseburger with bacon or a better butter tart. He makes all his own soups, all his own pies and all his own pizzas. He makes all his own fish and chips too, using nothing but the freshest halibut. He grinds all his own beef for the hamburgers. And he puts on a hot special every day at noon. Bikers on the Temiskaming Loop are told to stop here, and everyone else should do the same.

Open daily 6 am to 8.30 pm. Licensed. Master Card, Visa. ♿

MEDICINE HAT, Alberta   MAP 113
THAI ORCHARD ROOM   ☆
36 Strachan Court SE   **$90**
(403) 580-8210

This is a lovely room with orchids on every table, but if you're ten minutes late for your booking they fine you 10.00 a person. It's hard to see how they can get away with this, especially since on weekends you're allowed to book only eight of the nineteen tables. (The rest are for the walk-in trade.) Nothing but authentic Thai dishes appear on the menu. There are several lively vegetarian items, most of them based on fried tofu or jasmine rice. There are red, green and yellow curries with beef, chicken, pork or seafood. Recently they've added a number of stir-fries and grills. Sounantha and Ken Ross started out twelve years ago on Bow Island and later moved to Medicine Hat. Here they have a variety of loose teas and a handful of wines; they work hard and make few mistakes.

Open Tuesday to Thursday 11 am to 9 pm, Friday 11 am to 10 pm, Saturday 4.30 pm to 10 pm, Sunday noon to 9 pm. Closed on Monday. Licensed. Amex, Master Card, Visa. ♿

MEDICINE HAT   MAP 113
TWIST   👉
531 3 Street SE   **$65**
(403) 528-2188

Twist was sold in 2012 to two sisters, Melissa and Cheryl-Lynn. They intend to stay with the menu that made Twist's name in the first place. Melissa used to work in the restaurant and she knows all the ropes. The list of tapas dishes has survived intact, though last fall they added a soup and several salads. There are a number of important main dishes. The panko-crusted salmon has been replaced by salmon Spanish-style and the herb-stuffed chicken is now filled with dilled goat-cheese. The butter chicken, the house paella, and the triple-A beef tenderloin are all exactly as they used to be. Melissa makes the sweets now and they're all lovely.

Open Monday to Saturday 11 am to 11 pm. Closed on Sunday. Licensed. Amex, Master Card, Visa. &

MIDDLE WEST PUBNICO, N.S.   **(MAP 223)**
RED CAP   ☆
1034 Highway 335   **$95**
(902) 762-2112

The Red Cap has been in business for 68 years and it's changed hands only once in all that time. You'll find the village on the South Shore, about 30 miles east of Yarmouth, which makes it a two-hours' drive from the Digby ferry. The Pubnicos still have an active fishing fleet; in fact the dollar value of their catch is the highest east of Montreal. Amy Scott has every kind of fish and shellfish at her door, and the fish on her menu is always stunningly fresh. Nearly every ingredient she uses is local—something that's more of a necessity than a fash-ion in this part of the world. She grows her own herbs and buys her vegetables from local farmers. She uses nothing but grain-fed chicken and beef, and makes every-thing from scratch—the sauces, the stocks, the soups and even the onion rings. She likes to cook such Acadian dishes as rappie pie, which in season will become wild-blueberry pie or bread pudding. Most of the wines come from Grand Pré or Peller, but if you like you can bring your own bottle. There's no corkage fee.

Open daily 11 am to 9 pm from 1 May until 25 December (shorter hours in winter). Licensed. Amex, Master Card, Visa. &

MIDLAND, Ontario
EXPLORERS CAFE
345 King Street
(705) 527-9199

MAP 115

☆☆

$100

Maybe the menu here should change more often, but the fact is that nothing else in town can compare with it. The cooking, the presentation and the service are all superb. The decorations are intriguing, the walls hung with treasures from Rob and Jennifer's travels. The menu shows the influence of just about every cuisine in the world. The salmon comes in a maple-chipotle glaze, the Passage-to-India curry comes with raita and naan. We like to start with the lamb salad, served on a bed of Asian greens, and go on to the curry. At the end of the meal there's a fine peanut-butter pie with chocolate. The wine-list is one of the best anywhere north of Toronto.
Open Monday to Saturday noon to 10 pm, Sunday 4 pm to 10 pm from mid-June until mid-October, Tuesday to Saturday noon to 10 pm from mid-October until mid-June. Closed on Sunday and Monday in winter.

MIDLAND
See also PENETANG.

MILL BAY, B.C.
AMUSE ON THE VINEYARD
2915 Cameron Taggart Road
(250) 743-3667

(MAP 58)

☆

$125

Amusé Bistro has moved from Shawnigan Lake to Mill Bay and acquired a new name. The restaurant now occupies an old farmhouse next to the Unsworth vineyards. Dinner starts with shellfish broth or apple-and-parsnip soup. Qualicum Bay scallops are served as a main course, as well as wild sockeye salmon with a beet-and-radish salad. For sweet there's an apple cobbler that makes you feel at home in the farmhouse setting. There are also table d'hôtes of three, four and five courses. The wines all come from the Unsworth vineyards.

Open Wednesday to Sunday 5 pm to 9 pm. Closed on Monday and Tuesday. Licensed. Master Card, Visa. Book ahead in summer. &

MILL VILLAGE, N.S. (MAP 191)
RIVERBANK CAFE
8 Medway River Road **$45**
(902) 677-2013

This little café is located in the Riverbank General Store in Mill Village, which is just off Exit 17A on Highway 103. The General Store sells everything from penny candy to tools. The café itself offers nothing but lunch. They always have a soup, however, several salads and a choice of sandwiches and wraps. Sweets (crumbles, pies and bread pudding) are all made on the premises. Before you leave, drive through the village and admire the old houses along both sides of the river.

Open daily 11.30 am to 2.30 pm. Master Card, Visa. No liquor. Book ahead if you can.

MIRAMICHI, N.B. MAP 118
BISTRO 140
295 Pleasant Street **$60**
(506) 622-2221

Miramichi is a depressed area where everything that happens happened in the past. So we were pleased to come across Bistro 140, housed in what used to be the town square. The place seats 150 and they're planning to enlarge the lounge area. It was voted the people's choice for several years. Then everybody started talking about O'-Donaghue's Irish pub at 1606 Water Street (telephone (506) 778-2150, in what used to be known as Chatham. O'Donaghue's is really a gastropub operating in a lovely old heritage building. It's a gay and lively place with a very long menu. Meanwhile, at Bistro 140 you can begin with a smoked-salmon taco and go on to boneless breast of chicken stuffed with spinach and feta cheese. There's always some fresh fish, usually haddock, as well as linguine with local lobster in white wine. The vegetables are all fresh and the sweets are all made in-house.

Open Monday to Thursday 11 am to 9 pm, Friday 11 am to 10 pm, Saturday 4 pm to 10 pm. Closed on Sunday. Licensed. Master Card, Visa.

MONCTON, N.B. MAP 119
L'IDYLLE ☆☆☆
1788 rue Amirault **$225**
Dieppe
(506) 860-6641

Emmanuel Charretier and Hélène Legras run the best restaurant this side of St. Andrews. It's in Dieppe, a suburb of Moncton. Look for L'Idylle three and a half miles south of Main Street (here called rue Champlain) on Highway 106. The dining-room is elegant, the menu daring, the cooking superb. Dinner begins with garden-fresh tomato soup with an olive-and-basil mousse, say, followed by ravioli stuffed with seasonal vegetables. The fish course may be salmon served in a sauce *du chef*. Charretier is proud of his rabbit stew, but we haven't tried it. On a recent visit we had a delightful *amuse-bouche* of shredded greens on a bed of foam, but everything Charretier touches is delicate and lovely. Wine service brings you a glass of carefully chosen wine with every course and costs only 30.00 a head. Every reader of this guide should make their way to L'Idylle at least once a week.

Open Tuesday to Saturday 5 pm to 10 pm. Closed on Sunday and Monday. Licensed. All cards. &

MONCTON MAP 119
THE WINDJAMMER ☆
Hôtel Beauséjour **$180**
750 rue Principale
(506) 854-4344

The Windjammer is a likeable place. It's formal and dignified, but it's very friendly. It has free valet parking and an interesting menu. And it has good cooking. You can spend a lot here if you like—on sturgeon caviar, for instance, which costs 162.50 a serving or, for that matter, on foie gras served with apple and rhubarb icewine for 22.95. But you don't need sturgeon caviar or foie gras. House-smoked salmon is yours for only 14.95, six oysters for only 15.95. (We ourselves can never resist the splendid lobster bisque for a dollar or two more.) The trio of lamb is generally the best of the main courses. It's about the most expensive item on the list, but it's local and tender and full of flavour. There's loin of wild boar for 31.95 and beef tenderloin, grandly flamed at your table for 43.95. The wines are all sold at favourable prices, and the Liberty School cabernet sauvignon comes for just 45.00, which is a real bargain.

Open Monday to Saturday 5.30 pm to 10 pm. Closed on Sunday. Licensed. All cards. Valet parking. Book ahead if you can.

MONTAGUE, P.E.I. (MAP 39)
WINDOWS ON THE WATER ☆
106 Sackville Street **$100**
(902) 838-2080

If you're tired of Windows on the Water you're tired of life, as Dr. Johnson once said of London. Lilian Dingwell has a lovely old house (built in about 1880) with a wraparound deck overlooking the Montague River. The cooking is old-fashioned and features things like boiled carrots, but everything is perfectly fresh and generously served. The prices are all very fair. The seafood linguine, for instance, offers an abundance of seafood (mussels, haddock, scallops and lobster) for just 22.00. Every noon there's a lobster quiche, a garden salad, a haddock bake and blue mussels in a white-wine mirepoix. We usually order the mussels, because they're the best the Island has to offer. In the evening they pair scallops with beef tenderloin and serve salmon with maple syrup. Lilian's sweets are famous, especially her apple crisp and her blueberry cake with brown sugar. The wine-list, however, is lamentable.

Open daily 11.30 am to 9.30 pm from early June until mid-

October. Licensed. All cards. Book ahead if you can. ♿

MONTREAL, Quebec   **MAP 121**
LA CHRONIQUE   ☆
104 avenue Laurier o   **$295**
(514) 271-3095

When Normand Laprise and Marc de Canck arrived in
Montreal a generation or so ago, the local restaurant
scene had little to cheer about. But before long the two
men had turned on all the lights in the city. Over the
years, however, Marc de Canck has lost some of his original excitement, though his restaurant is still as expensive
as ever. It's a good idea to come at noon, when prices are
lower. The lunch menu starts with venison tartar, seared
scallops, cured salmon and foie gras de canard, and goes
on to a side of beef, a fillet of red snapper and a chine of
pork. There may no longer be a lot of real excitement in
this kitchen, but there are precious few mistakes either.
The cooking is correct. The dining-room is small but
well served. Marc's stepson, Olivier de Montigny, is now
in the kitchen as well, and regulars like to argue about
which is the better of the two. (We think the answer is
Marc.)
*Open Tuesday to Friday 11.45 am to 1.45 pm, 6 pm to 9 pm,
Saturday and Sunday 6 pm to 9 pm. Closed on Monday. Licensed. All cards. Book ahead if you can.*

MONTREAL   **MAP 121**
LE CLUB CHASSE & PECHE   ☆
423 rue St.-Claude   **$225**
(514) 861-1112

The Club Chasse & Pèche is well appointed and extremely well served. The menu is small and very choice.
It starts with oysters on the half-shell, chilled octopus,
seared scallops and black cod, which is rarely seen as an
appetizer. Then come partridge two ways, Gaspé char
with salmon caviar and sea-bass. The sea-bass is elegantly
cooked, with crisp skin and moist flesh. The meal ends

with a lovely lemon-meringue tart, full of wonderful flavour. The wine-list, which is impressive in every area, is at its best with its stunning array of wines by the glass. These aren't just house wines; there's a delightful, sunny sancerre from the Loire and a magnificent St.-Emilion grand-cru from one of the oldest vineyards in Bordeaux. *Open Tuesday to Thursday 6 pm to 10.30 pm, Friday 11.30 am to 2 pm, 6 pm to 10.30 pm, Saturday 6 pm to 10.30 pm. Closed on Sunday and Monday. Licensed. Amex, Master Card, Visa. Book ahead.* ♿

MONTREAL   **MAP 121**
LE COMPTOIR   ☆
4807 boulevard St.-Laurent   **$145**
(514) 844-8467

This is really just a boîte, but it has a prepossessing menu featuring such things as fennel soup with truffle oil, cod tart with yellow beets, a jarret of pork and spaghetti with anchovies and pimento. In the evening they add charcuterie, sweetbreads and braised squid, as well as a lovely treatment of rhubarb with strawberry yogurt. The kitchen makes much of mustard with cumin and smoked paprika, seeking always the daring and the unusual. In spite of this, the prices are quite low. A bottle of brouilly costs only 50.00, sancerre 52.00, barbera d'Asti 56.00. Le Comptoir is Montreal at its most genuine.
Open Monday 5 pm to midnight, Tuesday to Friday noon to 2 pm, 5 pm to midnight, Saturday 5 pm to midnight, Sunday 10.30 am to 2 pm (brunch), 5 pm to midnight. Licensed. Master Card, Visa. No smoking Book ahead if you can. ♿

MONTREAL   **MAP 121**
DOMINION SQUARE TAVERN
1243 Metcalfe Street   **$150**
(514) 564-5056

The Dominion Square Tavern was opened in 1927 and later restored, so it still looks much the same as it did 85 years ago. It's a long room with bare tables and hard chairs and a bar running the whole way from front to back. The chef is Eric Dupuis, formerly of Pullman and Leméac. Here he serves traditional pub food in the Parisian style, which really means Montreal-style. The menu starts with smoked mackerel, salmon gravlax and pork terrine, and continues with a Ploughman's Lunch of fish or beef. The beef and fish are both admirable, but we think the braised beef with mashed potatoes is usually better than either. Every Sunday night they put on a dinner roast between 4.30 and midnight. On weeknights there's a lovely lemon tartlet and a wonderfully light sticky-toffee pudding. They have a massive list of red wines, but we think it's usually more fun (and much cheaper) to have a glass of one of their eight on-tap beers. The service is leisurely— allow two hours, even for lunch.

Open Monday to Friday 11.30 am to midnight, Saturday and Sunday 4.30 pm to midnight. Licensed. All cards. No smoking.

MONTREAL MAP 121
LES 400 COUPS ☆☆
400 rue Notre-Dame e **$160**
(514) 985-0400

Marc-André Jetté buys his ingredients wherever he can find them and prepares his meals as the spirit moves him. He cooks his octopus, for instance, with green strawberries, his lobster with a sabayon of cider, his Arctic char with daikon. His halibut comes from the Pacific, like all the best halibut. His sweetbreads are served with maitaki mushrooms. His magret of duck comes from Canardière Farm. His suckling pig is served with black trumpet mushrooms and comes from Gaspor Farm. His cooking is spectacular, his prices are high. The wine-list is big and expensive, but there's a lovely cru bourgeois médoc for 68.00. Tables are scarce and it's a good idea to book several days in advance. It took us two years to get one.

Open Tuesday to Thursday 5.30 pm to 10.30 pm, Friday 11.30 am to 1.30 pm, 5.30 pm to 10.30 pm, Saturday 5.30 pm to 10.30 pm. Closed on Sunday and Monday. Licensed. All cards. No smoking. Book ahead.

MONTREAL   **MAP 121**
HÔTEL HERMAN   ☆
5171 boulevard St.–Laurent   **$140**
(514) 278-1000

Don't come here looking for a room. The Hôtel Herman
is not, repeat not, a hotel. It's a boîte—a rough boîte with
a big table running the length of the dining area, plus a
few smaller tables. The Herman may be a rough boîte,
but there's nothing rough about the cooking, which is at
once adventurous and highly skilled. Meals start with
oysters from New Brunswick (six for 18.00), a lovely cold
corn soup that's bursting with flavour, bone marrow with
a coulis of mashed potatoes, marinated trout, smoked eel,
sunny-side-up duck eggs, venison tartar and braised head
of duck. The main dishes are rather less exciting. There
are sweetbreads with zucchini flowers and coffee mushrooms, seared halibut with fava beans, leg of lamb with
roasted carrots and terrine de foie gras. We haven't yet
tried the lamb, always having been tempted by the sweetbreads and the terrine, both of which are outstanding
dishes. The wine-list may be thin on wines by the glass,
but it has several interesting wines by the bottle, among
them a Beaune premier-cru and a chassagne-montrachet.
Both are very expensive, but the restaurant itself is not.
Open Monday and Wednesday to Sunday 5 pm to midnight.
Closed on Tuesday. Licensed. Master Card, Visa. No smoking.
Book ahead.

MONTREAL   **MAP 121**
JOE BEEF   ☆
2491 rue Notre–Dame o   **$175**
(514) 935-6504

Joe Beef takes some getting used to. It's small and packed
with people. There's often a lineup at the door and if you
have a booking (as you should), that doesn't seem to matter. There's no printed menu or wine-list. The food and
wines are chalked up on big blackboards that are hard to
read in the dim light. Relax. They have oysters from the

east and west coasts, and the best are from New Brunswick. They have smelts, cod (on a bed of potato mash), spaghetti with lobster (at a great price) and whole trout. You won't be able to see any of these items on the wall, but never mind, you have this guide in your hand. Anyway, the trout is the thing to have. There's no use looking for a wine of your choice. Simply ask for the house white or the house red—they're both good, drinkable wines. Joe Beef is real Montreal and David McMillan probably knows more about food and wine than anyone else in the city. Talk to him if you can—he's the big man on the scene.

Open Tuesday to Saturday 6.30 pm to 10 pm. Closed on Sunday and Monday. Licensed. Master Card, Visa. You must book ahead. &

MONTREAL   **MAP 121**
LAWRENCE   ☆
5201 boulevard St.-Laurent   **$140**
(514) 503-1070

Lawrence is all big windows and hard chairs. You take a seat, notice the elegant servers and pick up the menu. Immediately you see things like marinated trout with a potato cake, ox tongue in a green sauce, smoked sausage with endive and fried veal with potato salad. In the evening there's braised octopus, sablefish with green cabbage and bone-marrow pie. A few minutes later you start to notice the cooking, which as it happens is brilliant. Be sure to ask for the marinated trout, which is wonderful. Don't miss the ox-tongue either or the bone-marrow pie. All this on a corner lot in the far reaches of boulevard St.-Laurent. All this and more. Try the tarte tatin to follow. It's baked fresh and brought to the table piping hot.

Open Wednesday to Friday 11.30 am to 3 pm, 5.30 pm to 10 pm, Saturday and Sunday 5.30 pm to 10 pm. Closed on Monday and Tuesday. Licensed. Amex, Master Card, Visa. No smoking. Book ahead. &

Nobody but nobody can buy his way into this guide.

MONTREAL MAP 121
LEMEAC ★★
1045 avenue Laurier o **$190**
(514) 270-0999

Leméac is back at the top of its form this year. The menu is full of interest; the cooking is excellent, the service charming. There are tartars of beef and salmon to start with, Toulouse sausage and ravioli stuffed with wild mushrooms, beef short-ribs, rack of lamb and hanger steak to follow. Everything is exactly as it should be. Every table is full. Nobody hurries. The wine-list is large, ambitious and well chosen. If you want to go cheap, ask for the sancerre from Henri Bourgeois—it's a great buy at 58.00. If you have money to spend, ask for a solaia, a sassicaia or a petit mouton from Mouton-Rothschild, yours for $194. Or, in a different mood, you can have a lovely glass of fresh-squeezed orange-juice for just 6.00. Marie-Per Morin and Rémi Brunelle have made this a remarkable restaurant.

Open Monday to Friday noon to midnight, Saturday and Sunday 10.45 am to 3 pm (brunch), 6 pm to midnight. Licensed. Amex, Master Card, Visa. No smoking. &

MONTREAL MAP 121
THE LIVERPOOL HOUSE ★
2501 rue Notre-Dame o **$160**
(514) 313-6049

The Liverpool House, like Joe Beef, is a restaurant made for men. It's *masculin*. It's Italian. There's plenty of noise. There are attractive waitresses. The menu is chalked up on a blackboard. David McMillan believes in integrity and integrity is what these two restaurants are all about. But if you sit down beside him, Macmillan will tell you frankly, "I'd never eat here. It's too noisy." Noisy it certainly is, crowded and noisy. But that isn't all he has to say. "I have the most sophisticated clientele in North America," he'll tell you. "New York? New York is one big steak house. I have sweetbreads on my menu. I have tripe, heart and cheeks. Others offer some of these things. They offer them for show, but I *sell* them." He also offers speck with melon, ears and tails of bison, chicken under a brick, sea trout and lobster spaghetti (for 49.00). Everything on the menu is prepared casually but with genuine style. Helpings are big, too big for most women, but there's always plenty to drink—the wine-list covers one whole wall.

Open Tuesday to Saturday 6 pm to 10 pm. Closed on Sunday and Monday. Licensed. Master Card, Visa. No smoking. You must book ahead. ♿

MONTREAL   **MAP 121**
MAISON BOULUD   ☆☆
Ritz-Carlton Hotel   **$195**
1228 Sherbrooke Street W
(514) 842-4224

The new dining-room at the Ritz-Carlton, which opened in late 2012, is called Maison Boulud. Daniel Boulud came to Montreal by way of New York, after a brilliant but unsuccessful stop in Vancouver, where he was briefly in charge of the kitchen at Lumière. At the Ritz he has a sumptuous space—all pale teak, overstuffed chairs and a sensational gas-burning fireplace. His menu is cautious to a fault, offering things like Bayonne ham, smoked salmon, ravioli, terrine de foie gras, Arctic char, black cod and grilled entrecôte. The most spectacular dish, oddly enough, is wild fresh snails in garlic butter. Garlic butter is a familiar enough treatment, but wild snails are a rarity. The cooking is light and delicate, the portions small, the service graceful and well informed. As for the wine-list, it's magnificent. The still wines by the glass are not impressive, but for the same money you can have a glass of Roederer champagne from Anderson Valley in California. The list of bottled wines starts with such good things as Grgich Hills and Stag's Leap and ends with a number of premier-cru Mouton-Rothschilds at appropriate prices. If you like, you can take a table at the bar and have a plate of oysters on the half-shell (six for

21.00) or a duo of salmon, with a glass or two of champagne, for only 17.00.

Open daily noon to 2.30 pm, 5 pm to 10 pm. Licensed. Amex, Master Card, Visa. No smoking. Book ahead. ♿

MONTREAL   MAP 121
LE MAS DES OLIVIERS
1216 rue Bishop   **$160**
(514) 861-6783

If you want something comfortably old-fashioned, this is it. The Mas des Oliviers is charming inside and out and has friendly service. (For instance, when we admired the carrot-and-ginger soup they brought us a second bowl—for free.) You've seen everything on their menu before. Dinner starts with consommé, vichysoisse or soupe du jour, and continues with Bayonne ham, smoked salmon, escargots de bourgogne and brochette of mussels. Charcuterie is the only concession to the late twentieth century, or the twenty-first. They follow this with crêpes Suzette, which they offer for 22.00 for two. But after all, crêpes Suzette were a lovely experience a hundred years ago, and so were escargots de bourgogne. This place may be old-fashioned, but it's also very likeable. It has a convenient location and it's not expensive. Have a glass of muscat de Beaumes de Venise with your crêpes Suzette and be happy.

Open Monday to Friday noon to 2 pm, 5.30 pm to 10 pm, Saturday and Sunday 5.30 pm to 10 pm. Licensed. Amex, Master Card, Visa. ♿

MONTREAL   MAP 121
NORA GRAY
1391 rue St.-Jacques   **$150**
(514) 419-6672

Emma Cardarelli is the chef at Nora Gray, and Ryan Gray, the owner, decided to couple her grandmother's first name with his own family name. Emma Cardarelli's menu is rich and strange, featuring such things as boulettes, tripe, braised short-ribs, salt-crusted sea-bream, rabbit stuffed with walnuts, risotto of squid and, of course, boudin noir. The most successful dish, however, happens to be the plain char-grilled pork chop. The cooking can be sensible or merely startling—it all depends on your luck. Be careful to listen to the daily specials, because they're often the best things on the menu. The stuffed clams, for instance, are more appealing than either the boulettes or the rabbit. There's a big list of bottled wines, but there aren't many wines by the glass. The dining-room is comfortable, even elegant, and if you like you can have dinner at the bar.

Open Tuesday to Saturday 5.30 pm to 11.30 pm. Closed on Sunday and Monday. Licensed. Amex, Master Card, Visa. No smoking. Book ahead. &

MONTREAL   **MAP 121**
PASTAGA   ★★
6389 boulevard St.-Laurent   **$125**
(438) 381-6389

Pastaga is still fairly new to the Montreal scene, but already it's established itself as a restaurant with an inconvenient location and wonderful food. Where else can you get oysters from the Magdalen Islands, small, plump and full of flavour? Who else has scallops that are grilled on the outside and unbelievably tender on the inside? Where else can you get lacquered pork belly like this? Everything at Pastaga is served on small plates—the marinated Atlantic salmon, the Atlantic halibut, the tuna tataki, the beet salad, the endives, the charcuterie, the tarte tatin. They have a big wine-list, featuring numerous wines priced in the forties and fifties, most of them unfamiliar to the average diner. Many are unfiltered, several are organic. By Montreal standards, Pastaga is cheap. Quebec cheeses, for example, sell for twelve cents a gram. Pastaga just made it to this guide in its first year; now it has two stars. How's that for excitement?

Open Monday to Thursday 5 pm to 11 pm, Friday noon to 2 pm, 5 pm to 11 pm, Saturday and Sunday 10 am to 2 pm (brunch), 5 pm to 11 pm. Licensed. Amex, Master Card, Visa. No smoking. &

MONTREAL **MAP 121**
LA SALLE A MANGER ☆☆
1302 avenue du Mont-Royal e **$150**
(514) 522-0777

The Salle à Manger may not have any table-cloths, and they may set their tables with a knife and fork and no spoon, but make no mistake, it's a first-class restaurant with an exciting menu, good service and excellent cooking. They start dinner with such things as foie gras with cranberries, tartar of duck with crème fraîche and salmon tartar with wasabi cream—a brilliant dish served with a delicate array of tiny turnip leaves. The meal continues with sweetbreads, clams steamed in beer, pork tongue, blood sausage, salt cod and pot au feu with bone marrow. Ask for a glass of gewurztraminer with your dinner. It usually goes better with dishes like this than either chardonnay or cabernet sauvignon. For us, the Salle à Manger was an important find.
Open daily 5 pm to midnight. Licensed. Amex, Master Card, Visa. No smoking. &

MONTREAL **MAP 121**
TOQUE! ☆☆☆
900 place Jean-Paul-Riopelle **$225**
(514) 499-2084

Normand Laprise and Christine Lamarche have always been known for the remarkable quality of their ingredients and for the daring originality of their kitchen. They still live in a world of unexpected pleasures: strawberry blossoms mixed with parsnip-and-apple soup, fine-ground seaweed with smoked sturgeon, beets and beer with pork tenderloin, calvados with cavatelli, endive with calf's liver and sea-buckthorne with carrots. Even the sweets (caramelized lemon tart) and digestifs are remarkable—the digestifs made with chantilly cream and maple sugar instead of the customary chocolate. There are no disappointments at Toqué! The service is perfect and so is the setting. The wine-list, with its magnificent clarets and burgundies, to say nothing of its sassicaias and its solaias, is equally impressive. Laprise and Lamarche have come a long way from the rue St.-Denis.

Open Tuesday to Friday 11.30 am to 1.45 pm, 5.30 pm to 10 pm, Saturday and Sunday 5.30 pm to 10.30 pm. Licensed. Amex, Master Card, Visa. Book ahead. ♿

MONTREAL   MAP 121
LES TROIS PETITS BOUCHONS   ☆☆
4669 rue St.–Denis   **$180**
(514) 285-4444

This is a crowded, noisy, happy place. They have a long shared table and a number of smaller tables for two or three people. Audrey Dufresne is still in charge of the kitchen; the other two work in the front of the house. No money has been spent on the interior, which could be called shabby. But the cooking is good, very good. The menu, which is posted on a blackboard, changes every night, but usually starts with oysters on the half-shell (21.00 for Pacific oysters, 18.00 for Atlantic). The calamari are wonderfully tender. The tartine of wild mushrooms comes with beautiful greens. The tartelette of reblochon is dressed with one of the best cheeses from the Haute Savoie. The foie gras is generously served for only 22.00—in fact the only expensive dish on the menu is the côte de boeuf, which costs 80.00 for two. This is not the place for a côte de boeuf; have the pintade in Jura wine instead, or the risotto of mussels. The wine-list offers a number of unusual wines, the best of which is the Mittnacht grand cru from Alsace.

Open Monday to Saturday 6 pm to 11 pm. Closed on Sunday. Licensed. All cards. No smoking. Book ahead.

Every restaurant in this guide has been personally tested. Our reporters are not allowed to identify themselves or to accept free meals.

MONT TREMBLANT, Quebec   MAP 122

LE CHEVAL DE JADE   ★★★
688 rue de St.-Jovite   **$200**
Saint-Jovite
(819) 425-5233

All is well in St.-Jovite. It's been a hard year for Canadian restaurants, but Olivier Tali and Frédérique Pironneau have stuck to their guns. They put all they had into this old farmhouse in St.-Jovite and within a few years they won the Table d'Or, Quebec's most prestigious honour. Tali is also the only Canadian winner of the Ordre des Canardières, which came to him for his caneton à la Rouennaise, the signature dish of the Tour d'Argent in Paris. It means pressed duck and it's on the menu at the Cheval de Jade every night of the week. It has to be ordered the day before and it costs 99.00 for two. They make their bouillabaisse with seafood they import from France and serve the same day. Olivier aims to have the freshest and best fish to be had anywhere in the Laurentians and he probably does. He always has a fish soup, a fillet of striped bass en papillote, scallops with vanilla beans and paradise seeds. They buy everything locally, and we especially admire their red deer, their truffled duck and their foie gras. The presentation is always gorgeous, and there's a very good wine-list. The Cheval de Jade is pure magic.
Open Tuesday to Saturday 5 pm to 10 pm. Closed on Sunday and Monday. Licensed. Amex, Master Card, Visa. Book ahead.
♿

MONT TREMBLANT   MAP 122

MILLE PATES
780 rue de St.-Jovite   **$85**
Saint-Jovite
(819) 717-3830

The Cheval de Jade is the best restaurant in St.-Jovite, as everyone knows. But perhaps you'd like a change. Mille Pâtes is a small shop selling pasta. They also have a table where you can sit down and order whatever pasta's fresh from the oven that day. It's a Mum-and-Pop operation, with a short list of house-made soups, salads and sweets, and a table d'hôte priced at only 22.00. We remember their ravioli, which is wonderfully light. Everything here is made by a couple who take pleasure in what they do, and hope you do too.

Open Monday to Wednesday 9 am to 4 pm (lunch), 4 pm to 6 pm (dinner), Thursday to Sunday 9 am to 4 pm, 4 pm to 9 pm. Licensed. Master Card, Visa.

MONT TREMBLANT
See also VAL-MORIN.

MORRISTON, Ontario   (MAP 79)
ENVER'S   ☆
42 Queen Street   **$130**
(519) 821-2852

Morriston is little more than a scattering of houses along Highway 6, but for more than 30 years there's been a restaurant here good enough to take its place with the best of Stratford and Toronto. Look for an old grey-brick store front with neo-Gothic windows and doors. Enver was a one-man band, doing almost everything himself. Terri Manolis, who bought the place from Enver many years ago, was happy to sell a share of the business to the chef, Ken Hodgins. Hodgins does his best to cater to all comers. His fish, usually Lake Huron pickerel, is always fresh. His game is all organic. He features bison and On-tario lamb, either roasted or stewed in wellington stout. There's a good appetizer plate to start with, followed by pheasant or bison and at least four sweets. Last winter people were talking about the sticky-apple upside-down cake with cream and brown sugar. The wine-list is no longer small; it's grown enormously and now covers most of the New World and the Old.

Open Tuesday to Friday 11.30 am to 3 pm, 5 pm to 8.30 pm, Saturday 5 pm to 8.30 pm. Closed on Sunday and Monday. Li-censed. Amex, Master Card, Visa. Book ahead if you can. ♿

NANAIMO, B.C.   MAP 123
BISTRO AT WESTWOOD LAKE   ☆☆
2367 Arbot Road   **$135**
(250) 753-2866

Gaetan Brousseau has closed the Wesley Street Cafe and reopened under a new name on Westwood Lake, next door to the tennis club. Here he has a handsome dining-room with a fireplace and high ceilings. He also has excellent service and about the best cooking in town. Lunch means a marvellous quiche, with a cup of homemade soup or a mixed salad, for only 12.00. Dinner means scallops with a sweet-pepper and citrus relish or breast of duck with colcannon and raspberries, followed by a dark-chocolate cheesecake or vanilla crème brûlée.
Open Tuesday to Saturday 11.30 am to 9 pm, Sunday 11 am to 3 pm (brunch), 5 pm to 9 pm (dinner). Closed on Monday. Licensed. Master Card, Visa.

NANAIMO   MAP 123
CROW & GATE PUB
2313 Yellow Point Road   **$70**
(250) 722-3731

In 1972 Jack Nash, an Englishman, built the Crow & Gate on ten acres of scenic property in Cedar, near Nanaimo. The Crow & Gate was the first neighbourhood pub in the province. The place is pure Yorkshire, with its low wooden ceilings, oil paintings and wood-burning fireplaces. There's no deep fryer here, no fish and chips. What they have is country-style meat pies, the best of which, of course, is the steak-and-kidney pie. There are other good things too, like the oyster stew, the crab-cake, the stilton quiche, the English trifle and the sticky-toffee pudding. You order and pay up front and the food is brought to your table, so there's no waiting ever.
Open daily 11 am to 11 pm. Licensed. Master Card, Visa. ♿

If you use an out-of-date edition and find it inaccurate, don't blame us. Buy a new edition.

NANAIMO
GATEWAY TO INDIA
202 4 Street
(250) 755-4037

MAP 123

$85

The premises on 4 Street have been restored and redecorated, and everything is now trim and bright. The restaurant has a good wine-list and a sensible menu, offering
such familiar things as shrimp pakoras, aloo gobi, palak
gosht, mutter panir and tandoori chicken. The sweet lassi
is disappointing, but they have a good Indian beer
(Kingfisher) and several wines. If you like, you can drink
Kim Crawford's sauvignon blanc or perhaps a bottle of
Caymus Conundrum, with your tandoori chicken. The
naan is light and lovely, the service obliging.
*Open Monday to Friday 11 am to 9 pm, Saturday and Sunday
4 pm to 9 pm. Licensed. Master Card, Visa.* &

NANAIMO
THE HILLTOP
5281 Rutherford Road: Unit 102
(250) 585-5337

MAP 123

☆

$135

At the Hilltop we usually start with either the smoked-
halibut croquettes served with crème fraîche, saffron and
roasted tomatoes or the Humboldt calamari with grilled
shishitos. After that we recommend the Qualicum Bay
scallops with braised organic chard, chorizo and horseradish, the Arctic char with prawns and mussels in a
chilli-and-saffron broth and the braised bison short-ribs
with shallots and mashed potatoes. Ryan Zuvich has a
rare talent and if you find yourself in Nanaimo you
should come and see what he has to offer.
*Open Wednesday to Sunday 5 pm to 11 pm. Closed on Monday
and Tuesday. Licensed. Master Card, Visa. Book ahead if you
can.*

We accept no advertisements. We accept no payment for
listings. We depend entirely on you. Recommend the
book to your friends.

NANAIMO

MAP 123

THE NEST BISTRO
486A Franklyn Street
(250) 591-2721

$120

The Nest is a newcomer to Nanaimo. Nick Brawn and
Jen Ash make all the pasta in-house, as well as the spinach
gnocchi. Their prices aren't high. Most of the appetizers,
even the wild-mushroom tart with brie and the flash-
fried prawns in phyllo, cost less than 10.00. The lamb
shank is about the best of the entrées. Afterwards there's
a wonderful chocolate-ganache cake and a fabulous warm
ginger cake with whipped cream and caramel sauce.
There are only about ten tables, so it's a good idea to book
ahead.
Open Wednesday to Friday 11 am to 2 pm, 5 pm to 9 pm, Sat-
urday and Sunday 5 pm to 9 pm. Closed on Monday and Tues-
day. Licensed. Master Card, Visa. Book ahead if you can.

NANAIMO

MAP 123

TWO CHEFS AFFAIR
123B Commercial Street
(250) 591-4656

The Two Chefs closes in mid-afternoon, but they have a
very good breakfast, unless you want champagne with
your omelette. Most people order the eggs benedict with
a light and lemony hollandaise sauce, but we generally
find ourselves asking for the French toast, which is made
with rich egg bread, pumpkin and cinnamon topped with
maple syrup. For lunch we suggest the local mussels
steamed in apple cider or the crab-and-snapper fishcake
on a bed of lettuce with a dressing of lemon and orange.
We like both.
Open Tuesday to Friday 8 am to 4.30 pm, Saturday 8 am to 3
pm, Sunday 9 am to 3 pm. Closed on Monday. No liquor. Mas-
ter Card, Visa.

NANAIMO
See also CEDAR.

We've been writing about the All Seasons Café at 620 Herridge Lane (telephone (250) 352-0101) for so long that we find it pretty hard to say now that we can no longer recommend it. Nelson is a picturesque town, restored to look much as it did during the Gold Rush, and we've been looking hard for other places to eat. We can tell you that The Full Circle at 402 Baker Street: Suite 101 (telephone (250) 354-4458) has a fabulous breakfast. It's open Monday to Saturday 6.30 am to 2.30 pm, Sunday 7 am to 2 pm, but it doesn't serve dinner. We're still looking for a place that does.

NEW GLASGOW, N.S.   MAP 125
BaKED FOOD CAFE   ☞
209 Provost Street   **$60**
(902) 755-3107

This is a delightful little café that makes the most of the local, the seasonal, and the healthy. They have a great number of vegetarian dishes and make all their sandwiches with homemade bread. At noon there may also be a butternut-squash quiche, perhaps served with curried chick-peas. All the helpings are small and the sweets are really small—really small but very good. (The best of the lot is the chocolate-banana marquis topped with hazelnuts.) The coffee is made with freshly ground beans, one cup at a time. In the early morning they serve a fine breakfast that starts with an omelette, made with a variety of fillings, among them ham, peppers, green onions, mushrooms and cheese.

Open Tuesday to Saturday 8 am to 5 pm. Closed on Sunday and Monday. Licensed. Master Card, Visa.

NEW GLASGOW   MAP 125
THE BISTRO   ☆☆
216 Archimedes Street   **$115**
(902) 752-4988

The French chef who opened the Bistro later sold it and

returned to France. It was bought by Robert Vinton and his wife, Heather Poulin. They closed the place for the better part of a year while everything was renovated. Meanwhile, the couple became involved with the local art community and every three months they put on a display of work in progress. There's always a public reception, with an abundance of appetizers supplied by the kitchen. Vinton's meat is all organic and local, and one often sees him in town shopping for one of his daily specials—a soup, perhaps, or some meat or fish. He's particularly good with fish, especially salmon, scallops and mussels, which never leave the menu.

Open Tuesday to Saturday 5 pm to 9 pm. Closed on Sunday and Monday. Licensed. All cards. Book ahead.

NEW GLASGOW
See also PICTOU, STELLARTON.

NIAGARA-ON-THE-LAKE, Ontario   MAP 126
THE CHARLES INN   ☆
209 Queen Street   **$150**
(866) 556-8883

The Charles Inn occupies a splendid old house right on the main street. The house was built almost a hundred years ago. Now restored, it has twelve comfortable bedrooms and a handsome dining-room. Weather permitting, breakfast is served on an open verandah filled with light and air. Inside, Steve Sperling has a rather grand tasting menu that offers home-smoked Arctic char, seared Quebec foie gras, pan-fried diver scallops, tenderloin of triple-A beef, cheese and a sweet, all for 95.00 a head or 135.00 with appropriate wine pairings. The regular à la carte is good too, and cheaper. Dinner begins with foie gras with a garnish of foraged mushrooms and goes on to chinook salmon, whitefish or beef tenderloin, ending with a lemon-meringue tart or four-year-old cheddar or a piece of Waltzing Matilda, which means soft buffalo cheese ripened in balsam ash. They have a generous selection of Niagara wines (Lailey, Thirteenth Street,

Malivoire and Tawse). The Tawse is probably the best of these, but it costs 110.00 a bottle. If you have any money left, there are four good icewines, all sold by the glass.

Open daily noon to 2.30 pm, 4 pm to 8.30 pm from 1 May until 31 October, Monday to Friday 4 pm to 8.30 pm, Saturday and Sunday noon to 2.30 pm, 4 pm to 8.30 pm from 1 November until 30 April. Licensed. Amex, Master Card, Visa. Book ahead if you can.

NIAGARA-ON-THE-LAKE   MAP 126
EPICUREAN
84 Queen Street   **$140**
(905) 468-0288

The Epicurean is that rare thing: a good, cheap restaurant in an expensive town. People line up at the door for thick, made-to-order sandwiches and a glass of wine, which most of them eat outside under the huge butternut tree. But there's more to the Epicurean than a sandwich and a glass of wine. Every evening they serve steak frites, lamb shanks and rainbow trout, as well as a number of quiches. You can also count on a selection of charcuterie and cheese, and there's always plenty of good drinking from the Niagara Region and a surprising sangria by the glass.

Open daily 9 am to 5 pm (lunch), 5 pm to 8 pm (dinner). Licensed. Amex, Master Card, Visa. &

NIAGARA-ON-THE-LAKE   MAP 126
LIV   ☆
White Oaks Resort   **$160**
253 Taylor Road
(800) 263-5766

Liv has a lavish setting in a resort complex on the outskirts of Niagara-on-the-Lake. Good cooking is the last thing one would expect. But so it is: the menu is surprising and so is the cooking. For instance, they have a water list, offering bottled water from Voss as well as San Pellegrino. They have 24 wines by the glass and countless draft beers. Most of the wines come from the Niagara Region, but there are several also from California, Australia, New Zealand, Chile and Argentina. The soup of the day may be spiked with bourbon, and there's an avocado salad with chèvre and black beans as well as mussels in dark ale. After that there's lobster agnolotti, grilled Atlantic salmon, Berkshire pork, rack of lamb and, for 42.00, a ten-ounce striploin steak. To top all this off, if you have 50.00 to spare you can drink yellow-label Veuve Cliquot champagne with your meal.

Open Sunday to Thursday 5 pm to 9 pm, Friday and Saturday 5 pm to 10 pm from 1 May until 30 September, Tuesday to Thursday 5 pm to 9 pm, Friday and Saturday 5 pm to 10 pm from 1 October until 30 April. Closed on Sunday and Monday in winter. Licensed. Amex, Master Card, Visa. &

NIAGARA-ON-THE-LAKE   MAP 126
RAVINE VINEYARD
1366 York Road   **$90**
St. David's
(905) 262-8463

The beauty of the Ravine Vineyard is that it's open all day. All their soups come from local gardens, and the same is true of their salads. They have a fine charcuterie platter, all of it home-smoked and garnished with home-made preserves. It comes with half a dozen or more Canadian cheeses, from Riopelle to Thundering Oak. Daily specials run to things like chicken-liver parfait, pan-seared whitefish, Cornish guinea-hen, smoked scallops, *sous-vide* lamb and dry-aged beef. The best of the sweets are the lemon-meringue pie and the rhubarb panna cotta. There aren't many wines, most (but not all) from the Ravine vineyard at the door.

Open daily 11 am to 9 pm. Licensed. Master Card, Visa. &

The price rating shown opposite the headline of each entry indicates the average cost of dinner for two with a modest wine, tax and tip. The cost of dinner, bed and breakfast (if available) is shown in parentheses.

NIAGARA-ON-THE-LAKE

MAP 126

STONE ROAD

☆

Garrison Plaza

$145

218 Mary Street
(905) 468-3474

Stone Road has been discovered, and prices have risen dramatically. The menu used to be all about soups, salads and sandwiches. Nowadays they're more ambitious. There's prosciutto with melon (a charming if familiar dish), foie gras poutine, mussels, charcuterie, steak frites and meatballs made of the best beef from Cumbrae in Toronto. The sweets too are surprisingly elaborate—cloudberry crème brûlée and brandied-cherry clafoutis. There are three craft beers to drink, several wines by the glass and at least one good gewurztraminer by the bottle. And they still have a lively oyster bar where you can sample several varieties of oyster, among them Kusshis from the Pacific and Malpèques from the Atlantic, all served in the half-shell with preserved lemon and horseradish.
Open Tuesday to Friday 11.30 am to 2 pm, 5 pm to 9 pm (later on Friday), Saturday 5 pm to 10 pm, Sunday 5 pm to 9 pm. Closed on Monday. Licensed. Master Card, Visa. Book ahead.
&

NIAGARA-ON-THE-LAKE

MAP 126

TRIUS AT HILLEBRAND

1249 Niagara Stone Road

$175

(905) 468-7123

Trius is committed, they tell you, "to working with passionate farmers, growers and producers, who remind us daily why it is so rewarding to follow nature in the kitchen." All restaurants say the same, of course, and what really counts is what the kitchen does with the produce local farmers (passionate or not) bring to the door. Some things they do well here—the corn soup with buttermilk espuma, for instance, the albacore tuna with chiogga beets and sea asparagus and the diver scallops with maple and bacon. But the Perth County lamb with pressed tomato and candied onions is an indifferent dish and the wines that come from the Hillebrand vineyards (as most of them do) are not really good enough. The five-course tasting menu is better. For 75.00 you can have salmon cured in icewine, foie gras with icewine jelly and dark-chocolate ice cream. But aside from that Trius is not quite what it used to be.

Open daily noon to 2.30 pm, 5 pm to 8 pm. Licensed. Amex, Master Card, Visa. Book ahead if you can. &

NORANDA, Quebec
See ROUYN.

NORRIS POINT, *Newfoundland* (MAP 164)
JUSTIN THYME BEAN & BISTRO
216 Main Street   **$100**
(709) 458-2326

Justin George and his wife, Lynn, spent sixteen years working in the hotel business before opening their own place in Norris Point. Here they have a blackboard that changes every day. The place looks pretty basic, but everyone speaks highly of their fish chowder and their mussels. Not that Justin is content with that. He also serves lamb, beef, chicken and two sweets—one a mandarin orange cake, the other a deconstructed tiramisu. Just in Thyme is open all day every day in summer, but has shorter hours in winter. They have a licence and take all cards. &

NORRIS POINT (MAP 164)
NEDDIE'S HARBOUR INN
7 *Beach Road*   **$150**
(709) 458-3089

Norris Point is on Bonne Bay in the heart of Gros Morne National Park. Neddie's Harbour is a small boutique hotel with stunning views of the bay and the mountains beyond. The dining-room is good if rather expensive. The menu is short. Beef tenderloin is served with a stilton crust and figgy duff comes with molasses. Cod, halibut, scallops and mussels are all generally available. The kitchen orders fresh fish every day and if the chef doesn't like what the suppliers send him, he just serves Arctic char instead. You can start with an heirloom-tomato soup with coconut and cilantro, a confit of Valley Hill pork with polenta or an apple-and-parsnip salad with a sea-buckthorne gastrique. Everything is made from scratch and the service is very professional.

Open Tuesday to Sunday 7.30 am to 10 am, 5 pm to 8.30 pm from 15 June until 15 September. Closed on Monday (Monday and Tuesday from 15 May until 14 June and from 16 September until 30 November). Licensed. All cards. &

NORTHEAST MARGAREE, N.S.   (MAP 151)

THE DANCING GOAT
6335 Highway 19   **$45**
Cape Breton
(902) 248-2308

The Dancing Goat is a real find. It's always full, though now that they've enlarged the dining area you can usually find a chair. There's no table service. You go up to the counter, choose what you want from the blackboard and take a number to your table. Every day they have two homemade soups—curried chicken, perhaps, or broccoli with coconut. There's always a quiche and there are also a number of sandwiches, all made on thick, home-baked bread with crusts on. There's usually some Black Forest ham, some roast beef, some egg salad and (the best of the lot) some bacon with avocado. There's espresso and caffe latte to go with your sandwich and they're both good. There may be no liquor but there's just about everything else. Recently the Dancing Goat has opened a second restaurant, at 15933 Central Avenue in Inverness (telephone (902) 258-3520). It has table service and so far the critics have all been extremely favourable.

Open Monday to Wednesday 7.30 am to 5 pm, Thursday and Friday 7.30 am to 8 pm, Saturday 7.30 am to 5 pm, Sunday 8 am to 5 pm. No liquor. Master Card, Visa. &

Nobody but nobody can buy his way into this guide.

NORTH RUSTICO, P.E.I. (MAP 39)
THE PEARL ★★
7792 Cavendish Road **$160**
(902) 963-2111

The Pearl is on an especially lovely stretch of Highway 6 between North Rustico and Cavendish, right in the heart of *Anne of Green Gables* country. Maxine Delaney has been winning awards for the Pearl almost from the day she opened. Local people love the place and regularly book it for private parties in September and October. She did most of the interior design herself and ever since she's kept up a charming garden. But she's always found it hard to keep chefs from one year to the next—which is why we can't be specific about her menu. But we do know that this year the chef will be Rob MacDonald, who comes from the Pelican in Ottawa. Last year there was a three-course table d'hôte for 45.00 a head, and this year you can probably count on Kim Dormaar's smoked salmon, as well as fresh oysters from Raspberry Point. Soups all come straight from the garden, and both lobster and scallops appear on the menu from time to time. Warm weather brings local asparagus, and triple-A beef tenderloin is seldom off the menu. The Pearl today is as good as anything in the province.

Open daily 5 pm to 9 pm from mid-May until mid-October. Licensed. Master Card, Visa.

OKANAGAN CENTRE, B.C. (MAP 92)
GRAPEVINE
Gray Monk Estate Winery **$140**
1055 Camp Road
(250) 766-3405

Here it's hard to choose between the venison meatloaf in a reduction of red wine with house-made pear chutney and the Fraser Valley duck confit with cranberry-onion marmalade and homemade spaetzle. Don't hesitate. Despite appearances, the venison meatloaf is much the better of the two. The sweets are all lovely, especially the cheesecake topped with fresh seasonal fruit. Grapevine is still run by Willi Franz and René Haudenschild, and they're as good as ever.

Open daily 11.30 am to 4 pm, 5 pm to 9 pm from 1 April until 31 October. Licensed. Master Card, Visa. &

OLIVER, B.C. (MAP 92)
MIRADORO
Tinhorn Creek Vineyard **$135**
32830 Tinhorn Creek Road
(250) 498-3742

Miradoro is run as a partnership between Manuel Ferreira of the Gavroche in Vancouver and the Tinhorn Creek Winery. It's elegantly modern and overlooks the whole of the southern Okanagan. The menu is Mediterranean and draws inspiration from such countries as Italy, Spain and Portugal. The wine-list offers wines from many local wineries as well as Tinhorn Creek. You can start with wild-boar carbonara, a traditional Italian dish, or any one of a number of first-class pizzas. Typical of these are the pizza bresaola and the Neapolitan pizza rucula, topped with arugula, prosciutto and fresh lemon. In the evening they have an unusual combination of albacore tuna and sweetbreads, served with semolina, tomato agridolce and heirloom carrots or, if you're uneasy with surf and turf, organic chicken with wild mushrooms, caramelized onion and potato gnocchi. For sweet, you can experiment with the hazelnut cake with summer fruit and praline.

Open daily 11 am to 3 pm, 5.30 pm to 9 pm. Licensed. Master Card, Visa. &

OLIVER (MAP 92)
TERRAFINA
Hester Creek Estate Winery **$135**
887 Road 8
(250) 498-2229

Terrafina is on the Golden Mile Bench, right in the heart of some of the best wine country. They serve Tuscan-style dishes, using nothing but fresh local ingredients, in a rustic and informal setting. We like the marinated duck carbonara with green beans, pancetta and white truffle oil. Others prefer the pappardelle with braised lamb, tomato and mint chiffonade. The best of the main courses, we think, is the roasted chicken with a risotto of squash, or perhaps the braised-beef short-ribs with a reduction of wild mushrooms and sundried tomatoes. If you'd like to drink a wine from Hester Creek with your dinner, there's a free evening shuttle from Osoyoos.

Open Wednesday to Saturday 11.30 am to 9 pm, Sunday 10 am to 4 pm. Closed on Monday and Tuesday. Licensed. Master Card, Visa. ♿

ORANGEVILLE, Ontario   MAP 132
FORAGE
163 1 Street   **$95**
Credit Creek Plaza
(519) 942-3388

Restaurant One 99 has both ambition and style, but right now it's being made over and it'll be some time before it's open again. Meanwhile, there's Forage. Forage is pretty noisy and you certainly have to book ahead, because Matthew Jamieson and his wife, Wendy, brought a lot of people with them when they moved here from the Hockley Valley. It's quieter at noon, when it seems casual and even comfortable. The cooking is simple, but everything is professionally plated, fresh and carefully foraged. The prices are fair and all the wines are sold by the glass as well as the bottle. They go out of their way to accommodate vegetarians. We keep ordering the crab-cakes, but others prefer the seafood stew. Admittedly, the kitchen is good with fish, even the squid and the tuna tataki. Wendy makes all the sweets, the best of which, we think, is the flourless-chocolate cake with salted caramel. There are six craft beers, as well as several wines.

Open Monday to Saturday 11 am to 9 pm. Closed on Sunday. Licensed. Amex, Master Card, Visa. Book ahead if you can. ♿

ORILLIA, Ontario MAP 133
WEBERS
8844 Highway 11 N **$25**
(705) 325-3696

After all these years, Webers still gives everyone a feeling of real excitement. Nobody waits too long, nobody is disappointed. Children play, lovers touch each other, tired drivers sit down, at peace, under a tree, somebody goes to the bathroom. Everyone is happy. Webers now has sixteen flavours of ice cream, and if you want a real, old-fashioned milkshake you can get it at the ice-cream counter. They're still using Illy coffee beans to make their espresso. Webers beef is all pasteurized by exposing it to a steam-blanket in a pressurized chamber at a temperature of 185°F; it's then stored at 30°F, ground fresh daily and cooked to a temperature of 160°F. Each week in summer they process and sell more than three tons of ground beef—50 tons a summer. Their fries all come from potatoes grown, cut and packed in Prince Edward Island. Teenagers take your order, make change and see that you get what you want within two minutes, no matter how long the lineup may be. On the first Tuesday in August there's free corn on the cob for all comers. There's rock music on the soundtrack and free parking for hundreds of cars on both sides of the highway, with an overhead bridge that connects the southbound lot to the restaurant.

Open daily 10.30 am to 7 pm from 11 until 21 March, Friday to Sunday 10.30 am to 7 pm from 22 March until 14 April, daily 10.30 am to 7 pm (later on weekends) from 15 April until 26 May, daily 10.30 am to 9 pm from 27 May until 23 June, daily 10.30 am to 10 pm from 24 June until 5 September, daily 10.30 am to 7 pm from 6 September until 10 October, Friday to Sunday 10.30 am to 7 pm from 11 October until 10 November. No liquor, no cards. &

Every restaurant in this guide has been personally tested. Our reporters are not allowed to identify themselves or to accept free meals.

OSHAWA, Ontario MAP 134
BUSTER RHINO'S ☞🖐
28 King Street E **$60**
(905) 432-8750

We've come a long way from the elegant dining-room at the Robert McLaughlin Gallery, where good cooking and reasonable prices couldn't deliver a durable tenant. But Darryl Koster, who has worked rough in both Whitby and Oshawa, has opened a first-class restaurant here on downtown King Street. It may not take reservations, but it does have a licence and comfortable seating. The menu offers a poutine of beef brisket, pulled pork, slow-cooked for sixteen hours, which makes it tender and full of flavour, and wonderful smoked ribs rubbed with spices and then slow-cooked until the meat falls off the bone. There's a new kitchen now, so the menu will be expanding. Meanwhile, the cooking is just getting better and better.

Open Monday to Thursday 11 am to 9 pm, Friday 11 am to 11.30 pm, Saturday and Sunday 11 am to 9 pm. Licensed. All cards. No reservations. ♿

OTTAWA, Ontario MAP 135
ALLIUM
87 Holland Avenue **$140**
(613) 792-1313

Lunch at Allium is simple and straightforward: chicken-fried snails, squid with pickled red onions, steak frites with smoked chilli, burgers with chipotle, shrimp wrap and roasted breast of duck. Dinner is more elaborate and on Monday they offer a big selection of tapas—wild salmon (sometimes overcooked), duck confit (with excellent accompaniments), scallops (often with pea purée and red peppers), sometimes potato-and-cauliflower soup. The wine-list is full of good buys, most of which, like the Stanners chardonnay, come from the Niagara Region. Allium is at its best on Monday nights, but if you come then you have to book ahead.

Open Monday 5 pm to 10 pm, Tuesday to Friday 11.30 am to 2 pm, 5 pm to 10 pm, Saturday 5 pm to 10 pm. Closed on Sunday. Licensed. Amex, Master Card, Visa.

OTTAWA   **MAP 135**
ATELIER   ☆
540 Rochester Street   **$450**
(613) 321 3537

When the celebrated restaurant elBulli closed in Catalonia, we thought the world had said goodbye to molecular gastronomy. Not so. Marc Lepine has made his name at Atelier in Ottawa using many of the same procedures. He offers a tasting menu of twelve courses served either on small plates or in test tubes. The menu is coy, but the waiters are both knowledgeable and friendly, and if you have 450.00 to spare this may be a good place to spend it. (If you're over 30, perhaps not.) The new Canadian food, as Lepine calls it, is all hyper-modern. It's dehydrated, frozen, then put back together again. This is what Ottawa needs? Sadly, we're over 30.

Open Tuesday to Saturday 5 pm to 10 pm. Closed on Sunday and Monday. Licensed. All cards. You must book ahead. &

OTTAWA   **MAP 135**
BECKTA   ☆
226 Nepean Street   **$185**
(613) 238-7063

Michael Moffatt is cooking better this year. He handles steelhead trout and lobster with equal assurance, and sells the lobster at bargain prices. He serves duck from Quebec, wall-eye from Lake Erie and beef from Wellington County, all with easy competence. His oysters come from New Brunswick or Prince Edward Island and are served in the half-shell, though without the benefit of grated horseradish. His foie gras is wonderful and he has a seldom-seen dry riesling from Lincoln Lakeshore in Niagara, but if you're having the beef you'll find some good drinking among the reds from France, Italy or Australia.

The setting on Nepean Street is quiet and serene and the service is poised and elegant.

Open daily 5.30 pm to 9.30 pm. Licensed. Amex, Master Card, Visa. Book ahead. ♿

OTTAWA   **MAP 135**
THE BLACK CAT   ✩✩
428 Preston Street   **$160**
(613) 569-9998

Patricia Larkin is cooking as well as ever, though her menu keeps changing. She now takes her stand on Richard's Angus burger (prepared with cheddar cheese, smoked bacon and a secret sauce), Black Angus striploin with peppercorn bordelaise and maître d'hôtel butter, steelhead trout with sunflower sprouts, blue mussels in coconut both, loin of lamb with goat-cheese, sockeye salmon (with beets, radishes and horseradish) and seared Qualicum Bay scallops with cauliflower purée and shiitake mushrooms. The flourless-chocolate cake has, sadly, disappeared, but they still offer a French lemon tart and a variety of Quebec cheeses. There are several unusual wines by the glass and the bottle, among them Frog's Leap cabernet sauvignon from the Napa Valley. If you can't afford the Frog's Leap, ask for the cabernet franc from Organized Crime. It's good.

Open Monday to Saturday 5 pm to 10 pm. Closed on Sunday. Licensed. Amex, Master Card, Visa. Book ahead. Free parking. ♿

OTTAWA   **MAP 135**
EIGHTEEN   ✩✩
18 York Street   **$195**
(613) 244-1188

Matthew Carmichael made Eighteen the best restaurant in Ottawa. When he left last year to open his own restaurant we were concerned about the future of his kitchen. It turned out that Eighteen under Carmichael's sous-chef, Walid El-Tawel, has lost little (perhaps none) of its for mer polish. The menu is still extraordinary, offering such things as salt-roasted beet salad, grilled octopus, tuna sashimi, bison cheeks, lobster consommé and steak tartar. These are all perfectly cooked and the tuna sashimi is easily the best in the city. The butter-poached lobster that comes next has few equals, though the lacquered black cod is also a marvellous dish. The venison can be tough, and you may be safer with the rack of Ontario lamb. If the enoki mushrooms from Le Coprin are on offer, be sure to ask for them; they're rare and wonderful. The sticky-toffee pudding is lighter than most and better than any of the crème brûlées. The wine flights are now available only on special occasions like New Year's Eve, but there are many good buys on the regular wine-list. Inside, the restaurant is exciting, but the service is leisurely. Allow two hours for dinner.

Open Monday to Saturday 5 pm to 10.30 pm. Closed on Sunday. Licensed. Amex, Master Card, Visa. Book ahead.

OTTAWA   MAP 135

THE ELMDALE OYSTER HOUSE
1084 Wellington Street W   **$150**
(613) 728-2848

The Elmdale Oyster House is named after the pub that used to operate on the same site. Owned by Whalesbone, it features oysters on the half-shell. If you're lucky, these may be from Shemogue, though Shemogues aren't well known outside the Atlantic Provinces. There's also a nice treatment of albacore tuna crudo with cucumber, sesame and ginger, but the clam chowder lacks flavour. As for the lobster dumplings with chilli and walnuts, we haven't yet tried them. The so-called clamghetti is a surprising dish, stuffed as it is with clams, pecorino cheese and roasted red peppers. There are a couple of sweets, and the dirty-sailor chocolate mess is much the better of the two. To drink, there's a light, clean chardonnay from Butterfield Station for 10.00 a glass.

Open Monday and Tuesday 5 pm to 11 pm, Wednesday 11.30 am to 11 pm, Thursday 11.30 am to midnight, Friday and Sat

urday 11.30 am to 11 pm (oysters only 11 pm to 2 am), Sunday
11.30 am to 11 pm. Licensed. Master Card, Visa. Book ahead
if you can. &

OTTAWA   **MAP 135**
FRASER CAFE   ☆
7 Springfield Road   **$140**
(613) 749-1444

You can usually get a table here in the late evening, which
is something to remember. After 9 o'clock you can often
find a place to sit down to a first-class plate of charcuterie
and a dozen oysters on the half-shell from St.-Simon, impeccably cleaned, chilled and served with horseradish.
Earlier in the evening they like to serve such things as
Pacific halibut with chick-peas, B.C. salmon with white
beans, house-smoked trout with beet-root and mustard
and albacore tuna with savoy cabbage. The menu changes
with the seasons, but you can usually count on beef with
fries, wild salmon, Cornish game hen, halibut, pork belly
and tuna, as well as cheese and charcuterie. On Monday
evening they put on a special dinner at Table 40 next
door. A typical table d'hôte there might start with raw
oysters, go on to pork tenderloin and a tomato salad and
end with a rhubarb Danish.
Open Monday to Friday 11.30 am to 2 pm, 5.30 pm to 10 pm,
Saturday 10 am to 2 pm (brunch), 5.30 pm to 10 pm, Sunday
10 am to 2 pm (brunch). Licensed. Amex, Master Card, Visa.
Book ahead.

OTTAWA   **MAP 135**
GEZELLIG
337 Richmond Road   **$150**
(613) 680-9086

Gezellig (Dutch for convivial) is all about small plates,
pulled pork, sautéed snails and seared scallops from
Alaska. All of these are cheap and they all make a perfect
lunch. If you come in the evening they have grilled
shrimp with popcorn, pan-roasted Pacific halibut, braised

rabbit and coffee-cured leg of duck, all of course at higher prices. Coffee-cured leg of duck is a new idea and so are Alaskan scallops and, for that matter, shrimps with popcorn. The wine-list covers a lot of ground—from Creekside sauvignon blanc for 30.00 to Sleepy Hollow for 105.00, from Cave Spring gamay noir for 35.00 to Painted Rock for 135.00. A number of wines are offered by the glass and there are a couple of draft beers as well. Gezellig is fresh and new and very well served.

Open Monday to Friday 11.30 am to 2 pm, 6 pm to 10 pm, Saturday 6 pm to 10 pm, Sunday 10.30 am to 3 pm (brunch). Licensed. Amex, Master Card, Visa. &

OTTAWA   MAP 135
MURRAY STREET
110 Murray Street   **$120**
(613) 562-7244

This place started out as a charcuterie, but it was (and still is) open all day, which means that you can come in at 10 o'clock and have some elk kielbasa with a glass or two of wine. In the years since then they've started serving other things as well—things like chicken pot-pie, falafel, charcoutine (fried kielbasa with black-pepper sausage, bologna and homemade spaetzle), corned beef, pulled pork and potato gnocchi. But we suggest that you stick pretty closely to the charcuterie, most of which is made right on the premises. It's good and so are the cheeses (riopelle and bleu d'Elizabeth). The other things are not. The pickerel, for instance, may come from Whalesbone, but it's buried in lentils and flavoured improbably with tartare sauce. The corned beef is served with pickled onions on rye bread, which comes from the Rideau Bakery. The dining area is dark and solemn, and it would take more than a bowl of fries with mayonnaise to make it seem bright and lively.

Open daily 11.30 am to 2.30 pm, 5 pm to 10 pm (11 pm for charcuterie). Licensed. Amex, Master Card, Visa.

Nobody but nobody can buy his way into this guide.

OTTAWA   **MAP 135**
NAVARRA   ☆
93 Murray Street   **$175**
(613) 241-5500

René Rodriguez grew up in Mexico and at Navarra today he's cooking in the Mexican style. That means salmon cured with ancho, scallop ceviche with lime and a dungeness-crab salad with red grapefruit. The crab salad is certainly a wonderful dish. After that ask for the Oaxacan black mole, which is made in the traditional way with coffee and chocolate. There are other good things too, like the pig's cheeks with bufala mozzarella, lamb's belly with chilli torcados and rabbit confit with fried mushrooms. The bread is a lovely treatment of sweet potato, served warm with herb butter. On the wine-list there's a chardonnay and a cabernet franc from Prince Edward County. Both are bottled especially for Navarra and both are cheap and pleasant. The sauvignon blanc from Appleby costs more and is better. There are only three red wines from Spain and two white, which is disappointing. After all, the restaurant is called Navarra.
Open Tuesday 4 pm to 10 pm, Wednesday to Saturday 5.30 pm to 10 pm, Sunday 10.30 am to 2.30 pm. Closed on Monday. Licensed. Amex, Master Card, Visa. Book ahead.

OTTAWA   **MAP 135**
SIDEDOOR
18B York Street   **$115**
(613) 562-9331

Sidedoor was opened as a cheaper alternative to Eighteen. Like Eighteen, it's all rough stone and glass. The menu is basically Mexican, though the tacos aren't made with corn. They're white and soft and at noon that's about all there is. In the evening there are two or three tacos, served as appetizers, followed by black cod with soya, mirin and truffle oil, white-tuna sashimi, sockeye-salmon ceviche, salt-and-pepper squid, seared scallops, pork belly with mango, cashews and chillies and braised panaeng

179

beef. The beef and the black cod tend to be overcooked, though the sauces, on which the kitchen lavishes a lot of care, are usually pretty good. There's an ambitious wine-list as well as several sakes. There's nothing else like Side-door in Ottawa.

Open daily 11.15 am to 2 pm, 5 pm to 10 pm. Licensed. Amex, Master Card, Visa.

OTTAWA   **MAP 135**
SIGNATURES   ☆☆
453 Laurier Avenue E   **$160**
(613) 236-2499

Signatures occupies the fine old mansion at the east end of Laurier Avenue that once housed the Cercle universitaire. It's run nowadays by the Cordon Bleu school of cooking, and the price for an elaborate and well-served dinner is less than you'd expect. The meal begins with a well-designed beef tartar or a tartar of salmon with ginger and daikon, or perhaps with a goat-cheese tart or braised pork belly with mustard. It continues in a similar vein with seared scallops with tomato and truffle oil, fillet of cod with garlic, breast of duck with semolina or seared white tuna with madeira and baby bok choy. Tuna with madeira? Scallops with truffles? Despite appearances, these dishes actually do work. (If you don't think so, order the Black Angus with calvados, which is a much more conservative dish.) The meal ends in gay and lively style with a passion-fruit semifreddo. The wine-list emphasizes wines from Canada and Italy, though the best of the lot—the Rule cabernet sauvignon—is from Napa and costs only 65.00 for a bottle or 14.00 for a glass.

Open Wednesday to Friday 11.30 am to 1 pm, 5.30 pm to 9 pm, Saturday 5.30 pm to 9 pm. Closed Sunday to Tuesday. Licensed. Amex, Master Card, Visa. Free parking. Book ahead. &

The map number assigned to each city, town or village gives the location of the centre on one or more of the maps at the start of the book.

OTTAWA MAP 135
SUPPLY & DEMAND
1335 Wellington Street W **$150**
(613) 680-2949

Supply & Demand is a new restaurant and it's widely regarded as the best in the city. This is hardly the truth,
though the place does hold considerable promise. The
menu is awkward. There are sections devoted to raw
dishes, small plates, pasta, meat and fish. If you want an
appetizer and a main course, you'll have to go looking
for them. They have oysters on the half-shell and lovely
treatments of albacore tuna crudo and a crudo of sea scallops with pomegranates and celery. But if you start your
meal that way you'll be left with only two or three main
dishes—mackerel with boudin noir, octopus with rye
berries and porchetta of duck for two. The octopus
comes with the leg of a chicken and if you don't like surf
and turf you should ask instead for the squid-ink rigatoni,
the black-pepper spaghetti or the ceviche of razor clams.
The scallops and tuna are both superb, but the mackerel
with boudin noir is usually not. There's plenty of good
drinking, however, on the wine-list. There's a fine sauvignon blanc from Napa, a chardonnay from Prince Edward County and a riesling from Thirty Bench. The best
of the reds, we think, is the Laughing Stock from the
Okanagan.
Open Monday 5 pm to 9.30 pm, Tuesday to Saturday 5 pm to
10 pm, Sunday 5 pm to 9.30 pm. Licensed. Amex, Master
Card, Visa. Book ahead.

OTTAWA MAP 135
TAYLOR'S GENUINE FOOD & WINE BAR
1091 Bank Street **$140**
(613) 730-5672

People (including the editors of this guide) have often
spoken highly of Taylor's cheese and charcuterie, but the
fact is that you'll do better nowadays if you turn the page
and order from the regular à la carte. There you'll find

many good things, like braised pig's-cheek croquettes and smoked black-cod rillettes. The main dishes are almost equally inviting. There's pan-roasted breast of duck with squash, mushrooms, baby beets and wilted greens and pan-seared sablefish with young spinach and lemon-meringue gnudi. There are other things too—beef short-ribs and pork tenderloin, for instance—but it's probably better to settle for the duck and the sablefish. The wine-list starts with five or six wines chosen by the house, and they're all good. Try the cabernet from Dirty Laundry while it lasts, or perhaps the merlot from Burrowing Owl. The mulled wines served in the winter are considerably cheaper and if it's cold outside they're a good choice.

Open Monday to Saturday 11.30 am to 2 pm, 5.30 pm to 9.30 pm, Sunday 5.30 pm to 9.30 pm. Licensed. Amex, Master Card, Visa. Book ahead if you can.

OTTAWA   **MAP 135**
WELLINGTON GASTROPUB
1325 Wellington Street W   **$135**
(613) 729-1315

The Wellington Gastropub may be simple, but it's very cheap. Christopher Deraiche is an accomplished chef, but it's hard to do a lot with prices like these. St.-Simon oysters (among the best) come (without ice, lemon or horse-radish) for 11.00 for four, shrimp tempura for a dollar more, loin of pork for 26.00, sea scallops in fish chowder for 27.00, Pacific halibut on a bed of lentils for 28.00 and flat-iron steak for 27.00. The best of these is probably the sea scallops in fish chowder. Most of the others come to the table with black beans or (too many) lentils. Adriana makes first-class ice cream and there's always some fine artisanal cheese. They actually make several of their own beers and one of them, the Eddie Double D, contains 9.2 percent alcohol, which is double what you get in the commercial product. They also have eight beers in cask as well as those they have on tap. So far as we know, there's nothing else like this in Ottawa.

Open Monday to Friday 11.30 am to 2 pm, 5.30 pm to 10 pm.
Saturday 5.30 pm to 10 pm Closed on Sunday. Licensed. Amex,
Master Card, Visa. Book ahead if you can.

OTTAWA   MAP 135
WHALESBONE
430 Bank Street   **$140**
(613) 231-8569

Whalesbone is one of a kind. It's very small and very noisy. It's rough and doesn't pretend to be anything else, but they supply oysters to most of the restaurants in the city. The menu is short, prices higher than you might expect. Lobster risotto with sweet peas and greens costs about 45.00, hanger steak 33.00, wall-eye clams 30.00. On the other hand, a pound of mussels from Prince Edward Island with coconut and Thai basil costs only 12.00. People come here and order 30 oysters and are happy. Scallop ceviche is served with smoked olive-oil, albacore tuna with sweet soy and sesame; crisp clams come with spicy mussels and smoked oysters. They have a lovely, light sweet—churras with chocolate sauce. The wine-list is big and strong, and everything is priced at 12.00 a glass or 48.00 a bottle. For that they'll give you a glass or a bottle of the Lailey unoaked chardonnay or the Bogle petite syrah. It's a steal.

Open daily 11.30 am to 2 pm, 5 pm to 11 pm. Licensed. Amex,
Master Card, Visa. ♿

OTTAWA
See also CHELSEA.

OWEN SOUND, Ontario   MAP 136
THE FLYING CHESTNUT
199 Pellisier Street   **$100**
Flesherton
(519) 924-1809

To get to Flesherton, turn off Highway 26 at Thornbury and drive south on Highway 13 almost as far as Highway

4. This is the heart of Blue Mountain country, where you can go fishing on Lake Eugenia or visit Eugenia Falls, second only in height to the falls at Niagara. Shawn Adler has installed a big wood-burning stove in his kitchen and dedicated it to regional, organic cooking—even his beer and wine are local. Every night three appetizers and three main dishes are written up on a blackboard. Usually there's one fish, one meat and a vegetarian dish. The menu changes every week, but dinner usually ends with bread pudding, butter tarts or a fruit crumble. The Sunday brunch offers omelettes, pancakes and waffles for about 15.00, and portions are very generous.

Open Thursday to Saturday 5 pm to 10 pm, Sunday 11 am to 2 pm (brunch), 5 pm to 10 pm. Closed Monday to Wednesday. Licensed. No cards. Book ahead if you can.

OWEN SOUND   MAP 136
THE ROCKY RACCOON   ☆
941 2 Avenue E   **$95**
(519) 374-0500

Robin Pradhan plans to concentrate on Owen Sound from now on, even if only because that's his wife's home town. Pradhan and Shelley Bentz first met in Europe. Together they came to Canada and began working for the Rocky Raccoon in Dyers Bay. Before long they had taken the place over and moved it to Gore Bay on Manitoulin Island. Soon they moved again, this time to Wiarton, then finally to Owen Sound. In Owen Sound their menu is, as always, a marriage of Asian cuisine and the profusion of fresh produce available on the Bruce Peninsula. They offer fresh fish from sustainable stock, which means whitefish and line-caught lake trout. They get their lamb, wild boar, bison and pheasant from nearby farms. In the evening they serve a lot of Bengali and Burmese curries with hand-crafted chutneys. At noon they put on a buffet lunch, featuring a variety of French crêpes and Nepalese dumplings. Shelley makes a wonderful chocolate mousse and a great tiramisu. The wines all come from Niagara and even the craft beers are local.

Open Monday to Saturday 11 am to 11 pm. Closed on Sunday. Licensed. All cards. &

PAPINEAUVILLE, Quebec   MAP 137
LA TABLE DE PIERRE DELAHAYE   ☆
247 rue Papineau   **$125**
(819) 427-5027

Pierre Delahaye and his wife, Jacqueline, realized a dream back in 1985, when they bought this old house, built a century earlier. Pierre came from Normandy and liked the dishes he'd grown up with. He intended to buy everything locally. And he believed that to cook well you need to be a happy man, which he was. So people now drive 40 miles from Ottawa for brunch here, knowing they'll have a good time. The menu doesn't change much. There are always snails with apples and calvados, and sweetbreads braised with apples and finished with apple cider. There's a three-course dinner for 31.50 that features a fish course, snails with garlic butter and a French pastry. The pick of the sweets, of course, is the French apple tart.
Open Wednesday to Saturday 5.30 pm to 9 pm, Sunday 11.30 am to 2 pm (brunch), 5.30 pm to 9 pm. Closed on Monday and Tuesday. Licensed. Master Card, Visa.

PEMBROKE, Ontario   MAP 138

There are a couple of new places in Pembroke this year that we think you should know about. One is the Nook Crêperie at 26 Pembroke Street W (telephone (613) 735-4800). They offer ten savoury crêpes and thirteen sweet crêpes. You can make a dinner out of the lox crêpe or the Michelangelo, which comes with a spicy Italian sausage. If you order the Voltaire you get marinated beef with asparagus and goat-cheese plus soup or a salad for just 23.00. Janna's Gallery Café at 20 Pembroke Street W (telephone (613) 631-0443) is famous for its coffee, and on Saturday there's an all-day breakfast for 5.50. The service is great. Finally there's Ullrich's on Main at 214 Pembroke Street W (telephone (613) 735-6025), but they serve nothing but lunch. They usu-

ally have two soups, a quesadilla, a few salads and a number of sandwiches. Keep an eye out for the maple-syrup tart and the chocolate torte—they're both very good. You'll find Ullrich's in the corner of a butcher shop. All three restaurants are open all day six days a week. They all have a licence and take most cards. ⅋

PENETANG, Ontario (MAP 115)
FROTH CAFE ☆
102 Main Street: Suite 1 **$50**
(705) 549-7199

The Olympia Gardens has unexpectedly closed, so Penetang is left with the Froth Café, which happens to have an excellent kitchen. They have superb coffee but, more important than that, they have at least 30 different varieties of bread—hazelnut with pears and figs, pumpkin, apple pecan—all of them irresistible. People buy their bread by the armload, giving loaves to anyone they can think of. They make a very good breakfast too and a fine lunch of soups, sandwiches, quiches and some really remarkable salads. The best of these is the garden salad with a poppyseed dressing or the salmon salad in a honey-lemon vinaigrette. You won't be disappointed in their sweets either. They have a carrot cake, and a lovely strawberry-rhubarb pie as well.
Open Tuesday to Saturday 8 am to 6 pm, Sunday 9 am to 4 pm. Closed on Monday. Licensed. No cards.

PERCE, Quebec MAP 140
AUBERGE LE COIN DU BANC ☆
345 route 132 e **$150**
(418) 645-2907

The Coin du Banc occupies an old frame building four miles north of Percé on route 132. The place is littered with hurricane lanterns, ships' models, wood stoves and primitive artwork. It's open all day and has a wonderful breakfast that features pain doré, foie de morue and the lightest of crêpes, served with real maple syrup. Every day they put on a simple lunch featuring salade des crevettes and croque monsieur. In the evening they add such things as escargots de bourgogne, smoked salmon and a shrimp omelette, followed by cod three ways, scallops with tartare sauce and steamed lobster. If you come in summer and order the *repas complet*, you can even expect cods' tongues, which are a rarity nowadays. There's a short list of familiar wines and a handful of half-bottles, of which the best is probably the riesling Willm.

Open daily 8 am to 10 pm from 1 June until 30 September. Licensed. Amex, Master Card, Visa.

PERCE

See also ST.-GEORGES DE MALBAIE.

PETERBOROUGH, Ontario	**MAP 141**
ELEMENTS	☆☆
140 King Street	**$130**
(705) 876-1116	

Elements would probably be the best restaurant in Peterborough even if most of the others hadn't already shut their doors. For one thing, they have a great wine-list, because they buy limited quantities of wine from local wineries. They also offer a broad selection of dessert wines and digestifs, something that's not all that common. Nobody brings supplies to the door, so the owner, Norman Howard, does his own foraging. He changes his menu every few weeks, so summer's pollo pepitoria (chicken in a sauce of almond, saffron and garlic) becomes autumn's pollo con pimento (chicken with roasted red peppers). The vegetables, however, are always pommes William and rainbow carrots (orange, yellow and purple). If you want a steak, they have a very good one—triple-A with brandy. Otonabee pork tenderloin is stuffed with pears, walnuts and sundried cranberries and served with hard cider. Fresh fish comes in daily. And they make all their own sweets. Our favourite is the torta de Santiago, a honey-almond cake made with fresh plums. When you book, it's a good idea to ask for a table on the patio, which overlooks a garden shaded by spreading locust trees.

Open daily 11.30 am to 11 pm. Licensed. All cards. &

PICTON, Ontario
BLUMEN GARDEN
647 Highway 49
(613) 476-6841

MAP 142
☆
$140

The Blumen Garden is a few miles from Picton on High-way 49. It's owned and run by Andreas Feller. He has a short menu with five or six appetizers and eight or nine main courses. Start with seared scallops or a Jerusalem-artichoke vol-au-vent and go on to one of the traditional bistro main dishes—things like breast of chicken, rack of lamb, rib steak and salmon, all carefully served with parsnip-and-potato mash. At lunchtime there are some smaller plates, a risotto perhaps, a quiche, crab-cakes, salads and sandwiches. The wines are mostly local and there are several local beers and local cider on tap.
Open Monday and Thursday to Sunday 11.30 am to 2 pm, 5 pm to 9.30 pm. Closed on Tuesday and Wednesday. Licensed. All cards. &

PICTON
GAZEBO
Waupoos Estate Winery
3016 County Road 8
(613) 476-1355

MAP 142

$145

This winery restaurant has proved so popular with sum-mer visitors that the old Gazebo has been expanded and the old patio enclosed. The view over the vines to the lake is as lovely as ever and, despite the fact that Jeff Wil-son has replaced Scott Ryan in the kitchen, the food is still very good. We admire the soups and the arugula salad with pears and candied pecans. At noon they also have a roast-chicken wrap with black beans and avocado, served with a green salad, as well as a number of sandwiches. Most of these dishes are available also in the evening. You can begin your dinner quite grandly with Quebec foie gras, followed by breast of duck, rack of Ontario lamb or roasted local chicken. The wines all come from the estate, even the icewines. The Geisenheim costs only 7.00 a glass, and that's a pretty good buy.

Open daily 11 am to 3 pm, 6 pm to 9 pm from mid–May until mid–October. Licensed. Master Card, Visa. Book ahead if you can.

PICTON   **MAP 142**
MERRILL INN   ☆
343 Main Street E   **$170 ($385)**
(866) 567-5969

Amy and Edward Shubert came here with impressive credentials, and before long they hired an equally impressive chef named Edward Sullivan. Sullivan's cooking is basically French. His menu is quite short and you'll be struck by the cleanness of all his dishes. Everything is beautifully plated, especially the salads. Market-fresh fish comes to the door every day, and we've always preferred it to the meat, but others feel the same about the beef tenderloin. The lamb is local, but it costs 38.00 a portion, which is a lot. The service, however, is civilized and the wine pairings are always appropriate. If you stay the night, the price includes a wine-tasting event as well as a spectacular breakfast. The cheese plate is very well maintained , and there's excellent drinking from Grange in Prince Edward County. The coffee is wonderful.

Open Tuesday to Saturday 5.30 pm to 9 pm. Closed on Sunday and Monday. Licensed. Amex, Master Card, Visa.

PICTON
See also BLOOMFIELD, WELLINGTON.

PICTOU, N.S.   **(MAP 125)**
MRS. MACGREGOR'S TEAROOM
59 Water Street   **$60**
(902) 382-1878

Mrs. MacGregor is a dab hand at selling herself. We've said it before and we say it again. She also, of course, knows how to cook and she runs a catering business summer and winter. At lunchtime she makes an excellent seafood chowder and a very good chicken soup, as well as a number of salads and sandwiches on homemade bread. There are also a couple of hot dishes such as quiche Lorraine and fishcakes. In the evening, coq au vin has taken the place of the turkey dinner and there's a vegetarian pasta as well as scallops and haddock. Mrs. MacGregor thinks her lobster roll is about as good as her sticky-toffee pudding, and that may very well be true. If you come for tea—this is a tearoom after all—you'll find that a slice of butterscotch pie goes well with any of the teas.

Open daily 11 am to 3 pm, 5 pm to 9 pm from 15 February until 23 December. Licensed. Master Card, Visa. Book ahead if you can. &

PICTOU (MAP 125)
STONE-SOUP CAFE
41 Water Street **$80**
(902) 485-4949

The Stone-Soup Cafe has been in business for only about four years, but already it's attracted a big local following. Barry Rundle and Camille Davidson have a generous menu that's served all day until 8 o'clock in the evening. Everything is prepared in-house except the bread and bread-rolls, which come in daily from a local bakery. For breakfast there's eggs benedict and a waffle, prepared on weekends by Barry and Camille's teen-age son. At lunchtime there's always a good soup, often cream-of-wild-mushroom. If there are no wild mushrooms on hand, ask for the seafood chowder. Next comes a variety of sandwiches—poached salmon on a bagel, perhaps, or a Thai-style chicken wrap. For dinner (if you come early) there's usually some fish and chips or a seafood bake. Sweets change daily—just look and see what they have. They're all good.

Open daily 7 am to 8 pm from 1 May until 15 October (shorter hours in winter). Licensed. Master Card, Visa. &

PLANTAGENET, Ontario   MAP 145
MARIPOSA FARM
6468 County Road 17   **$90**
(613) 673-5881

Nothing of importance has changed at Mariposa Farm in the last couple of years. Suzanne Lavoie and Ian Walker have been raising Embden geese and Barbary duck on their 175-acre farm east of Ottawa for almost 30 years. (Recently they've also been breeding a full complement of pigs—Berkshire, Tamworth and Saddleback.) They've converted an old barn into a small but charming dining-room, complete with white-linen table-cloths and a broad view of the surrounding countryside. Sad to say, the dining-room is open only two hours a week, on Sunday from 11 am to 1 pm. The chef, Matthew Shepherd, has a small menu—three appetizers, three main courses and two sweets (or a cheese plate), three courses for 45.00. Foie gras is always on the menu, along with either duck or goose and home-baked bread. Unfortunately, Mariposa Farm is not licensed, so the char-grilled breast of duck is marinated in fruit juice. The farm store is in the same building and it sells everything from duck and geese to homemade preserves, jams, jellies and pâtés. Look for the Mariposa Farm sign outside of town, just east of Wendover.

Open Sunday 11 am to 1 pm. Closed Monday to Saturday. (The store is open Friday to Sunday 9 am to 4 pm.) Master Card, Visa. Book ahead. ♿

LA POCATIERE, Quebec   MAP 146
CAFE AZIMUT
309 4 Avenue   **$120**
(418) 856-2411

The Café Azimut occupies an old house on 4 Avenue in La Pocatière, a few minutes from Exit 439 on Highway 20 west of Rivière du Loup. They don't really serve lunch any more—just pizza and pasta—but every day at about noon they put up a blackboard for the evening meal. It'll offer such things as mussel-and-shrimp soup en croûte, tartar of crab, ravioli of beets, feuilleté of shrimp and—best of all—smoked sturgeon. For sweet, there's usually a wonderful tarte au sucre. The wine-list is full of private imports, and among the open wines there's an R.H. Phillips cabernet sauvignon and a Kim Crawford sauvignon blanc. One could hardly hope for more.

Open daily 9 am to 11 am, 4 pm to 10.30 pm. Licensed. Amex, Master Card, Visa. &

POCOLOGAN, N.B. MAP 147
BAYBREEZE MOTEL
6410 Highway 1 **$50**
(506) 755-3850

The Baybreeze, which is on Highway 1 between Saint John and St. Andrews, is better than ever this year. John and Maria Lytras have always offered deep-fried clams and deep-fried scallops, and they're the best you'll find anywhere on this shore. But we usually ask instead for the lobster roll or the lobster stew. Others prefer the (excellent) grilled halibut. The vegetables, once quite indifferent, are now always fresh and seasonal. The fries are still frozen, but the coleslaw is homemade. The pastries are all prepared with a light hand, and the olives come from olive trees that grow on the Lytras property in Italy, where John and Maria spend their winters. Here in Pocologan, they have a spacious deck overlooking the Bay of Fundy where you can have a glass of wine before dinner.

Open daily 8 am to 9 pm from early May until late June, daily 7 am to 10 pm from late June until late August, daily 8 am to 9 pm from late August until late October. Licensed. All cards.

This is a guide to Canadian restaurants from coast to coast—the first ever published and the only one of its kind on the market today. Every restaurant in the guide has been personally tested. Our reporters are not allowed to identify themselves or to accept free meals.

PORT CARLING, Ontario   **MAP 148**
LOONDOCKS
98 Joseph Street   **$140**
(705) 765-5191

Loondocks is uphill from the small-boat lock in the heart
of Port Carling. They have a lovely open-air deck overlooking the water, but you need good eyes unless you get
there before dark. (The deck is poorly lit.) They have a
number of small plates—spring-rolls, local-mushroom
risotto and Yorkshire pudding stuffed with lamb. Of
these the Yorkshire pudding is probably the best. Among
the large plates is macaroni and cheese, which you probably haven't eaten since you were ten years old. There's
also fillet of trout with maple and merlot, halibut beurre
blanc and beef tenderloin with mushrooms and brandy.
The meal will end, if you're lucky, with a big wedge of
flourless-chocolate cake. The wine-list is small, but there
are a few good wines from California, Australia and the
Niagara Region, of which the best (we think) is the Tin
Barn cabernet sauvignon from Sonoma for just 47.00.
The bread all comes from the bakery next door, and it's
good.
Open daily 11 am to 8.30 pm from early May until late October.
Licensed. Master Card, Visa. Book ahead if you can. ♿

PORT CARLING   **MAP 148**
SHERWOOD INN
1090 Sherwood Road   **$190**
(705) 765-3131

The Sherwood Inn is deliberately old-fashioned—the
sort of place where your great-aunt used to spend the
summer. The dining-room is big and bare. The menu is
small, the prices high. But they do some very good
things. One of these are the scallops with spinach and
mango. Another is the rainbow trout from Manitoulin
Island. A third is the rack of fresh lamb from Australia,
served with balsamic vinegar. A fourth is the apple crisp,
made with northern Ontario spies—spies are rare nowa

193

days and they're hard to find. The wine-list concentrates on Niagara whites and California reds. The wines are expensive, but there are one or two very good buys. There's a Beringer cabernet sauvignon for 32.00 and a family-select chardonnay from Peller for a dollar less.

Open daily 11.30 am to 9 pm from early May until the middle of October. Licensed. All cards. Book ahead.

PORT CREDIT, Ontario (MAP 202)
BREAKWATER
Waterside Inn **$175**
15 Stavebank Road S
(905) 891-6225

The Waterside Inn is near the mouth of the river in the heart of Port Credit. The restaurant has big windows on three sides and the tables are widely spaced and laid with fine linen and silver. They have a tapas menu that features grilled chorizo with soft pumpkin, Yukon Gold potato with brie, shrimps sautéed with fresh ginger, salmon gravlax and terrine of foie gras. The main courses—châteaubriand, lamb shanks, pork wienerschnitzel and Alaska black cod—are (except for the black cod) less exciting. For sweet there's an apple tart tatin and an icewine crème brûlée. Ask for the crème brûlée every time.

Open Monday to Friday 7 am to 11 pm, Saturday and Sunday 8 am to 11 pm. Licensed. Amex, Master Card, Visa. Book ahead if you can. Free parking. &

PORT ELGIN, N.B. MAP 150
LITTLE SHEMOGUE INN
2361 Highway 955 **$125 ($325)**
(506) 538-2320

The bright-red house overlooking a marshy inlet of Northumberland Strait has been carefully restored and redecorated. Across the inlet, linked to the main house by a foot-bridge, there's a cottage with a spectacular interior. Ask for Room 8 in Log Point, as it's called, when you book. It's expensive, but there's nothing else like it in Atlantic Canada. Dinner is served every evening at 7 o'clock in one of three or four small dining-rooms, but the Sudbracks sold the place in the summer of 2012, so Petra is no longer in the kitchen and her husband, Klaus, no longer serves the wine. That makes all the difference. Over the years, Petra had become a gifted cook. Petra and Klaus—all that has gone now. Come to Little Shemogue, if you come at all, for a room in Log Point and the sight of the Great Blue Herons that fish in the shallows to the west.

Open daily at 7 pm by appointment only from 1 May until 31 October. Licensed. Master Card, Visa. You must book ahead. &

PORT HOOD, N.S. MAP 151
HAUS TREUBURG
175 Main Street **$125 ($250)**
(902) 787-2116

Georg and Elvi Kargoll bought this old house in 1984 and restored it from top to bottom. Their menu seldom changes, their prices never do. Dinner comes in four courses unless you book the seven-course *menu surprise* in advance. Normally you start with house-smoked salmon or flammkuchen, an Alsatian version of pizza, followed by soup or a Caesar salad. Then there's a choice of meat, fish or a vegetarian dish. The meat might be beef stroganoff or a pork schnitzel, the vegetarian dish might be lasagne. We ourselves usually prefer the fish. The poached Atlantic salmon is about as good as it gets, though they also usually have some haddock or halibut or even fresh lobster. The meal ends with a fine apple strudel, made to an old family recipe and topped with real whipped cream. If you spend the night—the bedrooms are immaculate—you'll come down in the morning to what they call a German Sunday breakfast, which means farm-fresh eggs, homemade sausages, cereals, grains, hot buttered toast and homemade yogurt. The Haus Treuburg has its own sandy beach and some of the warmest water in Eastern Canada.

Open daily by appointment only from 1 May until 30 November. Licensed. Master Card, Visa. You must book ahead.

PORT HOOD
See also GLENVILLE, NORTHEAST MARGAREE.

PORT STANLEY, Ontario   MAP 152
WINDJAMMER INN   ☆
324 Smith Street   **$125 ($250)**
(519) 782-4173

Kimberley Sanders has survived for eight years by virtue of hard work and hard work alone. Her house was built by a local ship's captain, Sam Shephard, in 1854 and it makes a fine place to stay. Kimberley has worked in several important Toronto restaurants and she certainly knows how to cook pastry. Her menu changes every six or eight weeks to make the most of fresh local produce. Fresh perch and pickerel are always on hand, the perch pan-fried and the pickerel barbecued. When it comes to the sweet course, Kimberley often simply improvises and ends up turning out something irresistible. Breakfast, which is served only to resident guests, is a glorious meal. Last year Kimberley opened a café with a bar and barman for the casual diner.
Open daily 8 am to 10 pm (shorter hours in winter). Licensed. Amex, Master Card, Visa. ♿

PORTUGAL COVE, Newfoundland   (MAP 174)
FERRY LAST-STOP CAFE   ☆
2 Loop Drive   **$85**
(709) 895-3082

Paulette King runs this little place with the help of her 85-year-old mother, Mercedes. Of this partnership Paulette says simply, "she is my life." The Café overlooks the ferry to Bell Island, and perhaps for that reason is one of a kind in Portugal Cove. The menu is short and seductive. Everything is fresh and organically grown. One diner writes that his salad of local greens was the best in

his memory. Bread is made in the kitchen every morning. All the soups and all the sweets are made in-house. If fresh cod is on the menu, be sure to ask for it—you'll be surprised when it comes to the table. There are fifteen to twenty wines on the list, most of them sold by the glass as well as the bottle. A couple of rooms upstairs are kept for travellers who want to stay for the night. (Those who do will find that breakfast is almost as good as dinner.)
Open Wednesday to Sunday 10 am to 3 pm, 6 pm to 9 pm from early May until early December. Closed on Monday and Tuesday. Licensed. Master Card, Visa.

PRINCE ALBERT, Saskatchewan MAP 154
AMY'S ON SECOND ☆
2990 2 Avenue W **$135**
(306) 763-1515

Amy's seems to be the only good restaurant that can survive in this town. Two by Dahlsjo opened to good reviews, but within a year it was reduced to catering. Amy always gave a little more than she had to, of course; she always listened to her customers and allowed for their preferences. When she began to get tired she found an able sous-chef in Klarke Dergoussoff, a graduate of the Stratford Chefs School. He and Amy have been offering bison and duck for so long that they now seem old hat. Fresh salmon has become a staple too, often served in a mango-butter glaze. Halibut and Arctic char come in once a week. Rack of lamb is often on the menu, though it's not Canadian—Canadian lamb is too expensive. The pastry chef has been with Amy for twenty years and makes at least eight different varieties of cheesecake, as well as wonderful crème brûlée. The Great West Coffee Company is gone, but Amy bought enough beans to last her for some time.
Open Monday to Saturday 11 am to 9 pm. Closed on Sunday. Licensed. All cards. Free parking. ♿

If you use an out-of-date edition and find it inaccurate, don't blame us. Buy a new edition.

PRINCE GEORGE, B.C.
THE WHITE GOOSE
1205 3 Avenue
(240) 561-1002

MAP 155
☆
$160

Ryan Cyre has at least one great asset: he loves what he's doing. What is he doing? Well, every year in February he orders four whole truffles from France. Six days a week he makes magnificent five-course dinners that sell for 85.00. All week he makes ten lunches and sells them for 10.00 each every ten minutes. The most popular of his dishes are his baked brie and his duo of duck (breast and confit of drumstick). We also like his bison risotto, his braised beef short-ribs with polenta, his crab-cakes and his golden-fried lobster ravioli. The weekly surprise dinner may be built around glazed salmon, goose, bison or ostrich. Cyre's mother still makes the chocolate cake to an old family recipe, and she doesn't intend to give it up. The wine pairings are chosen with great care, and the service is always exemplary.

Open Monday to Saturday 11 am to 2 pm, 5 pm to 9 pm. Closed on Sunday. Licensed. Master Card, Visa. ♿

PRINCE RUPERT, B.C.
COW BAY CAFE
205 Cow Bay Road
(250) 627-1212

MAP 156

$125

Adrienne Johnston was one of the most accomplished chefs in the province, and one of the most attractive. It was sad to see her leave the Cow Bay. Opa Sushi has bought the place and turned it into a high-end Italian restaurant. They make a lot of gluten-free pasta and there are always some interesting daily specials. The prices are higher than they used to be, of course, and it's still too soon for us to say what the future will bring. Further reports needed.

We accept no advertisements. We accept no payment for listings. We depend entirely on you. Recommend the book to your friends.

PRINCE RUPERT

MAP 156

OPA SUSHI
34 Cow Bay Road $90
(250) 627-4560

Customers at Opa Sushi are asking for sashimi these days instead of tempura. The kitchen is still offering kaiseki dinners every so often, but the chef is now more interested in his bi-weekly fresh sheet. A couple of new items will be on the sheet this year. One of these is the so-called Green Dragon, which means pickled asparagus with avocado, carrots and cucumber in barbecue sauce. The other is the Manila Vanilla, which is named after the Filipino chef. It combines crab with cucumber, avocado and curried honey. They never use anything in the kitchen but fresh local salmon, squid, octopus, eel and sweet shrimps, and they have the only sake bar in the Pacific Northwest. You'll find the place on the second floor of an old net loft, one of the last of its kind on this coast. It's right on the water and has 35 seats. If you take a table outside on the patio you should be able to watch sea-eagles nesting overhead.
Open daily 11.30 am to 2 pm, 5 pm to 9 pm. Licensed. Master Card, Visa.

PRINCE RUPERT

MAP 156

SMILE'S
113 Cow Bay Road $75
(250) 624-3072

You don't usually expect good cooking from a restaurant with a history like Smile's. There's been a café on this site, hidden away among railroad sidings and fish plants, for more than 70 years. People who used to come here with their children come today with their grandchildren. It's true, the cooks still use the old-fashioned deep-fry, but changes are on the way. Already, salmon, sole, red snapper and black cod can be had poached or pan-fried. Prince Rupert used to be the halibut capital of the world. Eventually the supplies ran out, but now halibut is once again on the menu at Smile's. Halibut is fiercely expensive at the moment, so they may be using snapper or cod in their fish and chips. They have excellent chowders too, as well as club sandwiches made with crab or shrimp. If you want an old-fashioned milkshake, this is the place to get it. Last year we were worried by talk of a complete renovation, but all that meant was a coat or two of fresh paint.

Open daily 10 am to 10 pm from early June until Labour Day (shorter hours in winter). Licensed. Master Card, Visa. ⅍

QUALICUM BEACH, B.C.   MAP 157
GIOVANNI'S
180 2 Avenue W: Unit 4   **$120**
(250) 752-6693

This place is the creation of Giovanni (the chef) and Helen Belcastro (the manager). Every evening in summer they serve a four-course tasting menu of Greek and Italian food in an attractive, comfortable setting. They start with an *amuse bouche* of a bruschetta that goes really well with the chianti riserva they have on the wine-list. (The fact is that a good chianti goes well with almost anything.) Steelhead salad comes next, then a trio of veal with prawns, scallops and sole. The sweet is usually tiramisu, which in our opinion comes in a poor second to the panna cotta. On the à la carte, veal is usually the best choice, though the rack of lamb is good too. The seafood, which is plentiful and correctly cooked, is all local. Recently, Giovanni has expanded his lounge, where he serves pizzas and light meals. Everything comes from the same kitchen—ask for the Italian Combo in the lounge and see for yourself.

Open Monday to Friday 11.30 am to 2 pm, 5 pm to 10 pm, Saturday and Sunday 5 pm to 10 pm from 1 June until 30 September, Monday to Thursday 11.30 am to 2 pm, 5 pm to 9 pm, Friday 11.30 am to 2 pm, 5 pm to 10 pm, Saturday 5 pm to 10 pm, Sunday 5 pm to 9 pm from 1 October until 31 May. Licensed. All cards. ⅍

QUALICUM BEACH
See also COOMBS.

QUEBEC, Quebec   MAP 158
APSARA
71 rue d'Auteuil   **$85 ($175)**
(418) 694-0232

The Apsara is now run by Chau Mouy Youk and her husband, a son of Beng an Khuong. Beng an Khuong es-
caped from Cambodia in 1975, leaving all his possessions
behind. Within two years of his arrival in Canada he had
bought this fine old house with his sixteen children, several of whom still work in the restaurant. Chau Mouy
Youk has been in charge of the kitchen for at least 30
years and she makes a virtue of consistency. The menu
includes Thai and Vietnamese dishes as well as Cambodian, and it seldom changes. Everything is amazingly
cheap. The lunch menu, which changes daily, costs just
12.95. Ignore the chicken brochette and look for one of
the shrimp dishes, which are always good. There's a
shrimp stir-fry, for instance, that comes to the table in a
nest of fried vermicelli. If you come with a companion,
there are several dishes on offer for two or more, among
them an appetizer of spicy pork with crisp noodles from
Thailand and a main course of oudong chicken stir-fried
with ginger. There are a number of Cambodian pastries
and some very good sorbets. They have a few wines, but
it's better, we think, to ask for a carafe of hakutsuru sake,
which is on draft. It comes cold and clear and it's great.
Open Monday to Friday 11.30 am to 2 pm, 5.30 pm to 11 pm,
Saturday and Sunday 5.30 pm to 11 pm. Licensed. Amex,
Master Card, Visa.

QUEBEC   MAP 158
L'INITIALE   ★★★
54 rue St.-Pierre   **$295**
(418) 694-1818

L'Initiale is one of only a handful of Relais & Châteaux

in Canada. Yvan Lebrun has two seasonal menus, one an eight-course tasting menu, the other a traditional à la carte. The à la carte offers medallions of venison, sea-bass, breast of duck and fresh lobster. Both menus end with a sweet *du jour* and a spectacular plate of fresh berries and cream with cake. The setting is beautiful, the service impeccable, the cooking rich but delicate. The wines are mainly French, with a small selection of Tuscans. Prices are high, but you can drink very well by the glass. Yvan Lebrun is once again at the top of his form.

Open Tuesday to Friday 11.30 am to 2 pm, 6 pm to 9 pm, Saturday 6 pm to 9 pm. Closed on Sunday and Monday. Licensed. All cards. Book ahead.

QUEBEC   **MAP 158**
LAURIE RAPHAEL   ☆☆
117 rue Dalhousie   **$260**
(418) 692-4555

There's no on-street parking and no valet parking at Laurie Raphael and the car park at the end of the street isn't easy to use, especially after dark. If you have trouble, ask for help at the front desk. The evening meal begins with white sturgeon or Raspberry Point oysters on the half-shell, followed by scallops from Maine and a ballotine of guinea-fowl from a local farm. At noon the menu is much simpler and considerably cheaper, featuring smoked salmon, wild-mushroom crostinis and oysters Rockefeller to start with, followed by curried shrimps, loin of pork and fish of the day. The smoked salmon is exquisite. It's smoked right here and served with ground sumac and cauliflower florets. The fish of the day might come from Hawaii, because Daniel Vézina doesn't limit himself to regional produce, though he uses it whenever he can. There's a well-made apple pie at the end of the meal, though we prefer the lemon cake. The wine-list is expansive, offering no fewer than 24 dessert wines, twelve ports and twenty champagnes, as well as the usual table wines.

Open Tuesday to Friday 11.30 am to 2 pm, 5.30 pm to 10 pm,

*Saturday 5.30 pm to 10 pm. Closed on Sunday and Monday.
Licensed. All cards. You must book ahead.* &

QUEBEC   **MAP 158**
PANACHE   ☆☆
Auberge St.-Antoine   **$250**
8 rue St.-Antoine
(418) 692-1022

Today, this once-great restaurant is but a shadow of its former self. Its menu is now quite small, its service less glamorous than it used to be, its wine-list impossibly expensive—there's no use in looking for an interesting wine at an affordable price, because there are none. (There is a Groth from Napa for 1700.00 and a pomerol from Pétrus for 3150.00.) Even a straightforward gamay noir from Tawse costs 180.00, a chardonnay from Mission Hill 145.00. As for the food, the squid with olives, tomatoes and lemon is disappointing. The salads are a better choice, as are the ris de veau with mustard and the duck from Saint Apollinaire with fresh blueberries. Visitors have also praised the ravioli stuffed with rapini and the foie gras with Jerusalem artichokes. But this is a short list of pleasures and it costs 125.00 a head. Further reports needed. *Open Monday to Friday 11.30 am to 2 pm, 6 pm to 10 pm, Saturday and Sunday 6 pm to 10 pm. Licensed. All cards. Free valet parking. Book ahead.* &

QUEBEC   **MAP 158**
LE PATRIARCHE   ☆☆☆
17 rue Saint-Stanislas   **$380**
(418) 992-5488

Stéphane Roth came to Canada from Switzerland and settled in Quebec with a passion for *terroir*. He serves every dish on his menu three ways. Duck, for instance, is served magret, ballotine and sausage. Everything is fresh and made from scratch in the kitchen—from the bread to the ice cream. There are three *prix-fixe* prices: 80.00, 90.00 and 105.00 a head. Game is the most expensive of the three: wild boar, guinea hen and venison, preceded by "a symphony of foie gras." Roth's flavours are rich and very intense and one has to bring a superb appetite to a meal at the Patriarche. The wine-list has grown to almost 3,000 bottles and 250 labels, some of them surprisingly cheap at 39.00 a bottle. The service is, of course, completely professional. The setting is lovely, but you need to be prepared: dinner will take three or even four hours. *Open daily 5.30 pm to 10 pm from 1 July until 31 August (shorter hours in winter). Licensed. All cards. Book ahead.* &

QUEBEC   **MAP 158**
LE SAINT-AMOUR   ☆☆☆
48 rue Saint-Ursule   **$250**
(418) 694-0667

Benoît Larochelle is the *chef de cuisine* here, which gives Jean-Luc Boulay more time to look after his own restaurant, Chez Boulay. But there's certainly been no loss of panache in the menu or the cooking at the Saint-Amour. Rather the reverse. The Saint-Amour may still have a two-star à la carte, but it now has a wonderful, three-star table d'hôte that costs 63.00 and changes every day. The soup with which the meal begins is good beyond belief, and everything that follows is carefully orchestrated, so that each dish comes to the table with an air of authority and grace. The à la carte begins with foie gras, long a specialty of Boulay's, and goes on to such things as lobster bisque, snow-crab ravioli, smoked and salted duck, seabass in a coulis of purple cauliflower, venison, squab and Alberta lamb. Why, one wonders, make so much of snow crab, which hasn't enough flavour to carry the ravioli? Why offer European sea-bass, which is always a disappointing fish? Such questions never arise on the table d'hôte, where the flavours are all compelling. The wine-list, of course, is extraordinary. There are three Lafites, two Latours, seven Mouton-Rothschilds and five Pétrus, one of which is now priced at 15,000.00. There are sensible wines too for ordinary drinkers, and most of them are fairly priced.

Open Monday to Friday 11.30 am to 2 pm, 6 pm to 10 pm,
Saturday 5.30 pm to 10 pm, Sunday 6 pm to 10 pm. Licensed.
All cards. Free valet parking. Book ahead.

QUEBEC   **MAP 158**
LA TANIERE   ✩✩✩
2115 rang Ste.-Ange   **$260**
(418) 872-4386

At La Tanière they offer three *prix-fixe* menus, the Discovery (ten courses for 75.00), the Sensation (fifteen
courses for 105.00 and the Revolution (twenty courses
for 135.00). If your companion shares your wine pairings
the evening will cost you 260.00. If not, you'll have to
pay 325.00. (If you don't accept the wine pairing and
choose your own wine, the price will be even higher.) We
have never tried the Sensation or the Revolution—the
guide doesn't pay us enough for that. The Discovery
menu begins with foie gras, black truffles, smoky fleur de
sel and chives in puff pastry, all served on a small mirror,
followed by salmon with baby zucchini and banana foam
on a warm pillow. Next comes a scallop in honey foam
and a morsel of guinea-fowl coated with cherry. Then
partridge with local vegetables in thyme jelly and duck
gizzard in parsnip purée. Finally, there's raw wapiti, bison
tongue, caramelized apple on a candy-cap mushroom and
a lavender macaroon. What can one say about such splen-
dours? If you have the money to spare, spend it here. If
you haven't, don't blame us.
Open Wednesday to Saturday 6 pm to 9 pm. Closed Sunday to
Tuesday. Licensed. All cards. You must book ahead. ♿

QUEBEC   **MAP 158**
TOAST   ✩✩
17 Sault-au-Matelot   **$175**
(418) 692-1334

Toast spends its summers in a big tent; in winter you eat
inside. Christian Lemelin is still in charge of the kitchen
and he has an exciting and unusual menu. It lists a dozen

small plates and customers usually choose two or three to share. There's tartar of venison, foie gras de canard, mushroom crostini, veal cheeks and entrecôte of bison. They're all cleverly cooked and presented with style. We particularly admire the veal and the bison. The menu is all in French, so if you have any allergies be sure to ask for an English translation. The wine-list, which is fairly priced, concentrates on wines from France and California, and there's an excellent Château Signac from the Côtes du Rhône for only 48.00.

Open Monday to Friday 11.30 am to 2 pm (summer only), 6 pm to 10.30 pm (later on Friday), Saturday 6 pm to 11 pm, Sunday 10 am to 2 pm (brunch), 6 pm to 10.30 pm. Licensed. All cards. &

QUEBEC
See also ILE D'ORLEANS, ST.-GEORGES-DE-BEAUCE.

RADIUM HOT SPRINGS, B.C.   (MAP 87)
HELNA'S STUBE
7547 Main Street W   **$160**
(250) 347-0047

Helna's is by far the best restaurant in Radium. The menu is German and offers an extraordinary variety of potato dishes. The cooking is essentially home-style, though there are always daily specials, which may be something unusual like elk with gin or venison with chanterelles. The kitchen is at its best, as you might expect, with wienerschnitzel, often served with cranberries. The restaurant seats 40 inside and 40 outside, but Radium is crowded in summer, so if you plan to come at that time of year be sure to book ahead.

Open Tuesday to Sunday 5 pm to 10 pm from 1 June until Thanksgiving, Tuesday to Saturday from Thanksgiving to 31 May. Closed on Monday in summer, on Sunday and Monday in winter. Licensed. Master Card, Visa. Book ahead.

Our website is at www.oberonpress.ca. Readers wishing to use e-mail should address us at oberon@sympatico.ca.

REGINA, Saskatchewan   **MAP 160**
LA BODEGA
2228 Albert Street   **$125**
(306) 546-3660

Adam Sperling is constantly trying out new ideas, which
he offers on what he calls his fresh sheet. There you might
find his jumbo shrimp in white wine, which has become
a specialty of the house. Sometimes he's way over the top,
as when he offers twenty ounces of beef spiked on a
sabre, and several of his tapas dishes are big enough for a
whole meal. But every Monday night there's a spectacular tasting menu. It consists of nine courses for 35.00 a
head, and it's one of the best deals in town. There aren't
a lot of wines, and you're meant to order one of their 80
martinis instead. Most people do just that.
Open Monday to Saturday 11 am to 2 am, Sunday 10.30 am
to 2 am. Licensed. Amex, Master Card, Visa. Book ahead if
you can. &

REGINA   **MAP 160**
TANGERINE
2234 14 Avenue   **$40**
(306) 522-3500

At Tangerine one whole wall is covered with a blackboard advertising what the kitchen has to offer on any
given day. They have a new pastry chef this year, which
means that you have a variety of new puddings, pies and
parfaits to choose from. Keep an eye out for their frosted
cherry chiffon cake and their fruit crumble. They still
have their salads and their sandwiches, of course, and
they still make a point of returning all their kitchen scraps
to their supplier of pork, which helps him to feed his
pigs.
Open Monday to Friday 7 am to 6 pm, Saturday 9 am to 4 pm.
Closed on Sunday. No liquor. Master Card, Visa. &

If you use an out-of-date edition and find it inaccurate,
don't blame us. Buy a new edition.

REGINA   **MAP 160**
WILLOW ON WASCANA   ☆
3000 Wascana Drive   **$160**
(306) 585-3663

This is the only place in Regina where you can have a meal overlooking Wascana, the artificial lake in the centre of town. Also, the kitchen is known for serving nothing but fresh regional produce, so there's always something like lamb or duck or one of several breeds of pig on the menu. Tim Davies likes to experiment, but on the whole most things seem to work, especially the bison. The new wine-list is quite large and easy to use.

Open Monday to Saturday 11.30 am to 9 pm. Closed on Sunday. Licensed. All cards. Book ahead. &

REGINA
See also VIBANK.

REVELSTOKE, B.C.   **MAP 161**
WOOLSEY CREEK CAFE   ☆
504 2 Street   **$135**
(250) 837-5500

In recent years Revelstoke has prospered, and they now have a really good restaurant, something that once seemed out of the question. We used to recommend Sylvia Bisson's three-cheese ravioli and little else. Now we can also recommend her butter-braised rabbit and her pork stew with black beans and chorizo. Sylvia buys organic fruits and vegetables whenever she can, and tries always to have some fresh fish on hand. Sometimes she can be quite expensive. Her rack of venison, for instance, costs all of 42.00. Her dark-chocolate cake is still available, as well as a five-cheese plate with figs and hand-made flatbread. And she has a couple of wines that you won't find in a liquor store.

Open daily 5 pm to 9 pm. Licensed. Master Card, Visa. Book ahead if you can. &

REVELSTOKE
See also HEDLEY.

RIMOUSKI, Quebec   MAP 162
LE CREPE CHIGNON   ☜🖝
140 avenue de la Cathédrale   **$90**
(418) 724-0400

This is one of the very few places to eat in Rimouski itself (see also Bic). Basically, it's a crêperie with a con-
science—everything is either recyclable or biodegradable.
The big, colourful menu offers fifteen or sixteen of their
favourite crêpes, as well as the crêpe Breton, for which
you choose your own filling from a list of several meats,
vegetables and cheeses. They make all their own jams and
their own yogurt and bake all their own bread. They also
make fine omelettes and several Mexican dishes, but
you're usually better with one of the crêpes. They have a
licence, and you can have a glass or two of Orpailleur if
you like, but we usually ask for the fresh-squeezed orange-juice or even a cup of the excellent coffee. The
Cathedral of Saint-Germain is just down the street and
the dazzling white interior looks like a painting by
Sanredam. It's worth a visit.
Open Monday 7 am to 9 pm, Tuesday to Thursday 7 am to 10
pm, Friday 7 am to 11 pm, Saturday 8 am to 10 pm, Sunday 8
am to 9 pm. Licensed. All cards. ♿

RIMOUSKI
See also LE BIC.

RIVIERE DU LOUP   MAP 163
CHEZ ANTOINE   ★★
433 rue Lafontaine   **$195**
(418) 862-6936

Chez Antoine gets better with every year that passes. The
wine-list is extraordinary, with its twenty tignanellos,
seventeen sassicaias, four solaias and four ornellaias. If
you're looking for something that costs less than 500.00,

ask for a bottle of the Nuits-Saint-George from Philippe and Vincent Léchenheaut. The cooking matches the wine. The feuilleté of escargots comes to the table with its snails enclosed in beautiful puff pastry. The carpaccio of beef is a delight and so is the ris de veau. The filet mignon is perfectly tender, the fillet of salmon is moist and very fresh. The service is always perfect.

Open Monday to Friday 11.30 am to 1.30 pm, 5 pm to 9 pm, Saturday and Sunday 5 pm to 9 pm. Licensed. All cards. &

RIVIERE DU LOUP   MAP 163
AU PAIN GAMIN
288-90 rue Lafontaine   **$35**
(418) 862-0650

When this place opened ten years ago we thought it was special, and we were right. It's been fixed up since and you can now sit outside under a big umbrella. But they've stuck to their last. The range of high-quality breads is amazing. If you order a ham sandwich you'll find that the ham comes from their own smokehouse. We always ask for the ham, but others speak highly of the smoked mackerel. Either sandwich, plus a bowl of homemade soup, costs just 14.95. They also make some great pizzas. The bakery opens right into the restaurant, which is always filled with the smell of freshly-baked bread. Even the coffee is good.

Open Monday to Friday 8 am to 6 pm, Saturday 8 am to 5 pm from late June until Labour Day, Tuesday to Friday 9 am to 6 pm, Saturday 9 am to 5 pm from Labour Day until late June. Closed on Sunday in summer, on Sunday and Monday in winter. No liquor. Visa.

ROCKY HARBOUR, Newfoundland   MAP 164
JAVA JACK'S   ☆
88 Main Street N   **$135**
(709) 458-3004

Java Jack's has the only espresso-maker in Rocky Harbour and perhaps the only kitchen without a deep-fry. Jacqui

Hunter knows what she's doing. She had a gardener before she had a restaurant, and there's still something from her garden on every plate she serves, even if it's just an edible flower. Her asparagus, all grown from seed, had a great year, and so did her lettuce. Salads are important to her. You'll still find mussels Thai-style, pan-seared cod and salmon en papillote on her menu. But what she's really interested in at the moment is moose meat. Now that moose meat is for sale, she's looking for a suitable entrée. Perhaps it'll be moose-meat shepherd's pie or maybe moose bourguignon. The big change last year was turning the downstairs space into a breakfast room. For breakfast there are now steel-cut oats and smoked-char scrambles with moose sausage. The wine-list is good and growing.

Open daily 9 am to 8 pm from 1 May until 30 June, daily 8 am to 9 pm from 1 July until 30 September. Licensed. All cards. No reservations.

ROCKY HARBOUR
See also NORRIS POINT, WOODY POINT.

ROUYN, Quebec   MAP 165
BISTRO JEZZ
117 rue 8   **$110**
(819) 797-4111

Bistro Jezz is named for the owner, Jézabel Pilote, whose nickname is Jezz. She has an interesting selection of locally-sourced produce, plus a good wine-list and a number of local beers. Dinner usually starts with beef, salmon, duck or bison tartar. Then comes a fillet of pork with dijon, a pavé of salmon with maple syrup, halibut poached in white wine and a fillet of beef. Jezz did her apprenticeship in lumber camps, where she got the idea of adapting traditional recipes to modern needs. Things don't always go as they should, but at least everyone is friendly.

Open Monday to Friday 11 am to 2 pm, 5 pm to 10 pm, Saturday 5 pm to 10 pm. Closed on Sunday. Licensed. Master Card, Visa. Book ahead if you can.

ST. ANDREWS, N.B.

MAP 166

ROSSMOUNT INN
4599 Highway 127
(506) 529-3351

★★★
$145

Chris Aerni is performing brilliantly again this year. He's particularly good with his pan-seared foie gras with cranberries, walnuts and balsamic vinegar, but you don't have to spend a lot to enjoy Aerni at his best. His most spectacular dishes are in fact among his cheapest: salmon tartar with cress, chives, cilantro, pickled ginger and wasabi. He's a master of vegetables, all of which come to the table garden fresh. As for his grand-marnier sabayon with strawberries and wild blueberries, it has few equals. Chris Aerni has a big wine-list. You can drink a sauvignon blanc from Oyster Bay quite cheaply, but only two wines on the list (a solaia and a sassicaia) cost more than 145.00 a bottle. The Rossmount and the Idylle in Moncton (see above) are without question two of the best restaurants in the country.

Open daily 5.30 pm to 9.30 pm from 9 April until 31 December.
Licensed. Amex, Master Card, Visa. Book ahead in season. ♿

ST. CATHARINES, Ontario

MAP 167

WELLINGTON COURT
11 Wellington Street
(905) 682-5518

★
$150

It's now almost 30 years since Claudia Peacock restored her father's charming little house on Wellington Street and started to run a small, choice restaurant with her son, Erik. Erik has now been on his own for almost ten years, developing an imaginative, even daring menu. The restaurant is plastered with vivid and ever-changing artwork. The service is knowledgeable and efficient; the cooking is reliable. Lunch runs to sandwiches and pizzas, but there's always a homemade soup (wild-mushroom, perhaps) and the fish of the day may be trout or perch or pickerel. In the evening there's homemade ravioli stuffed with Ontario lamb, pappardelle with veal cheeks and

212

chanterelles and confit of duck with white beans and sausage. (If you're looking for a steak, they've got a good one.) We've recommended the sticky-toffee pudding for years, but others think the almond cake with preserved strawberries is even better. Most of the wines come from the Niagara Region and they're all fairly priced. There are nine or ten wines by the glass and there's a fine Peter Lehmann shiraz by the bottle. You can bring your own bottle if you like, and the corkage fee is only 15.00. In summer Erik runs an outdoor restaurant at the Henry of Pelham winery at 1469 Pelham Road (telephone (905) 684-8423).

Open Tuesday to Saturday 11.30 am to 2.30 pm, 5 pm to 9.30 pm. Closed on Sunday and Monday. Licensed. All cards. Free parking. Book ahead in summer.

ST. CATHARINES
See also BEAMSVILLE.

STE.-FLAVIE, Quebec	**MAP 168**
LE GASPESIANA	
460 rue de la Mer	**$95 ($210)**
(800) 404-8233	

The cooking here may not be quite what it used to be, but the place is a godsend for anyone who comes to the Gaspé out of season. The bedrooms, all of which face the beach and the Gulf of St. Lawrence, are immaculate. The dining-room, which is open all year, is expansive and well served. The kitchen majors in fish and shellfish: clam chowder, shrimp bisque, cod meunière and bouillabaisse. They have a good sugar pie, but otherwise the cooking isn't distinguished. The wine-list, which is rather small and conventional, has two great buys: the Kim Crawford sauvignon blanc for 36.00 and the Liberty School cabernet sauvignon for 46.00. They're open Monday to Friday 11 am to 4 pm, 6 pm to 10 pm, Saturday and Sunday 6 am to 10 pm (shorter hours in winter). Licensed. Amex, Master Card, Visa. ♿

Our website is at www.oberonpress.ca. Readers wishing to use e-mail should address us at oberon@sympatico.ca.

ST.-GEORGES-DE-BEAUCE, Quebec (MAP 158)
MAISON VINOT   ☆☆
11525 2 Avenue   **$195**
(418) 227-5909

This old house—it was built in 1928—has been restored
and refitted as a restaurant. Raymonde and Philippe are
an enthusiastic and good-natured couple who like to
cook. They've been cooking for five years now and in
2011 were finalists in the Grand Prix du Tourisme. They
work with locally grown produce, which means fresh
vegetables of all sorts, but little fish. You'll be surprised
by the quality and freshness of everything on the menu.
The kitchen is particularly interested in grain-fed local
turkey, but they also make much of bison and emu and,
of course, of beef tenderloin, which must be ordered the
day before. At the end of the meal, you can expect Quebec cheeses and a number of first-class maple-syrup
sweets. Dinners are all *prix-fixe* and the price of the main
course includes an appetizer and coffee. Nothing is expensive except the beef, which is hard to get in these
parts. The wine-list consists mainly of private imports
and it keeps changing. The Maison Vinot is in a lovely
part of the Eastern Townships and it's well worth a visit.
*Open Tuesday to Friday 11.30 am to 1.30 pm, 6 pm to 9 pm,
Saturday 6 pm to 9 pm. Closed on Sunday and Monday. Licensed. Master Card, Visa. Book ahead.*

ST.-GEORGES DE MALBAIE, Quebec (MAP 140)
AUBERGE FORT PREVEL   ☜
2053 boulevard Douglas   **$115**
(418) 368-2281

The same chefs have been in charge of the kitchen here
for nearly ten years, the son taking over from the father.
The menu seldom changes, but the bouillabaisse is full of
beautiful lobster, cod, shrimps, salmon and scallops.
Many people admire the foie gras de canard, considering
it the best dish on the menu. The kitchen smokes its own
salmon and regularly offers Rivière-au-Renard shrimps

with white wine and dill. Salmon might come in a lobster coulis, cods' tongues with pancetta. All the seafood is perfectly fresh and in the fall there's usually some game as well. In season they always have plenty of fresh fruit. The hotel has a magnificent situation on a headland between Gaspé and Percé, with a beach, a swimming-pool, a tennis-court and a nine-hole golf-course. The dining-room itself is beautiful and there are several modern chalets.
Open daily 6 pm to 8 pm from mid-June until mid-September. Licensed. All cards. &

ST.-HYACINTHE, Quebec   MAP 171
LE PARVIS
1295 rue Girouard o   **$85**
(450) 774-0007

The Parvis occupies an abandoned church, built in 1878. Look in downtown St.-Hyacinthe for an old church painted brick red. Inside, it's very plain and one instinctively looks for the old box pews. But there are no box pews, only tables and chairs set out on a bare floor. Lunch is served five days a week, dinner six. Dinner starts with shrimps provençale or terrine of wapiti with cranberries in a peach coulis. A green soup comes next, then a bavette of beef, pavé of salmon with anise, chicken wings with green peppers or homemade pasta with sundried tomatoes and fresh pesto. Everything is table d'hôte and sweets are served buffet-style. Coffee comes with the meal.
Open Monday to Friday 11.30 am to 9 pm, Saturday 5 pm to 9 pm. Closed on Sunday. Licensed. Master Card, Visa.

ST.-JEAN-PORT-JOLI, Quebec   MAP 172
AUBERGE LE FAUBOURG
280 avenue de Gaspé o   **$120**
(800) 463-7045

This place has been around for ages, but in the last few years the cooking has gone up-market. The inn is right on the river and it has a handsome dining-room with an exceptional collection of wood carvings. If you want something more elaborate than the Boustifaille, this makes a useful alternative. Dinner is an ambitious meal, featuring fresh halibut, quail from Cap Saint-Ignace and Moroccan-style lamb. The most interesting appetizer is the guacamole of shrimps and sweet peppers.

Open daily 11 am to 2 pm, 5 pm to 9 pm (later on weekends) from 1 May until 15 October. Licensed. Amex, Master Card, Visa. Book ahead. ♿

ST.-JEAN-PORT-JOLI   MAP 172
LA BOUSTIFAILLE
547 avenue de Gaspé e   **$65**
(877) 598-7409

The Boustifaille opened in 1965 with the intention of providing *habitant* cooking at reasonable prices. After more than 45 years, the kitchen is still preparing things such as split-pea soup, tourtière, ragoût de pattes et boulettes, fèves au lard and, of course, sugar pie. Nowadays, the daily specials like chicken vol-au-vent are as good as ever, and the sugar pie may be better. But the dishes on the à la carte no longer possess their old magic, though the prices are still surprisingly low. (You can have a three-course table d'hôte for less than 20.00 a head.) They have a handful of serviceable wines and two or three draft beers. Maple syrup is always available to take out, and sometimes sugar pie as well.

Open daily 7 am to 11 pm from 1 June until 12 October (shorter hours in the spring and fall). Licensed for beer and wine only. Master Card, Visa. ♿

SAINT JOHN, N.B.   MAP 173
THE ALE HOUSE
1 Market Square   **$90**
(506) 657-2337

The Ale House is starting to get noticed right across the country. That's because Jesse Vergen is doing such a good job in the kitchen and behind the bar. He emphasizes local organic produce. His beef comes from Shipp Farms in Sussex; his fish mostly from New Brunswick. Some things are grown by Vergen himself in Quispamsis. Fish doesn't get any fresher than this and the beer-battered fish and chips is a steal at 9.45. The mussels, which come from Prince Edward Island, are also cooked with beer and the house-made pancetta and garlic are served with fries. Vergen has taken the bones out of his chicken but not the flavour, and his fried chicken fingers is one of the most popular items on the menu. Everything is cheap at the Ale House—everything, that is, but the lobster roll, which costs almost 40.00. They have the largest selection of beers in town, including drafts from Picaroon's in Fredericton and Pump House in Moncton. Every Thursday Moosehead sends them a cask of real ale, and there are people who will drink nothing else. There's an all-Canadian wine-list that offers wines from Nova Scotia as well as Niagara and the Okanagan. You can sit upstairs in the formal dining-room if you like or downstairs in the pub.

Open Sunday to Thursday 11.30 am to 10.30 pm, Friday and Saturday 11.30 am to midnight. Licensed. All cards. No reservations. ♿

SAINT JOHN   MAP 173
BILLY'S
City Market   **$140**
49-51 Charlotte Street
(888) 933-3474

The menu at Billy's has changed slightly in the last year or two. Traditional dishes have become more sophisticated: bacon-wrapped scallops, for instance, have become scallops with bacon jam. Aside from the scallops, there are calamari with a curry dip and local Beausoleil oysters on the half-shell at 26.00 for a dozen. The best of the salads is the spinach-and-beet, the best of the main courses the fish and chips, which is now as good as any. There's also cedar-planked salmon with maple syrup and a seafood pie in puff pastry. This is a seafood restaurant, but you can ask, if you choose, for a striploin steak. Billy's is a supplier as well as a restaurant and Billy Grant himself can often be seen behind the counter cutting up a whole halibut or a sashimi-grade tuna. He also has excellent sturgeon caviar—just ask.

Open Monday to Thursday 11 am to 10 pm, Friday and Saturday 11 am to 11 pm, Sunday (except in winter) 4 pm to 10 pm. Licensed. All cards. &

SAINT JOHN   MAP 173
SUWANNA   ☆
325 Lancaster Avenue   **$85**
(506) 637-9015

Suwanna has become an institution in Saint John. It's located out on Lancaster Avenue, where it overlooks the Saint John River. They serve traditional curries, stir fries and noodle dishes. There are red and green curries, priced from 17.50 for the pork to 21.50 for the fresh scallops. There's also a fine panaeng curry and a lovely, delicate Matsaman curry made with chicken, sweet potatoes and chopped shrimps. There are several noodle dishes, including the familiar pad Thai and a glass-noodle dish called poey sian. There are at least fifteen stir fries, some of which, like the squid with chillies and garlic, are quite unusual. The most attractive of the appetizers are the curry puffs, which are like potato samosas. Or you can just have a chicken satay with peanut sauce. There's a rudimentary wine-list and a Thai beer that goes well with any of the curries. That's the thing to drink.

Open daily 5 pm to 8 pm. Licensed. Master Card, Visa. Free parking. Book ahead.

SAINT JOHN   MAP 173
THE URBAN DELI   ☆
68 King Street   **$135/$50**
(506) 652-3354

The big news at the Urban Deli is that from Wednesday night to Saturday night it becomes a restaurant called Italian by Night. Liz Rowe hired Michelle Hooten as chef. Hooten is an old hand with bruschettas, ciabattas, terrines and cannellini beans. She also has an Italian sweet and an Italian cheese of the day. Italian by Night is very popular, so you have to book well in advance. Andrew Brewer continues to cook by day. He has a big menu, featuring such things as smoked-meat sandwiches, reubens, salmon burgers and a meatloaf. Usually there's also a quiche and macaroni and cheese in a double-cheese sauce. There are several local beers that go well with the lemon sour-cream pie.

Open Monday to Friday 11.30 am to 3 pm, Saturday 9 am to 3 pm. Closed on Sunday. Licensed. All cards. Book ahead if you can. & Italian by Night is open Wednesday to Saturday 5 pm to 9 pm. Closed Monday, Tuesday and Sunday. Licensed. All cards. Book ahead.

ST. JOHN'S   **MAP 174**
AQUA   ☆☆
310 Water Street   **$150**
(709) 576-2782

Mark McCrowe, the chef, has always been committed to serving the best and freshest of local produce. Every meal starts with focaccia and an *amuse bouche*, which is always interesting and often unusual. Nearly everything is served on small plates, which are meant to be shared. The fish is all perfectly fresh and the cod, served with mustard-pickle mash, salt-beef collard greens, pork scrunchions and pot-liquor beurre blanc, is marvellous. The pappardelle pasta is also a regular on the menu and is prepared in different ways in different seasons. The best of the sweets is the parsnip cake, which is a rare and wonderful dish.

Open Monday to Friday noon to 2 pm, 5.30 pm to 10 pm, Saturday and Sunday 5.30 pm to 10 pm. Licensed. All cards. Book ahead. &

If you use an out-of-date edition and find it inaccurate, don't blame us. Buy a new edition.

ST. JOHN'S

MAP 174

BASHO

☆

283 Duckworth Street

$160

(709) 576-4600

Basho is a Japanese fusion restaurant. The sushi is all prepared upstairs by Tak Ishiwata, who began by working for Nobu Matsuhisa in Tokyo. Tak brought many of Nobu's recipes with him when he came to Canada. His sushi is all superbly fresh, and he also has tuna tartar, snow crab and lobster sashimi. Everyone likes the tuna tartar, and the seasonal whitefish is also a delight. The green-tea ice cream is the most interesting of the sweets. We seldom recommend a martini, but at Basho the martinis are without parallel. People do say, however, that some of the waiters suffer from an attitude problem. We haven't noticed it.

Open Monday to Friday noon to 2 pm, 6 pm to 10 pm, Saturday 6 pm to 11 pm. Closed on Sunday. Licensed. All cards. Book ahead. ♿

ST. JOHN'S

MAP 174

BISTRO SOFIA

☆

320 Water Street

$125

(709) 738-2060

Sofia is a French-style bistro, just across the street from the Murray Premises. Gregory Bersinski, the chef, is Bulgarian and he makes everything in-house. His menu isn't large, but it's uniformly likeable, offering a glimpse of a relatively unfamiliar cuisine. At noon there's a shopska salad and free-range chicken with red wine on a ciabatta. In the evening there's blackened salmon with mango and braised lamb shanks with a vegetable mirepoix. The pastry chefs make what are said to be the best sweets to be had in St. John's. The restaurant has a mini-bakery on site and within a year they hope to have gluten-free options for most of their dishes. The coffee is outstanding.

Open daily 9 am to 11 pm. Licensed. All cards. ♿

ST. JOHN'S
CHINCHED BISTRO
7 Queen Street
(709) 722-3100

MAP 174
★★
$150

Chinched means full. When Michelle LeBlanc and Shaun Hussey first opened it wasn't so easy to fill every table. The charming little house, which isn't far from the strip-joints on George Street, has a dining-room upstairs. The menu is small and seasonal, but everything on the list is the best and freshest they can find. Start with the sweet-onion bisque with salt beef, but take a look also at the charcuterie platter. Hussey is a charcuterie chef and his charcuterie platters are always interesting. After that there's salt cod wrapped in potato, cornmeal-crusted chicken livers, slow-braised lamb shanks and sometimes an octopus stew. The sweets are all good and it's hard to choose among them, but we like the chinched pavlova with roasted apples, caramel and lemon. There aren't a lot of wines, but at least they're cheap.
Open Tuesday to Saturday 6 pm to 10 pm. Closed on Sunday and Monday. Licensed. Master Card, Visa. Book ahead.

ST. JOHN'S
GYPSY TEAROOM
315 Water Street
(709) 739-4766

MAP 174
★
$150

The Gypsy Tearoom has a big bar where people like to gather to have a drink and talk to friends. They're at their best with seafood. The fish is always fresh and never over-cooked. We like the blackened salmon; others praise the rack of lamb. The sweets are all made in house, and there's always something new and unexpected on the menu.
Open Monday to Friday 11.30 am to 3 pm, 5.30 pm to 10 pm, Saturday and Sunday 11 am to 3 pm (brunch), 5.30 pm to 10 pm. Licensed. All cards. Book ahead if you can.

Nobody but nobody can buy his way into this guide.

ST. JOHN'S MAP 174
THE HUNGRY HEART CAFE
142 Military Road **$45**
(709) 738-6164

The Hungry Heart is still one of the hottest places in town for lunch, so you need to book ahead. It's one of the enterprises run by Stella Burry Community Services, which means that everything is as cheap as possible. Not that Maurice Boudreau cuts corners. On the contrary, everything is perfectly fresh and locally sourced. Every day Boudreau offers soups, salads, sandwiches and one or two quiches. In his off hours he likes to fish for salmon or go foraging for chanterelles or blueberries. Recently he had a salmon sandwich that was made club-style with naturally cured bacon, wasabi and honey mayonnaise, all on homemade ciabatta bread. The menu has been designed to take care of people with allergies, and they even have a gluten-free chocolate pudding.

Open Monday to Friday 10 am to 2 pm, Saturday 10 am to 4 pm (brunch). Closed on Sunday. No liquor. Master Card, Visa. Book ahead. &

ST. JOHN'S MAP 174
INTERNATIONAL FLAVOURS
4 Quidi Vidi Road **$40**
(709) 738-4636

We dropped this place last year, because we objected to the fact that it served only one dish, the same dish day after day and week after week. But many of our readers disagreed, and so it's back in the guide this year. You can order their vegetable curry straight up, in which case it costs 9.50. Or you can have it with chicken, lamb or tofu for 10.50. It's a huge dish and it comes with some very good naan. If you want to drink something, help yourself to a bottle of water or a glass of mango juice from the cooler.

Open Tuesday to Saturday noon to 7 pm. Closed on Sunday and Monday. No liquor. Master Card, Visa. No reservations.

ST. JOHN'S
MAGNUM & STEINS
329 Duckworth Street
(709) 576-6500

MAP 174
★★
$150

Magnum & Steins moved to its current location during the winter of 2011. The restaurant offers two distinct dining experiences. Upstairs is formal and up-market; the bar downstairs is more casual. You can order anything you like upstairs; downstairs you can order only from the bar menu. Helpings are generous in both places. For instance, the fish soup comes with eight to ten ounces of seafood. The steaks weigh twelve to sixteen ounces. The main menu changes every four months and it always has five choices—beef, lamb, pork, chicken and salmon. The flavours are all amazing. After that there's an impressive flourless-chocolate cake, but sadly the triple-nut chocolate is gone. The waiters have all been there forever and the owner seldom leaves the premises. That's why the restaurant is worth two stars.

Open Monday to Friday noon to 2 pm, 6 pm to 10 pm, Saturday and Sunday 6 pm to 10 pm. Licensed. All cards. Book ahead. ♿

ST. JOHN'S
THE PANTRY
70 Chinch Crescent
(709) 722-8200

MAP 174
☜
$50

The Pantry is a social enterprise located in the Elaine Dobbin Centre for Autism. The menu changes daily, but there are always a couple of soups, several salads, two or three sandwiches and a number of specials, usually a quiche. Everything is made on site from scratch. The spinach salad is great and you should ask for it if it's available. The scallop cakes and the Newfoundland fish cakes are both good, though they're more filling. The Pantry is popular at lunchtime, so it's a good idea to book ahead.

Open Monday to Friday 10 am to 3 pm, Saturday 10 am to 2 pm (brunch). Closed on Sunday. Licensed. Master Card, Visa. Book ahead if you can.

ST. JOHN'S

RAYMONDS
95 Water Street
(709) 579-5800

MAP 174
☆☆
$250

Jeremy Charles and Jeremy Bonia met when they were both working at Atlantica in Portugal Cove. When they came here, they set out to create a high-end restaurant supplied by local farmers and fishermen. Their menu is impressive, their service impeccable. But if you're looking for a really good meal, choose from the tasting menu. You can sit in either the formal dining-room or the bar. Either way, the menu will open with oysters on the half-shell and go on to such luxuries as veal cheeks, belly of lamb or sweetbreads. The wines are all expensive, and even the wine pairing costs upwards of 75.00.

Open Tuesday to Saturday 5.30 pm to 10 pm. Closed on Sunday and Monday. Licensed. All cards. Book ahead. ♿

ST. JOHN'S

THE SPROUT
364 Duckworth Street
(709) 579-5485

MAP 174
☞
$50

The Sprout is the only vegetarian restaurant in St. John's. It's small and doesn't take reservations. It's popular at noon, so if you want to be sure of a table it's a good idea to get there early. They have many vegan and several gluten-free items. There are lots of sandwiches, lots of burgers and lots of salads, the best of which is the so-called townie taco, which comes with or without sour cream. The black-bean burrito is said to be excellent—it's made with black beans and sweet potatoes, all baked in a wholewheat tortilla. They're not really interested in sweets, but the sweet list is gradually getting better.

Open Monday to Wednesday 11.30 am to 8 pm, Thursday and Friday 11.30 am to 9 pm, Saturday 10 am to 2 pm (brunch), 4 pm to 9 pm. Closed on Sunday. Licensed. Master Card, Visa. No reservations.

ST. JOHN'S
See also PORTUGAL COVE.

ST.-LUNAIRE-GRIQUET, (MAP 6)
Newfoundland
DAILY CATCH
112 Main Street   **$75**
(709) 623-2295

This unassuming little restaurant is just a few minutes
drive from L'Anse-aux-Meadows (see above). It was
opened several years ago by Pearl Henderson and two of
her daughters. They specialize in such local dishes as pan-
fried cods' tongues with scrunchions and fish and chips
made with freshly-caught haddock. The chips are hand-
cut and deep-fried in the kitchen. Local beers come with
every meal and every meal ends with partridge-berry or
bake-apple cheesecake. They also have a small store
that sells locally-prepared bake-apple, blueberry and
partridge-berry jams at half the price they charge down
the road. If you plan to visit the Viking settlement
nearby, the Daily Catch is a handy place to know about.
Open daily 11 am to 9 pm from Victoria Day until 30 Septem-
ber. Licensed. All cards. &

ST. MARYS, Ontario (MAP 190)
WESTOVER INN
300 Thomas Street   **$175 ($350)**
(519) 284-2977

This is a lovely place to stay and it makes an ideal base for
the Stratford Festival. Stratford itself is only a few miles
away and St. Marys is one of the finest small towns in
Ontario. The Westover Inn occupies a wooded estate at
the edge of town. The main house was built a hundred
years ago of rough stone, and today the dining-room and
lounge fill most of the ground floor. The dining-room is
handsome and dignified and the service is friendly. But
the chef, Anthony Gosselin, doesn't ask enough questions. To him, lamb is lamb and bison bison, though ei-

ther or both may be tough or tasteless. He's at his best when he relies less on his suppliers. His green salad of baby spinach, for instance, and his ragoût of snails are both very successful dishes. His wines, however, are not cheap and there's nothing much to drink for less than 50.00 a bottle. The Westover Inn is cheaper than, say, Rundles in Stratford, but at 58.00 for a *prix-fixe* dinner it's still fairly expensive.

Open daily 11.30 am to 2 pm, 5 pm to 8 pm. Licensed. All cards. Book ahead.

ST. PETER'S, N.S.

MAP 178

BRAS D'OR LAKES INN
10095 Granville Street
(800) 818-5885

☆

$150 ($275)

Jean-Pierre Gillet ran a resolutely French restaurant in Kitchener before he moved to Cape Breton. Here he has an immaculate Inn and a spacious dining-room. Breakfast is a wonderful meal and there's plenty to choose from at dinner. The recipe for mussels changes daily; the fish sampler pairs a pan-fried fishcake with an assortment of smoked fish. Steamed local lobster comes with citrus butter, the scallops provençale are flamed in brandy, the half-rack of local lamb comes with rosemary from the garden. The pick of the sweets is still the apple pie with ice cream and caramel sauce. Most nights there's live gaelic music.

Open daily 5 pm to 8 pm from mid-May until mid-October. Licensed. All cards. Free parking.

ST. PETERS BAY, P.E.I.

(MAP 39)

THE INN AT ST. PETERS
1668 Greenwich Road
(800) 818-0925

☆

$160 ($280)

Wes Gallant left the Inn at the end of 2013, but his sous-chef, Sarah Forrester Wendt, has taken his place. She's into whole foods and macro cooking and shares Gallant's passionate commitment to local produce. She grows most of her own vegetables and her brother-in-law has an or ganic farm that can supply most things she can't grow herself. Mussels come from the bay and the scallops are local. There's North Shore lobster in season and halibut. Steerman's in Millview supplies her with high-quality pork, beef and chicken. She makes all her own ice creams and sorbets. The dining-room is too big for comfort, but the great windows offer a fine view of St. Peters Bay. The hostess, Karen Davey, can deal with almost any problem you may have—she's a wonder.

Open daily 5 pm to 8.30 pm from the beginning of June until the middle of October. Licensed. All cards. &

ST.-PIERRE-JOLYS, Manitoba   MAP 180
OMA'S SCHNITZEL STUBE
601 Sabourin Street S   **$55**
(204) 433-7726

If you call up this place to book a table, a voice will greet you. "Oma's still here," the voice will say. That's good news, because Oma is a gem. St.-Pierre-Jolys is a pretty village half an hour south of Winnipeg. The Stube is run by the Zimmerman family, who came to Canada from a small town near Frankfurt in 2007. Oma's has the best German food in the province and some of the lowest prices you'll find anywhere. In the last year or two the buffet price has crept up a dollar or two, so you may have to pay all of 17.00 (less if you're a senior) for rouladen (on Sunday), fresh pollock (on Friday), garlic shrimps with spaetzle (on Saturday) or one of the classic schnitzels, which are on the à la carte every day. After that there's apple strudel and schwartzwalder kirschtorte with cherry brandy or slivowitz. The coffee is great.

Open Wednesday to Sunday 11 am to 9 pm. Closed on Monday and Tuesday. Licensed. Master Card, Visa. &

SALT SPRING ISLAND, B.C.   (MAP 209)

Salt Spring Island has always been known for its lamb, its cheese and its mussels. More recently it's been known for its wineries, for its abundance of organic produce and for its bakeries. Try either

Barb's Buns at 21 McPhillips Avenue (telephone (250) 537-4491) for breakfast or the Embe Bakery at 174 Fulford-Ganges Road (telephone (250) 537-5611) for decadent cookies and pies. David Wood's celebrated goat cheese and sheep's-milk cheese can be found at the Cheese Farm Shop at 285 Reynolds Road (telephone (250) 653-2300). The best way to get to know what's available is to visit the Farmer's Market in Ganges, which is held every Saturday from Easter until Thanksgiving. (There's also an organic Farmer's Market every Tuesday.) If you drive north out of Ganges you'll soon come across the Garry Oaks and the Salt Spring Island wineries. Both offer tours and tastings. A third winery, Mistaken Identity, makes a number of organic wines. Smoked salmon and crab pâté are both available right in Ganges itself from Sea Changes. The restaurant in Hastings House (telephone (250) 537-2362) is, we think, too expensive for most readers. Piccolo's (see below, telephone (250) 537-1844) is closer to the mark and attracts visitors by the boatload.

SALT SPRING ISLAND (MAP 209)
HOUSE PICCOLO ☆☆
108 Hereford Avenue **$160**
(250) 537-1844

We think this is now the best place to eat on Salt Spring Island. Piccolo Lyytikainen used to price his meals as if the House Piccolo were the Hastings House. This year, however, he has reduced his prices, which makes the restaurant accessible to the ordinary traveller. Piccolo has no sea view, no open-air deck. He has nothing to offer but good food. The best of the appetizers is the gravlax marinated in brandy, though the local goat-cheese salad and the warm gorgonzola tart with red onions and port wine are both impressive dishes too. When it comes to the main course, diners have to choose between Grand Veneur venison with juniper and lingonberries and breast of Muscovy duck with green peppercorns—we usually ask for the venison. Piccolo is good with pastry and his Alsatian pear-and-almond tart is the best of his sweets. *Open Wednesday to Sunday 5 pm to 9 pm. Closed on Monday and Tuesday. Licensed. Master Card, Visa.*

SASKATOON, Saskatchewan   MAP 182
BOTTEGA   ☆
120 2 Avenue N   **$150**
(306) 954-2931

Bottega is a snappy new Italian restaurant with a first-class chef, Amedeo Vallati (who also happens to be the owner). The interior is all cool blacks and whites. The menu is long and ambitious, and everything is perfectly cooked. The kitchen starts with shrimps with sambuca, mussels with grappa (an interesting idea), squid with basil, pan-fried eggplant, Italian sausage and—now we become grand—Digby scallops flamed in brandy. The main courses are more substantial and rather less original. There's wild Atlantic salmon with mashed potatoes, Atlantic haddock with spinach and fresh halibut on a banana leaf. There aren't a lot of wines, but they're all carefully chosen. There's a lovely, clean orvieto classico from Ruffino and a fine brunello di Montalcino from Banfi, both sold by the glass as well as the bottle.

Open Monday to Thursday 11 am to 2 pm, 5 pm to 9 pm, Friday and Saturday 11 am to 2 pm, 5 pm to 10 pm. Closed on Sunday. Licensed. Amex, Master Card, Visa. Book ahead if you can.

SASKATOON   MAP 182
ST. TROPEZ
238 2 Avenue S   **$135**
(306) 652-1250

Regulars come here because they know exactly what they'll get. After all, the same chef has been in charge for twenty years, and his son has been here for at least ten. The chipotle shrimps and the chicken-liver pâté are both still on the menu. There have always been two salmon dinners and two chicken dinners (chicken Cajun-style and chicken with dijon). There's always filet mignon and curried lamb. The beef is local, the lamb often not. But everything is correctly cooked; the vegetables are fresh, the saskatoons hand picked every summer. At the end of the meal, crème caramel is always available. There are at least 70 labels on the wine-list. Almost all of them cost 100.00 a bottle or more, but if you pay cash they give you a 10% discount on your next meal. If you have tickets for the Persephone Theatre around the corner, they'll make sure you get there on time.

Open Wednesday to Sunday 5 pm to 10 pm. Closed on Monday and Tuesday. Licensed. All cards. &

SASKATOON   **MAP 182**
SUSHIRO   ☆
737 Broadway Avenue   **$75**
(306) 665-5557

Megan Macdonald moved to Vancouver last year and sold two thirds of the restaurant to her employees. That didn't sound like good news, but so far there haven't been any important changes. The fish is still beautifully fresh, and the sushi is about as good as it gets. The yam tempura is still a magical dish and the salads haven't lost their savour. Their seared tuna tataki with avocado and orange is still a memorable dish. They have Hakutsuru sake on draft, as well as two or three premium sakes by the bottle. Inside, the restaurant is decidedly contemporary and everything about the place is very chic indeed.

Open Monday to Saturday 5 pm to 10 pm. Closed on Sunday. Licensed. All cards. &

SASKATOON   **MAP 182**
TRUFFLES   ☆
230 21 Street E   **$125**
(306) 373-7779

Truffles is located in the old Birks building in downtown Saskatoon. Inside it's bright and *au courant*. This is one place where the table d'hôte could be regarded as the specialty of the house. There's almost always a first-rate eight-ounce striploin with wonderful truffled fries on it, or perhaps steelhead trout from Diefenbaker Lake. But Lee Helman is a trained French chef and there are those who think that it would be a mistake to stick to such things as steak or steelhead trout, even if they are cheap. If you feel that way, ask for the breast of duck or perhaps the house-made ravioli. Everything is made from scratch, even the tomato ketchup. He even makes all his own bread and all his own sweets. His wine-list, however, needs to be enlarged, especially the selection of wines by the glass. The service is all it should be.

Open Monday to Friday 11.30 am to 3 pm, 5 pm to 10 pm, Saturday 10 am to 2.30 pm (brunch), 5 pm to 10 pm, Sunday 10 am to 2 pm (brunch). Licensed. All cards. &

SAULT STE.-MARIE, Ontario MAP 183
ARTURO'S ☆
515 Queen Street E **$175**
(705) 253-0002

Arturo Comegna came from Abruzzo in Italy and established what may be the best of the many Italian restaurants in the Sault. That was at least 25 years ago. Now his sons, Thomas and Christopher, run the place. They have a pretty good kitchen, offering huge helpings in charming surroundings. The veal is all milkfed, the seafood all fresh. There's a daily catch every day, and often it's salmon or sea-bass, both perfectly cooked. We've liked the snails and the ravioli and we'd like the rack of lamb too if they didn't insist on giving you the whole animal. Most of the wines, of course, come from Italy, though there are also wines from Chile and elsewhere in the New World.

Open Monday to Saturday 5 pm to 10 pm. Closed on Sunday. Licensed. All cards. &

LA SCIE, Newfoundland MAP 184
THE OUTPORT TEAROOM ☞
Highway 414 **$45**
(709) 675-2720

This year the Outport Tearoom won the top award for cultural tourism, which inspired Valery Whalen to new

231

heights. She has often said that she and her husband, Larry, would entertain anyone who showed up at their door, no matter what the time of day. And it was true. She did the cooking while Larry played old Newfoundland tunes on his accordion. The Whalens had transformed their family homestead into a museum and then opened a tearoom on the spacious glass verandah that runs the length of the house. At first they just served fruit tarts, tea-buns and rhubarb crumbles. Later they enlarged the menu, adding such local dishes as crab-au-gratin and fishcakes. There's jiggs dinner on Thursday, pea soup on Saturday and codfish on Sunday.

Open daily 8 am to 8 pm from 1 June until 30 September. No liquor, no cards.

SHELBURNE, N.S.   MAP 185
CHARLOTTE LANE CAFE   ☆
13 Charlotte Lane   **$135**
(902) 875-3314

Kathleen and Roland Glauser have been operating this colourful little restaurant for many years now, and in 2013 it was named the best small restaurant in the province. Roland's food is rich, however, and he likes to serve such things as seafood crêpes with cream and cheese and lobster gratin with brandy, so it's a good idea to order the Arctic char instead. It's served very plainly with honey-mustard and maple for 22.95. The cooking is always innovative and the kitchen makes much use of such local ingredients as garden greens, red cabbage and asiago cheese. Lunch is essentially the same as dinner, though it also includes soups, salads and sandwiches. They do several theme nights during the season, of which the burger night is the most successful. The service is professional but friendly, and after dinner everyone feels they've spent the evening with good friends.

Open Tuesday to Saturday 11.30 am to 2.30 pm, 5 pm to 8 pm from the middle of May until late December. Closed on Sunday and Monday. Licensed. Master Card, Visa. Book ahead if you can.

SHELBURNE
See also CLARK'S HARBOUR.

SIDNEY, B.C. (MAP 209)
DEEP COVE CHALET ☆☆☆
11190 Chalet Road **$160**
(250) 656-3541

The Deep Cove Chalet is an hour by car from Victoria, but it's worth every mile, even in driving rain. Take Highway 17 from Douglas Street as far as the last exit before Swartz Bay and turn left there on Land's End Road. Pierre Koffel maintains a generous à la carte, but the table-d'hôte menus—there are three, priced from 32.50 to 60.00—offer most of his important dishes. For just 32.50 you can begin with a lovely lobster bisque, go on to a fine cheese soufflé and end with a wedge of flourless-chocolate cake, or, for a few dollars more, with a perfect tarte tatin or a soufflé grand marnier. Everything is perfect. The wine-list is extraordinary. There are eighteen Mouton-Rothschilds dating back to 1967, five Lafites from 1966 and four Latours from 1975. For realistic drinking, there's a useful list of Okanagan wines, of which the best buy is the pinot noir from Burrowing Owl, which is cheap at 60.00 a bottle. Pierre Koffel is no longer a young man and his cooking may not be as flawless as it used to be. But he still cooks as well as anyone on Vancouver Island, maybe better.
Open Wednesday to Sunday noon to 2 pm, 5.30 pm to 9 pm. Closed on Monday and Tuesday. Licensed. All cards. Book ahead. ♿

SINGHAMPTON, Ontario MAP 187
EIGENSINN FARM ☆☆☆
Townline 10 **$800**
(519) 922-3128

Michael Stadtländer and his wife, Nobuyo, have been running Eigensinn Farm for nineteen years. This year they plan to be open only on Friday and Sunday, and since there are only twelve seats in the dining-room you should book at least three months in advance and pay when you book. It's a long way to go from almost anywhere, even for an eight-course dinner. The price of a meal is 300.00 a head, plus tip and tax. As for wine, you must bring your own bottle. Michael Stadtländer ranks with the best chefs in the world. He was born the son of a farmer, and here he has a vegetable garden so big that he has had to employ a full-time gardener. He has two farm ponds, where he raises speckled trout and crayfish. He breeds ducks and sheep. He grows fruit trees. All these things eventually find their way onto his table. To get to Eigensinn Farm, head west from Singhampton on Townline 10 and remember, if you bring your own bottle there's no charge for corkage.

Open Friday and Sunday at 7 pm by appointment only. Closed Monday to Thursday and on Saturday. Bring your own bottle. No cards. You must book ahead.

SINGHAMPTON MAP 187
HAISAI ☆☆
794079 County Road 124 **$245**
(705) 445-2748

Michael Stadtländer designed this place for his son, Jonas. But before the job was finished, Jonas and his wife had left Canada for Japan. They've now returned, but not to Singhampton. Michael ran the place himself for a year or so, but the job left him little time for Eigensinn Farm, his main interest (see above). So he decided to hire a top chef from Japan every year—last year it was Min Young Lee. The farm continues to supply Haisai as well as Eigensinn, which means that all the produce used in both restaurants will still be organic and there will be no genetically modified food on either menu. They have a small à la carte, as well as two tasting menus, one at 70.00 and a second at 90.00. They also offer a variety of wood-oven pizzas, which they sell for 18.00 each. Haisai also has a short list of Niagara wines. Everything in the room is made by hand, even the wine-glasses and the furniture. But the fu-

234

ture is uncertain. Nobody can say when or even if Haisai will be open this summer.

Open Wednesday to Friday 5.30 pm to 9 pm, Saturday 1 pm to 3 pm (pizzas only), 5.30 pm to 9 pm, Sunday 11 am to 3 pm (brunch). Closed on Monday and Tuesday. Licensed. No cards. Book ahead.

SOURIS, P.E.I. (MAP 39)

21 BREAKWATER

21 Breakwater Street **$80**
(902) 687-2556

We liked the old Blue Fin in Souris, but 21 Breakwater is an upscale restaurant, where you can get a good meal while you watch the ferry to the Magdalens come and go. Breakwater opened in June of 2012 and quickly became so busy that you couldn't get in the door without a reservation. The menu is quite small, but everything on it is well and carefully cooked. Pedro Pereira and Betty MacDonald limit themselves to local favourites, plus a daily special or two. One cold winter night we remember that the special was a hot fish chowder, full of mussels, clams and hake. The chowder came with garlic bread and left no room for a sweet, not even the blueberry cobbler that was on offer that night. In the summer they have a splendid chicken salad, as well as fish and chips Portuguese-style. Prices are all reasonable—halibut with corn-on-the-cob costs only 15.95.

Open Monday to Saturday 11.30 am to 5 pm (lunch), 5 pm to 9 pm (dinner) from 1 June until 30 September, Wednesday to Saturday 11.30 am to 5 pm (lunch), 5 pm to 9 pm (dinner) from 1 October until 31 May. Closed on Sunday in summer, Sunday to Tuesday in winter. Licensed. Master Card, Visa. Book ahead. &

STELLARTON, N.S. (MAP 125)

ANDRE'S SEATS

245 Foord Street **$45**
(902) 752-2700

André started out with a pizza takeout at 243 Foord

Street, where business was so good that he expanded next door and opened a full-service restaurant with seats. The menu at André's Seats is enormous. Pizzas aside, there's lots of pasta and a number of salads. The chicken penne with maple is by far the best seller. In the evening they bring on salmon, haddock and several steaks. There are also two great salads: baked goat-cheese and André's salad. A fine oregano dressing comes with both. Most of the sweets are made in the kitchen, and the best of them is the three-layer carrot cake with real whipped cream. There are one or two good wines from Gaspereau, as well as numerous imports. The walls are lined with posters from the eras of Neil Young, Elvis Presley and the Dave Clark Five. The glass-topped tables are covered with ticket stubs from concerts of the time, and there's a real jukebox on the floor.

Open Monday and Tuesday 11 am to 8 pm, Wednesday and Thursday 11 am to 9 pm, Friday and Saturday 11 am to 10 pm, Sunday 4 pm to 8 pm. Licensed. All cards. &

STRATFORD, Ontario   **MAP 190**
THE PRUNE   ✩✩
151 Albert Street   **$260**
(519) 271-5052

Bryan Steele is doing a very good job at the Prune. The dining-rooms are lavish and lovely. The service is accomplished. The menu is exciting, the cooking everything it should be. Dinner is served table d'hôte and costs 75.00 a head. For that you have a choice of a lovely green-pea soup, lamb tartar or ravioli stuffed with ricotta and tomato butter. Poached trout comes next, with spinach and sorrel, and it's a superb dish. The lamb comes from Church Hill Farm, but it's no match for the braised veal cheeks. The meal ends well with a lemon semifreddo, which is usually a better choice than the chocolate crème brûlée. This summer all the wines will come from the Niagara Region. The best drinking will probably be the fumé blanc from Peninsula Ridge and the pinot noir from Flat Rock. If you still want to spend money, ask for a glass of the Reif icewine or, in a different mood, the Sarpa di Poli grappa.

Open Tuesday to Saturday 5 pm to 8 pm from late May until mid-October. Closed on Sunday and Monday. Licensed. Amex, Master Card, Visa. Free parking. Book ahead.

STRATFORD   MAP 190
RUNDLES   ☆☆☆
9 Cobourg Street   **$315**
(519) 271-6442

The interior (all white on white) is quiet and restful. The flowers are astonishing. The architecture is spectacular. The menu is small and well planned. The cooking (by Neil Baxter) is superb. Dinners (priced at 93.50) begin with white asparagus with King oyster mushrooms, scallop ceviche or dungeness crab with avocado—all elegant dishes prepared and served with dignity and restraint. Next come pan-fried pickerel, grilled breast of duck and roast rack of lamb. To end the meal there's lemon-poppyseed cake and frozen chocolate with milk foam, but we think the unpasteurized cheeses show the restaurant to greater advantage. The wine-list is short and surprisingly inexpensive. The Woolshed sauvignon blanc, the Cave Spring riesling, the Tawse chardonnay, the rioja and the valpolicella all cost 53.50 a bottle or 14.50 a glass. Take your pick—we like the Tawse. Rundles is the most expensive restaurant in town, and the best.

Open Tuesday 5 pm to 7 pm, Wednesday to Friday 5 pm to 8.30 pm, Saturday 11.30 am to 1.15 pm, 5 pm to 8.30 pm, Sunday 11.30 am to 1.15 pm, 5 pm to 7 pm from late May until late October. Closed on Monday. Licensed. Amex, Master Card, Visa. Book ahead. &

STRATFORD
See also ST. MARYS.

We accept no advertisements. We accept no payment for listings. We depend entirely on you. Recommend the book to your friends.

SUMMERVILLE BEACH, N.S. MAP 191
QUARTERDECK GRILL
7499 Highway 3 $115
(800) 565-1119

The Quarterdeck has one of the most spectacular seaside views to be found anywhere on the South Shore. There are sixteen tables, eight inside and eight outside, all overlooking the mile-long beach. The service is always cheerful and fairly quick, which means that you can have lunch and still have time for a swim. The cooking isn't remarkable and prices are quite high, but we can't find anything better within an hour's drive. The Quarterdeck is open all day every day from mid-May until mid-October. They have a licence and take all cards. &

SUMMERVILLE BEACH
See also MILL VILLAGE.

SUNDRIDGE, Ontario MAP 192
DANNY'S JUSTA PASTA ☆
367 Valleyview Road $90
(705) 384-5542

Sundridge is about halfway between Huntsville and North Bay. You need to know that, because Highway 11 has been altered to bypass Danny's old site. You now have to leave the highway and drive half a mile for some of the best pasta to be had anywhere in the province. Danny is a local fixture—he's had this place for at least 30 years and his parents ran the Sundridge Steak House for even longer. He has a lot of pasta dishes on his menu and they're all cooked to order. The flavours are clean and the spicing is always just right. Most people like the chicken penne, which comes with fresh vegetables in a curried cream sauce. We suggest you start with the snails or the bruschetta and finish with the tiramisu, if it's available. The sweets change every day.
Open Monday to Thursday 11 am to 8 pm, Friday and Saturday 11 am to 9 pm, Sunday 11 am to 8 pm from 1 April until 31 October, Thursday 11 am to 8 pm, Friday and Saturday 11 am

to 9 pm, Sunday 11 am to 8 pm from 1 November until 31 March. Closed Monday to Wednesday in winter. Licensed. All cards. No reservations. Free parking.

SYDNEY, N.S.   **MAP 193**
GOVERNORS
233 Esplanade   **$185**
Cape Breton
(902) 562-7646

Now that Amedeo is closed, the best place to eat in Sydney is Governors, which is just across the street from the Holiday Inn. They have a remarkable treatment of grilled squid, which is very tender and full of flavour. There's also a fine bone-in tenderloin of beef and a very inexpensive dish of pork back-ribs. Their scallops tend to be overcooked, so you'll usually do better with the fish and chips, made with haddock battered in beer. If you feel like spending more than that, ask for the Atlantic halibut with fresh fruit or the grilled salmon seasoned with maple. The meal ends with a lovely crème caramel for next to nothing. The wine-list offers three local reds and four local whites, one of which happens to be the wonderful sparkling wine from Benjamin Bridge. It's the Nova; it costs 51.00 and is worth at least twice that.
Open daily 11 am to 11 pm. Licensed. Master Card, Visa. ₭

SYDNEY   **MAP 193**
THE OLIVE TREE   ☜▯
137 Victoria Road   **$60**
Cape Breton
(902) 539-1553

This little pizzeria doesn't look much from the outside, but inside it's nicely done up. The menu is much too long and the prices much too low, but this is probably the town's best choice for either lunch or dinner. Everything is attractively presented and the service couldn't be friendlier. The menu offers a number of puréed soups, stuffed grape leaves, lamb souvlaki on a warm pita, chicken-mango stir-fry and, of course several pizzas with interesting toppings. There aren't many sweets, but there is at least a deep-fried cheesecake. The helpings are big, the soundtrack quiet.

Open Monday to Saturday 11 am to 9 pm, Sunday 4 pm to 8 pm. Licensed. Amex, Master Card, Visa. &

TANTALLON, N.S. (MAP 82)
WHITE SAILS BAKERY
12930 Peggy's Cove Road   **$45**
(902) 826-1966

Look for a bright-yellow building surrounded by a green lawn and a scattering of picnic tables. Behind is an inlet of the sea, in front is a parking-lot. The place is always packed with people filling up on smoked-meat sand-wiches. The sandwiches are Montreal-style, but they don't taste quite the way they did at Schwartz's. They also have sugar pies, though they don't come with real whipped cream. You won't do better, however, this side of Halifax.

Open Monday to Saturday 10 am to 7 pm, Sunday 10 am to 6 pm from 1 April until 31 December. No liquor. Master Card, Visa. &

TATAMAGOUCHE, N.S. MAP 195
GREEN GRASS RUNNING WATER
102 Main Street   **$45**
(902) 657-9393

Green Grass is a trim little café on the road to Tata-magouche from the west. It has an interesting art gallery displaying Indian prints and some fascinating furniture by Ken Pierson. The menu, which is posted on a black-board, offers a couple of homemade soups, a garden-fresh salad, a variety of sandwiches and three or four daily spe-cials—a quiche, smoked salmon, a taco and fishcakes. There are always sandwiches (egg, chicken, ham and tuna) as well as several homemade ice creams. If you ar-rive too late for lunch, or are looking for dinner, try the

Train Station Inn at 21 Station Road (telephone (902) 657-3222)). It's open late and it's a good place to spend the night.

Open daily 10 am to 4 pm. No liquor. All cards. &

TEMISCOUATA-SUR-LE-LAC, Quebec MAP 196
AUBERGE DU CHEMIN FAISANT ☆☆☆
12 rue Vieux Chemin **$225**
Cabano
(418) 854-9342

Cabano has now merged with Notre-Dame-du-Lac and become Temiscouata-sur-le-Lac. The Chemin Faisant has six bedrooms, all different and all decorated in the *art-déco* style. Hughes Massey won a number of prizes for his cooking when he was living in the Magdalen Islands and since he moved to Temiscouata he's been cooking better than ever. Every evening he offers an eight-course *menu de dégustation* priced at 50.00 for residents and 55.00 for non-residents. You can buy the wine service if you like or choose your own wine by the bottle. The menu changes regularly, but Massey likes to work with scallops and red deer, and he also uses a lot of foie gras. He gets his crab from the Magdalens and this summer plans to use more of it than usual. After dinner, he likes to play the piano, and he plays almost as well as he cooks.

Open daily 6 pm to 8 pm from 1 June until Labour Day, Sunday 6 pm to 8 pm from Labour Day until 31 May. Closed Monday to Saturday in winter. Licensed. All cards. &

TEMISCOUATA-SUR-LE-LAC MAP 196
AUBERGE MARIE-BLANC
2629 rue Commerciale s **$150**
Notre-Dame-du-Lac
(418) 899-6747

The Auberge Marie-Blanc was built in 1905 by a New York lawyer for his mistress, Mlle. Marie-Blanc Charlier, who lived here until her death in 1949. Guy Sirois and his wife, Jeannine, bought the place in 1960 and ran it for more than 40 years. Many people thought it was the only dependable place to break a journey from Fredericton to New York. The motel units were plain but tidy, and everybody had breakfast on their porch overlooking Lake Temiscouata. The evening menu was simple in its early days, but it grew over the years into a four-course table d'hôte. Finally Guy's daughter took charge of the kitchen. She had never heard of sweetbreads, but her father lived just long enough to teach her. Before long she hired Pauline Beaubien, a local chef who knew where to buy the best regional produce. Pauline may not be Guy Sirois, but she makes a very good seafood chowder and a perfectly satisfactory five-course table d'hôte. She has an ample wine-list, and her signature dish is said to be her sweetbreads!

Open Monday 8 am to 10 am, Tuesday to Saturday 8 am to 10 am, 5.30 pm to 8.30 pm, Sunday 8 am to 10 am from early June until mid-October. Licensed. Master Card, Visa.

TERRACE, B.C. MAP 197
DON DIEGO'S ☆
3212 Kalum Street **$85**
(250) 635-2307

Don Diego's flirts with Mexican cuisine, but it could never be described as a Mexican restaurant. (A Mexican restaurant wouldn't have lasted long in Terrace.) They do offer margaritas, but the menu as a whole offers whatever has worked well over the years. They do a lot of seafood, which is brought in from Prince Rupert. Shrimp is scarce on the Pacific coast, but keep an eye out for it, usually with chipotle and lime. Fresh fruit and vegetables are plentiful in Terrace, and stirling beef comes in from Alberta. The baby back-ribs are fall-off-the-bone tender. Sweets have always been a big thing here. At the moment the favourite is the chocolate-and-peanut-butter pie. The dining-room is small and it can be very noisy. Some people like it that way; others don't.

Open Monday to Friday 11.30 am to 9 pm, Saturday 9 am to 11.30 am (brunch), 11.30 am to 9 pm. Closed on Sunday. Li-

censed. Amex, Master Card, Visa. Book ahead if you can. ♿

THORNBURY, Ontario (MAP 49)
SIMPLICITY BISTRO ☆
81 King Street E **$140**
(519) 599-5550

This is an endearing little restaurant, decorated to match the season and offering fresh food cooked to order. That means that if you come in winter they'll give you Navy-bean-and-kale soup, shredded-cabbage salad with blue cheese, Brussels sprouts, boar sausages with apple and sage and sweet-potato fries. In summer there's likely to be wild blueberry and goat-cheese tarts, provimi liver, salmon or pickerel and an abundance of green vegetables. The helpings are never small—if you have three courses you'll know it. They like to pair their food with wines from one of the two local wineries, Georgian Hill and Coffin Ridge, both of which are too small to be found in the local liquor store. Local people like to compare Simplicity Bistro with some of the better Toronto restaurants. One thing, however, is different. It's cheaper.
Open Monday to Friday 11 am to 9 pm, Saturday and Sunday 10 am to 10 pm (brunch). Licensed. All cards. ♿

THUNDER BAY, Ontario MAP 199
BISTRO ONE ☆
555 Dunlop Street **$160**
(807) 622-2478

We've written about Bistro One a lot, but we've never mentioned their wine-list. In fact, they have several great and rare vintages, as well as many wines that aren't offered anywhere else. Their list of cheeses is also remarkable. Jean Robillard's menu touches all the bases of modern cooking, and it changes often. Nothing is ever overstated or overcooked. The rack of lamb now comes fresh from New Zealand, and it's served with gorgonzola butter. The confit of duck, which is cooked for at least five hours, is served with blackberries and brandy. Lamb may appear again in ravioli with minted sweet peas, or perhaps in a basil risotto with lamb sausage. Maria Costanzo, the *pâtissière*, has built up a big following over the years, so you know that her molten-chocolate cake will stay on the menu forever. (Recently she's also been offering sticky-toffee cake with bourbon crème anglaise.) And remember, their cheeses are wonderful.

Open Tuesday to Saturday 5 pm to 10 pm. Closed on Sunday and Monday. Licensed. All cards. &

THUNDER BAY   MAP 199
SCANDINAVIAN HOME
147 S Algoma Street   **$40**
(807) 345-7442

Scandinavian Home was opened to meet the needs of the Finnish community, where people were looking for comfort food at a fair price. Don't expect stylish cooking here. What you'll get is good, honest home-style meals. Hoito at 314 Bay Street (telephone (807) 345-6325) has always had a bigger reputation than Scandinavian Home, but we prefer the Scandia, as local people call it. There the soups are all homemade, the sandwiches made to order, the hollandaise sauce prepared from scratch. There are several fruit pies, among them apple, rhubarb and wild blueberry. There's no liquor, but the coffee is good.

Open Monday to Friday 7 am to 3.30 pm, Saturday 7 am to 2.30 pm, Sunday 9 am to 2 pm. No liquor. Master Card, Visa. &

THUNDER BAY   MAP 199
THE SILVER BIRCH
28 Cumberland Street N   **$150**
(807) 345-0597

Yes, this is where Armando used to hold court. He was always a happy man, but after 25 years he decided to give his wife a break and do a little travelling. Darlene Green ran a respected catering business before she opened here. It's supposed to look woodsy because the wallpaper was made from photographs of the birch trees in her garden. In the early days there were some rough days, but for almost a year now everything has been running smoothly. She brings in fresh fish from Lake Superior and her beef is all local. So are her rabbit, her mushrooms and her wild rice. The seafood chowder, which they call a bouillabaisse, comes in a tomato broth with fennel and fresh Prince Edward Island mussels. Everybody likes the thyme-roasted mushroom toast with parmesan and ricotta cheese. The pumpkin gnocchi got so popular that it became a fixture of the menu and has never been taken off. Darlene makes all the sweets, and if it's summer it'll be a lemon-raspberry torte. Nothing is really expensive except the latte, which costs too much at 4.00 a cup.

Open Tuesday to Friday noon to 2 pm, 5 pm to 10 pm, Saturday 5 pm to 10 pm. Closed on Sunday and Monday. Licensed. All cards. &

THUNDER BAY MAP 199
THE SOVEREIGN ROOM ☆
220 Red River Road **$110**
(807) 343-9277

This is a gastropub that stocks dozens of imported beers, including such greats as Innis & Gunn and Southern Tier. Sleeping Giant is always kept on tap. Stone-baked pizzas take up a lot of the menu, but we're more interested in the jalapeno empanadas, the nachos and the poutine of duck confit. They also have charcuterie, pork belly with romaine and braised short-ribs with potato purée. On Wednesday and Thursday they do a vegetable burger, though the regular burgers are about as good as they get. If you're driving, it's easy to miss the place, but that'd be a pity, because everyone seems to love it. They take no reservations, so come for lunch or early dinner. All the food is regional, the prices quite modest.

Open Tuesday and Wednesday 4 pm to 2 am, Thursday and Friday 11 am to 2 am, Saturday and Sunday 4 pm to 2 am. Closed on Monday. Licensed. Master Card, Visa. No reservations.

TOBERMORY, Ontario MAP 200

GRANDVIEW INN
11 Earl Street **$120**
(519) 596-2220

The Grandview Inn has been in business for almost half a century. It's not really a luxury hotel, but it has a great view of Little Tub Harbour, just at the point where the ferry crosses to Manitoulin Island. The Crowley family have always kept a good kitchen that's still known for its Georgian Bay whitefish, which they prepare in several different ways. (Most people choose the whitefish blackened Cajun-style.) The kitchen is at its best with seafood, including the orange-ginger salmon and the seafood fettuccine with shrimps, mussels and scallops. They buy most of their fish and vegetables from local organic suppliers. Everyone likes the brie baked in puff pastry with red-pepper jelly. A number of the pies are made to recipes that have been in the family for generations. This year they introduced live music, something they plan to continue in the future.

Open daily 5 pm to 8 pm from 1 May until Thanksgiving. Licensed. Master Card, Visa. Book ahead if you can.

TOFINO, B.C. MAP 201

SHELTER
601 Campbell Street **$150**
(250) 725-3353

Shelter is a great place for an outdoor meal in summer, provided it's not raining (as it often is). If you come for lunch, you'll find that they have a great seafood chowder, full of mussels, clams and smoked salmon. They also have a fine calamari plate and a first-class salad, made with local organic greens, sweet peppers, dates, pumpkinseeds, cucumbers and feta cheese. In the evening they bring on pan-seared wild salmon with fireweed honey, pan-roasted Pacific halibut with black truffles and a rib-eye steak in a green peppercorn sauce. After that there's a lovely darkchocolate mousse with fresh raspberries.

Open daily 11.30 am to 5 pm (lunch), 5 pm to 10 pm (dinner).
Licensed. Amex, Master Card, Visa. Book ahead if you can.

TOFINO   **MAP 201**
SOBO   ☆
311 Neill Street   **$130**
(250) 725-2341

Sobo stands for Sophisticated Bohemian, which is what
this place was when it was housed in a chip-wagon parked
by the side of the road. Today it occupies an elegant but
austere new building overlooking the harbour. Some
people think the food isn't as good as it used to be, but it
probably is—expectations are different now. The prices
seem high, but they are in fact comparable to other
restaurants in Tofino. We've tried many things—the
smoked wild-fish chowder, the West Coast seafood stew
and the braised duck thighs with wild local cranberries.
They use a lot of regional produce, so they have to
change the menu often.
Open daily 11 am to 5 pm (lunch), 5 pm to 9 pm (dinner). Li-
censed. Amex, Master Card, Visa. ♿

TOFINO   **MAP 201**
THE SPOTTED BEAR   ☆☆
120 4 Street: Unit 101   **$125**
(250) 725-2215

This small bistro gets full early, so it's important to book
ahead. The food is exquisite and the prices are reasonable.
Vincent Fraissange creates imaginative fusion dishes out
of the best local produce he can find. We like his mushroom risotto with truffle aioli and grainy mustard, which
goes beautifully with his beet salad and his splendid naan.
His beef short-ribs are good too and so is his albacore-tuna
pho. Of course, you can always have a shoulder of lamb
or a steak, which are said to be outstanding. There's a children's menu that offers pizzas and pasta, and this makes
the Spotted Bear an ideal place to bring your family.
Open Tuesday to Sunday 5.30 pm to 9 pm. Closed on Monday.

Licensed. Amex, Master Card, Visa. Book ahead. &

TOFINO   MAP 201
TACOFINO CANTINA   ☆
1134 Pacific Rim Highway $35
(250) 726-8288

If you really miss Sobo's old purple truck, look for the
bright-orange van of Tacofino Cantina. It's parked right
next to the Wildside Grill. Kaeli Robinsong is offering
what she calls "fast slow food, made from scratch with
no wait." There are picnic tables around the truck and
lots of sand and surf. They have huge burritos for 10.00,
and they're really good. But what makes Tacofino famous
is its Baja-style tacos. They have sustainable-tuna tacos,
beef tacos and halibut tacos. They're all great and bring
people from all over the province.
*Open Monday to Thursday 11 am to 5 pm, Friday and Saturday
11 am to 6 pm, Sunday 11 am to 5 pm. No liquor. Master Card,
Visa.*

TOFINO
See also UCLUELET.

TORONTO, Ontario   MAP 202
ARIA
Maple Leaf Square $160
25 York Street
(416) 363-2742

Aria has a stunning interior and marvellous architectural
views of the Union Station and nearby buildings. The
environment is exciting, the service poised and the cooking competent. Meals begin with a soup *del giorno*, fried
squid, carpaccio and prosciutto parmesan. There's breast
of chicken to follow, organic salmon and a beautifully
light tuna crudo. Many people simply order a frittata, but
the tuna crudo is more interesting. There's a whole page
of open wines, but the wine-list is really built around its
thirteen chiantis and its twelve valpolicellas. You can pay

up to 385.00 for one of the chiantis, up to an astonishing 950.00 for one of the valpolicellas. (The solaias and sassicaias are actually cheaper, and of course there are many affordable wines as well.)

Open Monday to Friday 11.30 am to 3 pm, 5 pm to 11 pm (later on Friday), Saturday 5 pm to midnight, Sunday 5 pm to 10 pm. Licensed. Amex, Master Card, Visa. Book ahead if you can. ♿

TORONTO **MAP 202**
BAR ISABEL ☆☆
797 College Street **$170**
(416) 532-2222

This is an extraordinary restaurant. It's dark, narrow and terribly noisy. But it's also the most exciting new restaurant in Toronto. Grant von Gameren's cooking is amazing. His kitchen thinks nothing of offering a plate of Iberican ham, a fine mussel escabèche, roasted bone marrow, albacore tuna, whole sea-bream ceviche and, most remarkable of all, whole grilled octopus. The whole octopus costs 59.00, but you can have a half-portion for just 34.00, because Bar Isabel is not really expensive. There's some salted dark chocolate for sweet and a wine-list that you've never seen before. If you're perplexed by what you see, just ask for a bottle of the rioja. It costs only 50.00 and is seldom seen in Toronto.

Open daily 6 pm to 2 am. Licensed. Amex, Master Card, Visa. You must book ahead.

TORONTO **MAP 202**
THE BLACK HOOF ☆
928 Dundas Street W **$115**
(416) 551-8854

Don't think of the Black Hoof as a place to fill up on bison or beefsteak—or horse-meat for that matter. It's a sophisticated restaurant that deals in all parts of the animal, even the blood. (One of their most celebrated dishes is the blood-and-brain terrine.) They have incomparable charcuterie and several excellent cheeses, and it's a good idea to order a platter of charcuterie and a second platter of cheese to share with your companion. Such a meal will cost less than 40.00 and it's pretty hard to beat. Of course, they also have such things as roasted bone marrow, tongue on a brioche, smoked sweetbreads and horse tartar. The wine-list is small—there are only three or four reds by the bottle and three or four whites, most of which cost about 80.00. We usually just settle for a glass or two of Blue Mountain gamay, which costs only 11.00.

Open Monday 6 pm to 11.30 pm, Thursday to Saturday 6 pm to 1 am, Sunday 6 pm to 11.30 pm. Closed on Tuesday and Wednesday. Licensed. No cards. No reservations.

TORONTO	**MAP 202**
BOULUD CAFE	☆
60 Yorkville Avenue	**$200**
(416) 964-0411	

After his failure in Vancouver, Daniel Boulud opened two successful restaurants, one in Montreal (see above), the other in Toronto. In Toronto, he's taken over the dining-room of the new Four Seasons Hotel, where his premises are luxurious and extremely well served. He has a table d'hôte every day at 32.00 for two courses, as well as an ambitious à la carte that starts with a soup (sunchoke, say) and goes on to a country terrine and seared albacore tuna, followed by such main dishes as speckled trout, loin of lamb, lobster salad, halibut and steak au poivre. The menu is full of surprises—in fact, surprise is what Boulud is really all about. Eggplant, zucchini, belly of lamb, crisp shreds of onion, cucumber, celery, shrimp, couscous, leeks and chorizo—they all make unexpected appearances on your plate. Would you believe, even the plain mashed potatoes come as a masterpiece of hot butter and cream? The sweets are on the whole less successful, but the wine-list is astonishing. The best drinking is on the list of old-world whites, where there's a Marc Brédif vouvray for only 69.00. (There's also a first-class cabernet sauvignon from Tin Barn in Napa that costs just 59.50.) If you really want to spend money, you can;

there's a good Lafite for 3640.00 a bottle.
Open daily 11.30 am to 2.30 pm, 5.30 pm to 10 pm (later on weekends). Licensed. Amex, Master Card, Visa. Book ahead if you can. &

TORONTO   **MAP 202**
BUCA   ☆
604 King Street W   **$120**
(416) 865-1600

Look for Buca at the north end of a lane off 604 King Street West. Rob Gentile is in charge of the restaurant here, which is all brick and stone and deep below ground. The cooking is modern Italian, which means things like lamb's brains wrapped in prosciutto, zucca (sugar pumpkin with prosciutto di Parma), scamorza (cured meat with cow's milk cheese), braised dandelions and, of course, salumi della casa. All the pasta is house made, but most of it is rather heavy, especially the bigoli (duck-egg pasta) with duck offal and Venetian spices. The wine-list is almost all Italian and there are no fewer than seventeen grappas. The sarpa di Poli is unexpectedly rough, so spend a few dollars more on the sassicaia di Poli, which is superb. Of the table wines, some are overpriced. Settle for a glass or a bottle of primitivo from Puglia. The service is young, handsome and very Italian.
Open Monday to Wednesday 11 am to 3 pm, 5 pm to 10 pm, Thursday and Friday 11 am to 3 pm, 5 pm to 11 pm, Saturday 5 pm to 11 pm. Closed on Sunday. Licensed. Amex, Master Card, Visa. Book ahead.

TORONTO   **MAP 202**
CAMPAGNOLO
832 Dundas Street W   **$150**
(416) 364-4785

Campagnolo is Italian and, like most Italian restaurants, it's warm and very friendly. The waiters laugh a lot and so does the chef, who spends much of the evening talking to customers. They have all the familiar things on the menu. There's spaghetti (all'amatriciana), tagliatelle (with water buffalo and honey mushrooms), fettuccine (with white truffles) and veal schnitzels (with sauerkraut). Actually, the two best things on the menu aren't recognizably Italian at all. One is the roasted bone marrow with oxtail and plum marmalade; the other is fresh burrata cheese with whole roasted grapes. (The roasted grapes are the talk of the town, and with good reason.) There's a sensible Norman Hardie pinot noir from Prince Edward County for 69.00); they also have an attractive primitivo from Puglia, but it costs 20.00 more.

Open Wednesday to Sunday 6 pm to 9 pm. Closed on Monday and Tuesday. Licensed. Master Card, Visa. Book ahead.

TORONTO   MAP 202
CANOE   ☆☆
Toronto–Dominion Centre $225
66 Wellington Street W
(416) 364-0054

Canoe, like Scaramouche (see below), lives on its view, and of the two Canoe's is probably the more interesting. The whole of Toronto Island is laid out before you from the 54th-floor south windows. The menu may not break important new ground, but the chefs make the most of every opportunity that comes their way. Meals start with maple-poached Pacific salmon, beef tartar and pan-seared Quebec foie gras, followed by skate wing, Alberta lamb and New Brunswick sturgeon, something seldom seen in Canadian restaurants. You can end the meal with panna cotta if you like, but the deconstructed tart is more fun. The wine-list is wonderful.

Open Monday to Friday 11.45 am to 2.30 pm, 5 pm to 9 pm. Closed on Saturday and Sunday. Licensed. All cards. Book ahead. &

The price rating shown opposite the headline of each entry indicates the average cost of dinner for two with a modest wine, tax and tip. The cost of dinner, bed and breakfast (if available) is shown in parentheses.

TORONTO   MAP 202
CAVA   ☆
1560 Yonge Street   **$150**
(416) 979-9918

At Cava Chris McDonald is running a tapas-style restaurant with a remarkable variety of Spanish food and drink. Cava has an exciting menu, especially if you spend a few extra dollars on the wonderful Iberican ham, which is much better than serrano ham. Carved off the bone in front of you, this is a dish of extraordinary delicacy and marvellous complexity. There are many other good things as well, though nothing that matches the Iberican ham. There's tiradito of tuna, a salt-cod cake with piperade, smoked octopus with wheat-berries, grilled sardines and roasted sablefish with black rice. The best wines are the riojas and most of them are very good indeed. So are the sherries from Pedro Ximenez, which make a perfect sweet course.

Open daily 5 pm to 10 pm. Licensed. Amex, Master Card, Visa. ♿

TORONTO   MAP 202
DIDIER
1496 Yonge Street   **$175**
(416) 925-8588

Didier Leroy cooks in Parisian style. His favourite dishes are omelettes, not foie gras He likes to work with flat-iron steak or merguez sausages. He's at home with fried mussels and snails in garlic butter—or perhaps snails bordelaise. If you give him 25 minutes, he'll make you a first-class soufflé or even a fine tarte tatin. He doesn't believe in big, showy wine-lists. He offers only a handful of wines—a few chardonnays and a sauvignon blanc, perhaps a cabernet or two. His prices are modest. These are old-fashioned virtues, simple, straightforward and dignified, like the man.

Open Tuesday to Friday 11.30 am to 2 pm, 5.30 pm to 9 pm,

Saturday 5.30 pm to 9 pm. Closed on Sunday and Monday. Licensed. Amex, Master Card, Visa.

TORONTO   MAP 202
EDULIS   ★★
169 Niagara Street   **$175**
(416) 703-4222

Local critics rated Edulis Toronto's best new restaurant in 2012. They have two *prix-fixe* menus, one priced at 50.00, the other at 70.00. The more expensive offers truffles from Périgord, the other starts with a Japanese salad of fish and shredded vegetables, followed by John Dory crusted with hazelnuts in a fish broth, shredded beef in a pita with mushrooms and green vegetables and Copper River salmon baked in cedar fronds and served with radishes and pea-shoots. The meal usually ends with a tiny bosc pear with walnuts and cream.

Open Wednesday to Saturday 6 pm to 9.30 pm, Sunday noon to 3 pm, 6 pm to 9.30 pm. Closed on Monday and Tuesday. Licensed. Amex, Master Card, Visa. Book ahead. &

TORONTO   MAP 202
ENOTECA SOCIALE   ★
1288 Dundas Street W   **$145**
(416) 534-1200

They have a new chef here, Kris Schlotzhauer, and that changes everything. The kitchen still specializes in Italian cooking and artisanal cheeses, but the menu has become more sophisticated, the cooking more agile. For instance, albacore tuna is now served with orange, black pepper and lovage, spaghetti with black pepper and sheep's-milk cheese. They also have a fine salmon platter, fried yellow perch, pork with polenta and a dandelion salad. They have a number of interesting wines—an Organized Crime gewurztraminer from Niagara, a chardonnay from Norman Hardie in Prince Edward County and a primitivo from Puglia. The wine-list, like everything else, has improved in the last year or two.

Open daily 5 pm to 11 pm. Licensed. Amex, Master Card, Visa. Book ahead.

TORONTO   **MAP 202**
FRANK
Art Gallery of Ontario   **$145**
317 Dundas Street W
(416) 979-6688

Frank is a casual, unpretentious place, at its best for a straightforward lunch before or after a visit to the gallery. They have a very good treatment of seared albacore tuna with onions, celery and sour cream, and there's an omelette and bangers and mash every day. Their fish and chips, made with halibut and spiced with wasabi and cardamom, is better than most, and so are the Brussels sprouts with onions, capers and chillies. There are a few good wines, among them the Tawse pinot noir and the Appleby sauvignon blanc. The Tawse, however, is quite expensive.

Open Monday to Friday 11.30 am to 2.30 pm, Sunday 11 am to 2 pm (brunch). Closed on Saturday. Licensed. Amex, Master Card, Visa. &

TORONTO   **MAP 202**
FRANK'S KITCHEN
588 College Street   **$175**
(416) 516-5861

This is an Italian kitchen serving classical Italian dishes, but it has none of the false cheer so common in restaurants of its kind. On the contrary, Frank's is quiet and serious. The cooking and the service are delicate and caring. The provimi veal is beautifully tender. The gnocchi is lightly scented with gorgonzola. The strip-loin of beef is dry-aged for three weeks. The ravioli is stuffed with lovely fresh lobster. There's a McManis cabernet sauvignon on the wine-list that sells for only 53.00. The Tawse chardonnay goes for a dollar more, and both are far better buys than the usual chiantis from Ruffino. The waiters are soft-spoken and attentive, and even the chefs show an interest in what goes on in the front of the house. Everybody likes Frank's.

Open Tuesday to Sunday 6 pm to 10 pm. Closed on Monday. Licensed. Amex, Master Card, Visa.

TORONTO   **MAP 202**

THE GALLERY GRILL
Hart House   **$140**
7 Hart House Circle
(416) 978-2445

The Gallery Grill may seem like a refuge for professors looking for dishes that were fashionable in the nineteen-seventies. Actually, it's not like that at all. The cooking is bright and lively and very much to the point. Suzanne Baby, the long-time chef, starts most of her meals with tomato soup laced with red peppers and goes on to such things as seared big-eye tuna with a superb tonnato of beets and hazelnut pesto. This is a striking dish and the best thing on a menu that also offers grilled octopus, turnip cake with shiitake mushrooms and quail with roasted sunchokes. The panna cotta that ends the meal, with its hibiscus crumble and wild blueberries, seems fresh and new. All the wines are sold by the glass, the half-litre and the bottle, and you won't do better than the viognier from Organized Crime or the pinot noir from Quail's Gate. The Gallery Grill is full of surprises, among them an array of cocktails, served every weekday from 4 to 7.30 pm.

Open Monday to Friday 11.30 am to 2.30 pm, Sunday 11 am to 2 pm (brunch). Closed on Saturday. Licensed. Amex, Master Card, Visa. &

TORONTO   **MAP 202**

GEORGE   ☆☆
111C Queen Street E   **$175**
(416) 863-6006

George is no longer really expensive. Nor is the menu

spectacular or the cooking without parallel, as it once was. But this is still a very competent kitchen, serving such delicacies as rack of lamb, Wagyu beef, Pacific halibut, wild salmon, duck confit, pork belly and ocean trout. The halibut is remarkable and the Wagyu beef is, well, Wagyu beef. There's an open kitchen and first-class service. The wine-list is surprisingly inexpensive and features such outstanding native wines as Tawse and Stannards.

Open Tuesday to Saturday 5.30 pm to 10.30 pm. Closed on Sunday and Monday. Licensed. Amex, Master Card, Visa. Book ahead.

TORONTO   MAP 202
THE GLOBE
124 Danforth Avenue   **$170**
(416) 466-2000

The kitchen here does some very good things—things like pork belly, gnocchi, smoked trout and Alaska black cod. The prices are modest and the service is attentive and friendly. But the great virtue of the restaurant is the wine-list, where everything is sold at half-price on Sunday. This puts almost all the wines within the reach of the ordinary diner. For instance, they offer an ornellaia from Bolgheri (a 280.00 value) for just 140.00. You can come to the Globe and have an unforgettable lunch of oysters from Prince Edward Island and a bottle of ornellaia. Or, if you don't feel like oysters, there's always smoked trout, pork belly and a house burger. And there are several wines from Niagara and Prince Edward County, and a few even from the Okanagan, as well as from Tuscany. You don't *have* to drink ornellaia.

Open Tuesday to Thursday 6 pm to 10 pm, Friday 11.30 am to 2 pm, 6 pm to 10 pm, Saturday and Sunday 11 am to 2 pm (brunch), 6 pm to 10 pm. Closed on Monday. Licensed. All cards. ♿

If you use an out-of-date edition and find it inaccurate, don't blame us. Buy a new edition.

TORONTO   **MAP 202**
THE GROVE   ☆
1214 Dundas Street W   **$150**
(416) 588-2299

The cooking here is deconstructive in spades. Even the parsley-root soup is filled with (overcooked) snails, bacon and fried bread. Cured salmon is more successfully paired with beetroot and apple, scallops (less successfully) with chicken and sunchoke. The main courses are usually more reliable. Cod comes with crab, cabbage and a (brilliant) treatment of black pudding, but the cod itself is seriously overcooked. Arctic char is on the plate with smoked potato and sherry vinegar. What, it has to be asked, does Arctic char do for sherry vinegar, or vice versa? Beef is served, more plausibly, with barley and horseradish. At the end of the meal there's one wonderful pudding. Ben Heaton's Eton mess is so much better than the same dish anywhere else that one wonders what other surprises he's got up his sleeve.
Open Sunday noon to 5 pm, Tuesday to Saturday 6 pm to 11 pm. Closed on Monday. Licensed. Amex. Master Card, Visa. Book ahead.

TORONTO   **MAP 202**
ICI BISTRO
538 Manning Avenue   **$140**
(416) 536-0079

Ici is a small, quiet bistro with a rather old-fashioned menu that features such things as lobster bisque, oysters on the half-shell, braised beef bordelaise, merguez sausage, escargots vignerons and squab with wild mushrooms. The lobster bisque is a fine example of its kind and the oysters from St.-Simon are superb. The torchon of foie gras is flattered by its beets, the squab by its wild mushrooms. There's steak tartar, served *au naturel*, and great charcuterie. Markups on the wine-list are modest, and there's a whole page of wines sold in three-ounce and six-ounce glasses.

Open Wednesday to Saturday 5.30 pm to 9.30 pm. Closed Sunday to Tuesday. Licensed. Amex, Master Card, Visa. Book ahead.

TORONTO   MAP 202
JABISTRO   ☆
222 Richmond Street W   **$140**
(647) 748-0222

JaBistro is new to Toronto. It's small and stylish, with scrubbed brick and an open kitchen. You don't come here for sushi, though you can have sushi if you like. But they'd rather sell you a house seafood platter or a house fish bowl, or perhaps a plate of shrimp, mackerel or salmon oshizushi. All of these are fine dishes, even the house soup, which is like no other. People have been known to have two or three cups of the soup, because it's marvellous. There are five junmai sakes, three junmai-ginjo sakes and three of the top-priced junmai daiginjo sakes, which can run to 50.00 a bottle. But a ten-ounce carafe of any of the junmai-ginjo sakes is good enough for anyone. All told, JaBistro is a pleasant surprise.
Open Monday to Friday 11.30 am to 2.30 pm, 5.30 pm to 11 pm (later on Friday), Saturday 5.30 pm to midnight, Sunday 5.30 pm to 11 pm. Licensed. Amex, Master Card, Visa.

TORONTO   MAP 202
JACQUES   ☞
126A Cumberland Street   **$120**
(416) 961-1893

Jacques does all the cooking himself at this charming, little upstairs restaurant, and he cooks well. His entrecôte maître d'hôtel is as good as you're likely to get anywhere. It's true that the vegetables are very plain and cooked hot raw, but if you like you can have a fricassee of snails with tomatoes and garlic instead. There's also a pretty good quiche *du jour*. The wine-list is small and rather predictable, but the prices are very low. In fact, everything at Jacques is cheap.

Open Monday to Saturday noon to 3 pm, 6 pm to 11 pm, Sunday 5 pm to 10 pm. Licensed. Amex, Master Card, Visa. Book ahead if you can.

TORONTO   **MAP 202**
KAJI   ☆☆☆
860 Queensway   **$325**
Etobicoke
(416) 252-2166

Mitsuhiro Kaji has been in a kitchen since he was thirteen years old. First he apprenticed in Japan for ten years, then he came to Canada in 1980. He's still in the kitchen today, working five nights a week, offering two seasonal omakase dinners, one featuring Wagyu beef, the other lobster tempura. Course after course appears at your table and everything is beautiful. The sushi is all flown to Canada the day the fish is caught and it's served in the restaurant the next day. It's all achingly tender. Kaji thinks the commercial soy sauce is too salty, so he makes his own. The vinegar is all imported from Japan. Before he goes home for the night he throws away all the leftovers. The toro tuna has been on his menu for years, as have the lobster, the abalone, the sea bream and the udon noodles. Spanish mackerel is a new delicacy. The menu keeps changing, so you never know just what's coming next. Come and see. A taxi from downtown Toronto costs 60.00, but you can avoid that by simply driving west on the Gardiner to Islington, turning north on Islington and east on the Queensway.
Open Wednesday to Sunday 6 pm to 9 pm. Closed on Monday and Tuesday. Licensed. All cards. Free parking. Book ahead.

TORONTO   **MAP 202**
LAI WAH HEEN   ☆
Metropolitan Hotel   **$125**
108 Chestnut Street
(416) 977-9899

The best time to come to Lai Wah Heen is at noon, when

Terrence Chan puts on his two *prix-fixe* dim-sum menus, one priced at 48.00, the other at 32.00. The cheaper of the two offers such things as crystal-shrimp dumplings, pan-seared Peking dumplings stuffed with lobster, foie gras and shredded duck. The other menu offers such costly things as dungeness-crab bisque, Wagyu beef in steamed dumplings and truffled lobster on a bed of noodles. No-one else serves dishes of such subtlety as Terrence Chan and few others maintain a dining-room of such formal elegance. Even the plates are special. They are Narumi bone china and the silver is weighty. The house tea is, however, without interest. It's best to take a look at the tea menu and order something better. And there's no choice of sakes. There's Gekkeikan, period, though there are a number of quite satisfactory wines.
Open daily 11.30 am to 3 pm, 5.30 pm to 10.30 pm. Licensed. All cards. Free parking. Book ahead if you can. &

TORONTO   **MAP 202**
LOIRE
119 Harbord Street   **$150**
(416) 850-8330

Loire is a cozy little bistro run with considerable skill by Charles Dupoire and Sylvain Brissonnet. Brissonnet is in charge of the front of the house, though he calls himself merely the *sommelier*. Dupoire is an imaginative chef who is at ease with such dishes as glazed pork jowl, grilled corn custard, braised belly of lamb and braised beef cheeks. His charcuterie board features a parfait of chicken livers and a homemade terrine. Prices are modest— butter-poached lobster costs only 26.00, belly of lamb only 24.00. The wine-list majors in such wines from the Loire as the vouvray from Gaudrelle and the sancerre from Hippolyte Reverdy, though there are also a couple of good red wines from Prince Edward County, one by Norman Hardie and one by Stanners. The cheese plate would be better if it had fewer French cheeses and more from Quebec. As it is, we usually ask for the spiced chocolate mousse.

Open Tuesday to Friday noon to 2 pm, 5.30 pm to 9.30 pm,
Saturday 5.30 pm to 9.30 pm. Closed on Sunday and Monday.
Licensed. Amex, Master Card, Visa. Book ahead if you can. ♿

TORONTO   MAP 202
MISTURA
265 Davenport Road   **$185**
(416) 515-0009

We've said it before and we say it again: the kitchen at
Mistura blows hot and cold. The prosciutto is wonderful,
but the pickerel is typically overcooked. The crisp fried
artichokes are lovely, but the escalope of veal is more beef
than veal. The goat-cheese-and-mushroom salad is perfect, but the octopus is tough. The wine-list, on the other
hand, unlike the menu, has all the important virtues. It
offers many of the best wines from the Old World and
the New. There are eight barolos priced from 85.00 to
295.00. There are countless super-Tuscans. There's a
Château Pétrus for 2750.00 and a Château Latour for
3600.00. There are, of course, several affordable wines,
most of them from the New World. One of the best of
these is the J. Lohr chardonnay, which costs only 49.00 a
bottle. The restaurant itself looks exactly like the interior
of a gentleman's club. As for the service, it's perfect.
Open Monday to Wednesday 5.30 pm to 10 pm, Thursday to
Saturday 5.30 pm to 11 pm. Closed on Sunday. Licensed.
Amex, Master Card, Visa. Book ahead if you can. ♿

TORONTO   MAP 202
MODUS
145 King Street W   **$180**
(416) 861-9977

Modus is on the ground floor of an office building in the
heart of downtown Toronto. It's predictably stylish and
well served. The menu has all the amenities of modern
Italian cuisine: beef carpaccio, tuna tartar, pan-roasted
halibut, pan-seared scallops with mustard and maple
syrup and salmon crusted with honey and hazelnuts. The

cooking is correct and to the point, the wine-list enormous. They have 33 cabernet sauvignons, 25 chardonnays, nine ports, five grappas and three sauternes. There's an impressive list of open wines, the best of which are the Columbia Crest cabernet sauvignon from Oregon and the Closson Chase chardonnay from Prince Edward County. Modus is expensive, the parking prohibitive.
Open Monday to Friday 11.30 am to 2 pm, 5.30 pm to 9.30 pm, Saturday 5.30 pm to 9.30 pm. Closed on Sunday. Licensed. Amex, Master Card, Visa. Valet parking on weekend evenings only. Book ahead. &

TORONTO   **MAP 202**
MOMOFUKU SHOTO   ☆☆
190 University Avenue   **$485**
(647) 253-8000

David Chang came from New York last year to open three new restaurants in Toronto: Momofuku Shoto, Daisho and Momofuku Noodle Bar. Momofuku Shoto is the flagship restaurant. Reviewers speak of it in hushed tones. They call it spectacular, which it certainly is. Some call it the best restaurant in town. Others speak of Susur Lee and Michael Stadtländer as they would of their grandfather, someone whose day is done. We're not quite so sure. Shoto still hasn't been open all that long. What will people think, in time, of all that grilled rice, all those crispy shrimps, all those veal cheeks with green chilli? Dinner for two costs around 485.00. Who will pay that much, when the novelty has worn off? Bookings have to be made on line at least two weeks in advance. Does Toronto really need David Chang that much? Some people, some very important people, think it does. We doubt it, but time will tell.
Open Tuesday to Saturday 6 pm to 9 pm. Closed on Sunday and Monday. Licensed. Amex, Master Card, Visa. Book ahead.

We accept no advertisements. We accept no payment for listings. We depend entirely on you. Recommend the book to your friends.

TORONTO   **MAP 202**
NORTH 44°   ☆☆
2537 Yonge Street   **$225**
(416) 487-4897

North 44° is as expensive as ever, partly because Mark McEwan insists on buying the best of everything. His red meats are all aged for six weeks. His oysters come from Raspberry Point or Malpèque Bay. His Kusshis may cost 4.95 each, but Kusshis are the best Pacific oyster there is. His foie gras is seared and served with stewed cherries; his shrimps are served tempura-style with yuzu, his lamb chops with curried yellow lentils and white asparagus. When it comes to tenderloin he prefers bison to beef—and he's dead right. There are occasional bargains—the black cod with kohlrabi costs only 40.95, the grilled lobster only 43.95. But it's with his wines that McEwan is at his best. He has 23 chardonnays and two whole pages of cabernet sauvignons, most of them from Napa, with a top price of 695.00 (for a bottle of Groth). Good buys are few and far between, though there's a dry riesling from Cave Spring for only 42.00 a bottle. The spacious dining-room is calm and well appointed, the service serene and very poised.

Open Monday to Saturday 5 pm to 10 pm. Closed on Sunday. Licensed. Amex, Master Card, Visa. Valet parking. Book ahead. ♿

TORONTO   **MAP 202**
NOTA BENE   ☆
180 Queen Street W   **$160**
(416) 977-6400

David Lee has found his feet at Nota Bene. His salads are exquisite and so are his hamachi ceviche, his big-eye tartar and his black-pig salumi. His main courses are on the whole less successful, perhaps because he feels free to ignore regional produce, buying his sea scallops in Digby and his ocean trout in Tasmania. There's a special every day of the week, and they're often the best things on the menu. We were last at Nota Bene on a Wednesday, when we were offered wild striped bass with truffles in a cauliflower purée, a fine, imposing dish. (On Saturdays you can have slow-roasted suckling pig.) The wine-list touches a lot of bases in the mid-price range, where there's a likeable sauvignon blanc from Map-Maker in Marlborough.

Open Monday to Friday noon to 2.30 pm, 5.30 pm to 11 pm, Saturday 5.30 pm to 11 pm. Closed on Sunday. Licensed. Amex, Master Card, Visa. Book ahead. &

TORONTO MAP 202
OLDE TOWNE BISTRO ☆☆
36 Wellington Street E **$145**
(416) 504-9990

We've always been fond of this restaurant, no doubt because Simon Bower has stuck to his guns through so many difficult years. He has lost his incomparable chef. He has given up his father's name. And now he has turned his restaurant into a bistro and oyster bar. In the last year or two there was, it's true, some criticism of Lucien, as it was called, but the Olde Towne Bistro has met with almost universal praise. They do just five or six entrées every night, one of which is always hand-made pasta. The new chef, Etienne Lemieux, adjusts his menu to what local suppliers bring to the door. Seafood usually takes up about a third of the menu and the shrimp tempura and the grilled octopus are both the equal of the same dishes in any Japanese restaurant. The oysters are as good as any and much cheaper at 15.00 for six. The wine-list is strong on chardonnays and cabernets from California, and the coffee is as marvellous as ever.

Open Monday to Saturday 4 pm to 10.30 pm. Closed on Sunday. Licensed. Amex, Master Card, Visa. Book ahead. &

If you wish to improve the guide send us information about restaurants we have missed. Our mailing address is Oberon Press, 145 Spruce Street: Suite 205, Ottawa, Ontario K1R 6P1.

TORONTO　　　　　　　　　　　**MAP 202**

ONE　　　　　　　　　　　　　　☆

Hazelton Hotel　　　　　　　　　**$220**

116 Yorkville Avenue

(416) 961-9600

One is spectacular and very well served. The menu is
expansive, the prices high—both hallmarks of Mark
McEwan's restaurants. You begin with raw oysters or
wonderful yellowfin-tuna sashimi with yuzu, coriander
and jalapeno. Then there's beef carpaccio with mustard
and pickled-honey mushrooms, grilled octopus in
tomato stew, calamari with red-pepper romesco and
seared foie gras with pain perdu. Main dishes—Alaska
black cod with miso and pickled kohlrabi, wild salmon
in vichysoisse with white turnips and white asparagus,
braised short-ribs and Australian leg of lamb—are rather
less exciting. There aren't many wines for less than 80.00
a bottle and even wines by the glass sell for 14.00 or
more—one, admittedly a tignanello by Antinori, for
56.00. People seldom criticize One, except for its prices.
*Open daily 11.30 am to 4.30 pm (lunch), 4.30 pm to 11 pm
(dinner). Licensed. Amex, Master Card, Visa. Book ahead.* &

TORONTO　　　　　　　　　　　**MAP 202**

ORIGIN

109 King Street E　　　　　　　　**$130**

(416) 603-8009

You don't go to Origin for foie gras, caviar or a bottle of
ornellaia. The tables are bare and there's a lot of noise.
Origin is essentially a tapas bar, which means that you
can have an adventurous meal at minimum cost. There's
also a raw bar where you can have oysters with yuzu, a
ceviche of shrimps with coconut and a tuna salad with
Asian pears and ponzu. If you opt for table service, you
can have chilled sweet-pea soup, crisp calamari with
caramelized peanuts and curried shrimps with hot naan.
Origin shows just what Claudio Aprile can do without a
table-cloth. Recently he's opened two more Origins, one

in Liberty Village, the other in Bayview.
Open Monday to Friday 11.30 am to 3 pm, 5 pm to 11 pm,
Saturday 5 pm to 11 pm, Sunday 10 am to 3 pm (brunch), 5
pm to 11 pm. Licensed. All cards. &

TORONTO　　　　　　　　　　　　　**MAP 202**
PANGAEA　　　　　　　　　　　　　　　　☆
1221 Bay Street　　　　　　　　　　　**$175**
(416) 920-2323

This lovely restaurant is seldom crowded and never noisy.
It has superb service and a large menu, featuring
Kunomoto oysters, provimi liver with pickled wild blueberries, Atlantic cod with chorizo, rack of lamb with preserved lemon, striped sea-bass with crushed potatoes and
striploin of beef. Martin Kouprie can make almost anything interesting and memorable. He also has a big wine-
list with some interesting drinking by the glass. Try the
Bogle from California or the Masson-Blondelet from the
Loire. Or you can order a cup of tea. They have leaf teas
from Kenya, Taiwan, Japan, Ceylon, India and China.
Open Monday to Saturday 11.30 am to 5 pm (lunch), 5 pm to
11 pm (dinner). Closed on Sunday. Licensed. All cards. &

TORONTO　　　　　　　　　　　　　**MAP 202**
PASTIS EXPRESS　　　　　　　　　　　☆
1158 Yonge Street　　　　　　　　　　**$145**
(416) 928-2212

The long-time owner, Georges Gurnon, is still in charge
of the front of the house at Pastis. His fish soup is unusually delicate and served with a proper rouille and gruyère
cheese. The ravioli is made in the kitchen and stuffed
with snails, garlic and herb butter—a nice idea. The entrées are on the whole less interesting. There's fish and
chips, steamed mussels, roasted breast of chicken, grilled
lamb chops, calf's liver and steak frites, all of which
you've often seen before. Ask instead for the beef ragoût
with spicy basil or perhaps the slow-roasted leg of duck
with a toulouse sausage. There are some choice sweets,

among them a lovely mango ice. The bottled wines are expensive and they need more wines by the glass.

Open Tuesday to Saturday 5.30 pm to 10.30 pm. Closed on Sunday and Monday. Licensed. Amex, Master Card, Visa. Book ahead if you can. &

TORONTO   MAP 202
RICHMOND STATION
1 Richmond Street   **$150**
(647) 748-1444

Richmond Station occupies a few feet of frontage not far from the old City Hall. Inside it's all black and white and thoroughly contemporary. The menu is quite small, offering little but several salads, smoked trout, carpaccio, Pacific halibut and a modern take on beef stroganoff. The vegetables are all splendid, especially the so-called pommes Kennedy, which are deep-fried in beef fat and served as croûtons. They also have oysters from St. Anne's and an excellent charcuterie board. There are no fewer than sixteen open wines (eight red and eight white), as well as a couple of dozen by the bottle, the best of which are from Organized Crime. Oysters, charcuterie and a glass of Organized Crime—where could you get a better lunch, especially when your waiter runs outside in his shirtsleeves (in January) to hail you a cab?

Open Monday to Friday 11 am to 10 pm, Saturday 5 pm to 10 pm. Closed on Sunday. Licensed. Amex, Master Card, Visa.

TORONTO   MAP 202
SCARAMOUCHE   ☆☆
1 Benvenuto Place   **$240**
(416) 961-8011

Scaramouche, as everyone knows by now, has a stunning view of the city by night. But there's a lot more to Scaramouche than the view. Keith Froggett is still in charge of the kitchen and he has a very handsome menu and does some beautiful things with it. His steak tartar, for instance, tastes exactly as it should, which is rare in Canadian restaurants. His grilled-octopus salad is a delight. And his yellowfin-tuna sashimi is wonderful. At his best, Keith Froggett is brilliant. But of course he's not always at his best. His warm lobster with ginger and sesame is a good example. Lobster is, of course, an important luxury, but it's hard to deal with, hard for a kitchen that wants to handle its dishes with real delicacy. Froggett's lobster is just like the lobster you'll get in any Maritime road house. But one has to admit that his pasta is all house-made, his sea-bass fresh and lightly cooked. As for his wine-list, it's long and very splendid. If money is a problem—and Scaramouche is certainly expensive—ask for a couple of half-glasses of the Proprietary bordeaux. It costs 23.00 for two half-glasses, which is cheap for a wine of this quality. If you insist on a whole bottle, we can't help you.

Open Monday to Saturday 5.30 pm to 9.30 pm. Closed on Sunday. Licensed. All cards. Free valet parking. Book ahead.

TORONTO   **MAP 202**
SIMPLE BISTRO
619 Mount Pleasant Road   **$125**
(416) 483-8933

Masaguki Tamaru has left the Simple Bistro and been replaced by Da Woon Chae, who so far is cooking about as well as his predecessor. The place is still cheap, though prices have gone up a little in the last year or two. The menu now features such appetizers as salt-cod and a charcuterie platter, followed by Berkshire pork, baked lamb shank and wild Atlantic scallops. The sticky toffee pudding is gone, but you can have a wedge of lovely lemon cake instead. The Norman Hardie wines from Prince Edward County have now priced themselves out of the market and right now the best buy on the list is the Peter Yealands sauvignon blanc, which is sold by the glass as well as the bottle. Simple Bistro is still quiet and extremely well served. All this for about half what you'd have to pay at many Toronto restaurants.

Open Monday and Tuesday 5.30 pm to 10 pm, Wednesday to

Friday 11.30 am to 2.30 pm, 5.30 pm to 10 pm, Saturday and Sunday 11 am to 2.30 pm (brunch), 5.30 pm to 10 pm. Licensed. All cards.

TORONTO   **MAP 202**
SPLENDIDO   ☆☆
88 Harbord Street   **$200**
(416) 929-7788

The all-new Splendido is back in form after a brief lapse. There's a new menu, of course, and meals now usually begin (and begin very well indeed) with green-pea soup with fresh herbs and croûtons. Then there's soft-shelled crab with pickled cucumber—another superb dish. The foie gras with quail is certainly expensive at 24.00, but it makes the most of its pickled beets, purple potatoes and crème fraîche. The rib-eye steak comes from Cumbrae Farms, which actually is no guarantee of quality, but they also have pastured veal from Haldimand County, sea-bass decorated with pea-shoots and preserved lemon, organic salmon with smoked peppers and (for a *supplément* of 9.00) Brussels sprouts in a wasabi vinaigrette. The wine-list offers a number of the best clarets, but if you can't afford any of these, try the V.Q.A. Tawse.
Open Monday to Saturday 5.30 pm to 10 pm. Closed on Sunday. Licensed. Amex, Master Card, Visa. Book ahead. Valet parking. ♿

TORONTO   **MAP 202**
YOURS TRULY
229 Ossington Avenue   **$220**
(416) 533-2243

Yours Truly inspires strong feelings and so does its chef, Lachlan Coljak. You either think they offer an inspired variety of dishes or you think that their recipes are way over the top. (We feel only that the noise level is almost beyond enduring, though some people think that's all part of the fun.) There are two menus. If you book two weeks in advance you can have the *carte blanche* menu, where there are more than twenty courses. Otherwise, there's a four-course menu for 55.00. Both menus are complicated and difficult, but the waiters are always ready to explain them. Even so, your choices, when they arrive, will not be anything like what you think you've ordered. It's all very artsy and playful, but the portions are tiny. We suggest you order the 55.00 menu, eat a lot of bread and drink a lot of wine. Otherwise you'll leave hungry.

Open Monday and Thursday to Sunday 6 pm to 9 pm. Closed on Tuesday and Wednesday. Licensed. Master Card, Visa. Book ahead.

TORONTO   **MAP 202**
ZUCCA
2150 Yonge Street   **$160**
(416) 488-5774

Zucca is Andrew Milne-Allan's creation and, after all these years, he's still in the kitchen. He still makes all the pasta every morning, even the ravioli stuffed with zucchini, ricotta and smoked scamorza. His specialty is whole fish grilled with fresh herbs, lemon and extra-virgin olive-oil. His beef, which comes from Cumbrae around the corner, is all dry-aged and simply grilled. His organic duck is served with spiced orange and wildflower honey. And he now has an impressive list of Italian wines, strong on barolos, barberas, brunellos and chiantis. There's even a tignanello from Antinori for 175.00 a bottle. Prices are modest, not just for the tignanello but for everything on the list.

Open daily 5.30 pm to 10 pm. Licensed. Amex, Master Card, Visa.

TORONTO
See also PORT CREDIT, WHITBY.

The map number assigned to each city, town or village gives the location of the centre on one or more of the maps at the start of the book.

TRINITY, Newfoundland

MAP 203

FISHER'S LOFT INN
3 Mill Road
Port Rexton
(877) 464-3240

☆☆
$175 ($295)

Fisher's has just one set dinner every evening, but travellers who have passed this way all say that their dinner here was better than anything else they had in Newfoundland. Trinity is the oldest settlement in the province. In 1615, only two years after Champlain founded Port Royal, Sir Richard Whitbourne held the first Admiralty Court here. The parish church of St. Paul dates from 1734, and the rest of the town looks much as it did two centuries ago. Fisher's Loft was opened in 1999 by John and Peggy Fisher. It's close to the start of the Skerwink Trail, which is a major destination for visitors. From the dining-room windows you can watch icebergs (and sometimes whales) in Trinity Bay. They now have a greenhouse as well as three open-air gardens where they grow herbs and vegetables for the kitchen. Dinner might begin with parsnip-and-caramelized-apple soup. Then there'll be garden greens in a partridge-berry vinaigrette. The main course might be cod with brown butter and puréed potato, the sweet, if you're lucky, lemon mousse with a wild berry sauce. They can get lobster from the middle of May until the middle of July and all summer long they forage for wild berries. The wine-list is short and simple; the service is impeccable. In the spring of 2013, John and Peggy Fisher turned the Loft Inn over to their sons, Luke and Gabriel. We're worried about the million-dollar Conference Centre they've built on the grounds, but we have no real reason to think that the dining-room is not as good as ever. We hope that the new developments will ensure their survival. Time will tell. *Open daily at 5.30 pm and 7.30 pm (two sittings) by appointment only from 1 May until 31 October. Licensed. Master Card, Visa.* ⚹

Nobody but nobody can buy his way into this guide.

TRINITY

MAP 203

THE TWINE LOFT ☆
Artisan Inn **$140**
57 High Street
(877) 464-3377

Tineke Gow has always been ambitious for the Twine Loft, which she has furnished with antiques. The dining-room is filled with whatever happens to be in season. Tineke's daughter, Marieke, is the *sommelier* and out of season she travels the world in search of the right wines at the right price. Two chefs work in an open kitchen preparing the table d'hôte dinners. Four courses cost 39.00 and feature lamb shanks braised in beer, cod provençale, coq au vin, salmon in a crust of hazelnuts and pork with rhubarb chutney. Tineke has always been interested in vegetarian dishes, but actually the kitchen is at its best preparing dishes for diets of every kind. Greens and herbs come fresh from the kitchen garden and rhubarb is cut daily for the rhubarb tartlets. Cod comes straight from the harbour and wild blueberries come from the surrounding hillsides. In winter they have a lot of roasted root vegetables, as well as first-class potatoes. The Twine Loft is only a few minutes from the summer theatre and they guarantee that you'll get there before the curtain rises.

Open daily 8 am to 10 pm (pre-theatre dinners at 5.30 pm and 7.45 pm) from 15 May until 15 October. Licensed. Amex, Master Card, Visa. Book ahead if you can. &

TYNE VALLEY, P.E.I.

(MAP 39)

DOCTOR'S INN
Highway 167 **$135**
(902) 831-3057

Tyne Valley is a pretty little village not far from the western shore of Malpèque Bay, where it's surrounded by some of the loveliest country on the Island. Paul and Jean Offer no longer rent rooms in their house, but they still serve dinner for up to six guests every evening but Friday.

Paul's passion is the two-acre organic vegetable garden behind the house. He may no longer cover the dinner table with vegetables, as he once did, but whatever he puts on your plate will be perfectly fresh. He grows more than 8 varieties of carrot and 28 varieties of lettuce, not to mention the tomatoes, cucumbers, cauliflower, zucchini, beets and onions that he raises to sell at the Farmer's Market in Charlottetown. Paul's wife, Jean, does all the cooking on an old wood stove that came with the house. Her salads are as good as her vegetables and her breads are all freshly baked. Entrées include scallops, Arctic char, salmon, sole and veal. Paul and Jean Offer are genial hosts, and a meal at the Doctor's Inn is a memorable experience. Dinner costs 60.00 a head and includes a bottle of wine that's appropriate to the meal.

Open daily except Friday at 7 pm Licensed for beer and wine only. Master Card, Visa. You must book ahead 24 hours in advance. ♿

UCLUELET, B.C. (MAP 201)
NORWOOD'S ☆☆
1714 Peninsula Road **$180**
(250) 726-7001

Richard Norwood travelled widely before opening this restaurant in Ucluelet. Here he works closely with farmers, fishermen and cheese-makers to design a menu based exclusively on local ingredients. The restaurant is small and seats only about 25 people. On one side there's an open kitchen; on the other is a small bar. Diners sit at tall tables made of slabs of local fir. Fishermen often call the kitchen a few hours before they reach port to let the chefs know whether they'll have salmon that day or halibut or even octopus. Dinner begins with the tenderest imaginable octopus on a bed of puréed potato with ginger and chilli. Or you can have curried mussels and dungeness crab-cakes with quinoa and lemon. For your main course, you get to choose between braised lamb shanks and albacore tuna wrapped in nori. There's also halibut on a bed of couscous and several steaks. Our favourite sweet is the chocolate mousse with caramel sauce. Wine can be bought by the half-glass, which means that you can have a chenin blanc with your octopus and a pinot noir with your steak.

Open daily 5 pm to 9 pm. Licensed. All cards. Book ahead in summer. &

VAL-MORIN, Quebec   (MAP 122)
AU MAZOT SUISSE
5320 boulevard Labelle   **$135**
(450) 229-5600

A few years ago a Swiss fondue was as common as bread and butter. Nowadays Au Mazot Suisse is one of the few places where you can get it. Take a table in the charming dining-room, order a glass of kirsch, which is the traditional drink with fondue, and wait for the cheese to melt. There are different kinds of fondue; there's cheese and there's chocolate. They all cost around 30.00, which includes an appetizer, a sweet and coffee. The wine-list offers several wines by the glass and the half-bottle, as well as a number of private imports.

Open Wednesday and Thursday 5 pm to 8 pm, Friday and Saturday 5 pm to 10 pm, Sunday 5 pm to 8 pm. Closed on Monday and Tuesday. Licensed. All cards. Book ahead.

VANCOUVER, B.C.   **MAP 207**
ACORN   ☆
3995 Main Street   **$110**
(604) 566-9001

Acorn has done the seemingly impossible. It's made vegan and vegetarian food fashionable. Located in the trendy area around Main and King Edward, Acorn fills up early and stays open late. For starters, try their potato-parsnip croquette, made with Okanagan apples, aged cheddar cheese and pale ale, or their ricotta gnocchi with a coffee-scented celeriac purée. Main courses are rather less inventive, but there are interesting treatments of king-oyster mushrooms with braised shallots, potatoes and car rot meringue. The sweets are all imaginative and the best of them is probably the compote of quince with mascarpone cheese, spiced walnuts and clover honey. We haven't yet tried their raspberry-cashew cheesecake with chocolate and an almond-coconut crust, but most people seem to like it.

Open Tuesday to Thursday 5.30 pm to 1 am, Friday and Saturday 5.30 pm to 2 am, Sunday 5.30 pm to midnight. Closed on Monday. Master Card, Visa. No reservations.

VANCOUVER   MAP 207
BANANA LEAF
1096 Denman Street   **$75**
(604) 683-3333

Malaysian cuisine is a blend of the Chinese, Indonesian and Thai styles of cooking. On the West Coast chefs use the extraordinary variety of fresh produce available to display each of these styles to its best advantage. At the three Banana Leaf locations they add great service and a warm atmosphere, and as a result all three have been immediate successes with the critics as well as the general public. Sadly, the Denman Street location doesn't take reservations, though it's always been a good place to recover from a hard walk in Stanley Park. At 820 W Broadway the best things on the menu are usually the dungeness crab with Singapore chilli, the rendang beef and the sambal beans. The beans are often cooked hot raw and if you don't like hot raw ask instead for the mixed seafood, which will bring you Malaysian versions of flat fish, scallops, shrimps, mussels, clams and squid. This is now a much better choice than the appetizer plate, which sometimes comes with soggy spring-rolls. The Kitsilano location, at 3805 W Broadway, has a splendid lunch that starts with roti canal and goes on to boneless shoulder of lamb, stewed in a cumin curry with fennel and coconut milk, or mixed seafood with lemon grass, ginger, garlic, chilli and galangal. In the evening they offer a large variety of fresh seafood—try the crab with garlic and black peppercorns, the prawns with sambal or the red snapper in Assam curry.

Open Monday to Thursday 11.30 am to 2.45 pm, 5 pm to 10.30 pm, Friday 11.30 am to 2.45 pm, 5 pm to 11 pm, Saturday 11.30 am to 11 pm, Sunday 11 am to 10 pm. Licensed. Amex, Master Card, Visa. &

VANCOUVER
BAO BEI
163 Keefer Street
(604) 688-0876

MAP 207

$75

Bao Bei is a post-modern take on the Chinese restaurants that once flourished all over Canada. It specializes in what they call schnacks, which in this case means marinated eggplant braised with soy, garlic and ginger, steamed prawn dumplings and pork won-tons with arugula in ham consommé. We particularly like their steamed buns with pork belly, bean-sprouts, preserved turnip and sugared peanuts, their beef tartar with preserved mustard root, crisp shallots, watercress and taro chips and their braised pork meatballs with cabbage in puff pastry. People write to us about the squid with Chinese sausage and baby bok choy and the crisp pork belly with sautéed turnip, Asian cucumber, chilli and garlic. After that there's Vietnamese coffee and mandarin oranges, or (even better) panna cotta with lemon gastrique and confit of kumquat. Bao Bei is still crowded, but it's not half so noisy as it used to be. Prices are close to their old lows.

Open Tuesday to Saturday 5.30 pm to midnight. Closed on Sunday and Monday. Licensed. Master Card, Visa. No reservations.

VANCOUVER
BIN 941
941 Davie Street
(604) 683-1246

MAP 207

$85

Very little has changed at Bin 941. They still offer West Coast fusion-style tapas, which have little in common with the real thing. It's a funky place, and when we go there we usually ask for free-range breast of duck with sundried cranberries, lamb sirloin with an heirloom-tomato salad or Digby scallops with bonito butter. Others tell us that they admire the portobello mushroom in a reduction of garlic and balsamic vinegar, the lemon salt-buttered halibut in a Japanese plum vinaigrette and the mussels steamed with coconut milk, lemon zest and garam masala. Some dishes, like the Yucatan breast of chicken with blue-corn bread and the Chinese five-spice duck with dragon fruit, fragrant pear, watercress and pecans, used to be offered only at Bin 942, which is now closed.

Open daily 5.30 pm to 1.30 am. Licensed. All cards. No reservations.

VANCOUVER

MAP 207
☆

BISHOP'S
2183 W 4 Avenue
(604) 738-2025

$175

John Bishop has always been known for his graceful, intimate interiors, his gorgeous flowers (orchids bigger and whiter than most) and his careful, competent service. But he hasn't been known, until now, for a masterpiece like his corn soup with black-pepper squid. His beet salad is such another, his terrine of wild boar still another. His rack of lamb, it's true, is no masterpiece, but it's a pleasing, likeable dish. So is his tenderloin of beef with kale and wild mushrooms. Everything or nearly everything served in the restaurant is organic. Nearly everything comes from nearby farms, many of which are named in the menu. Several of the wines come from either the old World or the Pacific Rim—of course they do. But the bulk of the list is grown next door, in the Okanagan. John Bishop has done an excellent job here on West Fourth, and sometimes he's inspired.

Open daily 5.30 pm to 10.30 pm. Licensed. All cards. No smoking, no cellphones. Book ahead. ♿

Nobody but nobody can buy his way into this guide.

VANCOUVER   MAP 207
BLUE WATER   ★★★
1095 Hamilton Street   **$200**
(604) 688-8078

Blue Water is a beautiful restaurant. They have a raw bar with fourteen varieties of oyster from B.C. (the Kusshis are the best), two from the State of Washington and four from the Atlantic provinces (the St.-Simon are the best unless you prefer the Malpèques for the sake of their reputation). There's a sushi bar, offering maguro red tuna, toro or tuna belly, hamachi or yellow-tail and ebi or shrimp, as well as a variety of sashimi. There's also a regular à la carte, which offers such classic dishes as Arctic char, scallops, sablefish, chinook salmon, Wagyu beef and white sturgeon. We always go for the raw bar, where we ask for six or eight St.-Simon oysters and two or three pieces of tuna belly. The Italian wines and wines from Pauillac are, of course, very expensive, but there are several good buys from the Okanagan. Or try a bottle of Little Farm from the Simulkameen. The 1911 vintage costs 69.00 and it's better than you'd expect.
Open daily 5 pm to midnight. Licensed. All cards. Valet parking.
&

VANCOUVER   MAP 207
LA BRASSERIE   ★
1091 Davie Street   **$145**
(604) 568-6499

We used to think of this place as a traditional French bistro, but these days it's getting to be more German than French. The best of the German dishes is the roast suckling pig with sauerkraut and schupfnudel. The best of the French dishes are the mussels in white wine, followed by the halibut cheeks with lemon, Israeli couscous, zucchini and cauliflower purée or the steak with mushrooms and fries. The sweets are rather predictable—there's little but crème brûlée and a chocolate mousse. But there are plenty of good German beers to drink.

Open Monday to Thursday 5 pm to 10.30 pm, Friday 5 pm to 11.30 pm, Saturday 11 am to 3 pm (brunch), 5 pm to 11.30 pm, Sunday 11 am to 3 pm (brunch), 5 pm to 10.30 pm. Licensed. Master Card, Visa. No reservations.

VANCOUVER   **MAP 207**
LA BUCA   ☆
4025 MacDonald Street   **$150**
(604) 730-6988

La Buca serves northern Italian food from a small storefront restaurant on the west side. They start with a specialty of the Friuli region, which is crisply baked Alpine piave cheese topped with a tomato fonduta and arugula. The mussels that follow are simply cooked in white wine and garlic. The tagliatelle is made with chestnut flour tossed with cabbage, speck and cheese. The Caesar salad features radicchio with Italian bacon, capers and anchovies. After that, ask for the panna cotta with brandied plums, if it's still on the menu. The wine-list is small but skilfully chosen.
Open Sunday to Thursday 5 pm to 9.30 pm, Friday and Saturday 5 pm to 10 pm. Licensed. Master Card, Visa. Book ahead.
&

VANCOUVER   **MAP 207**
CAFE KATHMANDU   👈
2779 Commercial Drive   **$85**
(604) 879-9909

Abi Sharma is the chef and owner of Café Kathmandu, and he's as good at talking to customers about politics as he is at preparing choilaa or shredded chicken with lemon, garlic, onion and fresh coriander. Sharma came to Canada after being arrested as a student protester in Nepal. Here in Vancouver, he serves such authentic Nepalese dishes as choilaa, aloo achaar or chilled sesame-and-lemon salad and jhingey maachaa, which means prawns sautéed in garlic. Sharma is at his best with dumplings stuffed with pork or vegetables and served with sesame and cardamom (or sometimes with tomato chutney). If you think that no meal is complete without meat, ask for the goat curry, served with yellow dal and a hot or sweet chutney. Sharma uses no dairy in any of these dishes, unlike most Indian chefs, who use gee for frying. At Kathmandu there's an abundance of such vegetarian dishes as cauliflower infused with turmeric and served with fenugreek potatoes simmered with bambooshoots. Nothing here costs more than 15.00.

Open Monday to Saturday 5 pm to 10 pm. Closed on Sunday. Licensed for beer and wine only. Master Card, Visa. &

VANCOUVER   MAP 207
CAMPAGNOLO
1020 Main Street   **$135**
(604) 484-6018

Campagnolo is a small, shabby Italian restaurant on Main Street. If you come with a companion, it's a good idea to order a salami platter, followed by Sloping Hills pork and the fish of the day, which if you're lucky may be beautifully undercooked trout. The salami is good, but if you don't like charcuterie you can have Sawmill Bay clams or a helping of beef tongue. There's a long list of red wines from Italy that rises unexpectedly to a tignanello for 140.00. On the way down the list there's a Bossi chianti classico for 75.00 and a Fontanafredda barbera for the unbelievable price of 38.00 a bottle. If you choose the barbera, you can spend the money you save on a glass of grappa. They have three grappas by Jacopo Poli, one of which costs only 24.00 a glass.

Open Monday to Friday 11.30 am to 2.30 pm, 5 pm to 11 pm, Saturday 11.30 am to 2.30 pm (brunch), 5 pm to midnight, Sunday 11.30 am to 2.30 pm (brunch), 5 pm to 11 pm. Licensed. Master Card, Visa. No reservations.

If you wish to improve the guide send us information about restaurants we have missed. Our mailing address is Oberon Press, 145 Spruce Street: Suite 205, Ottawa, Ontario K1R 6P1.

VANCOUVER　　　　　　　　　　　　**MAP 207**
CHAMBAR　　　　　　　　　　　　　　☆☆
566 Beatty Street　　　　　　　　　　　**$150**
(604) 879-7119

Chambar closed in May of 2014 and reopened a few
yards away at 566 Beatty Street, where it serves breakfast
and lunch as well as dinner. The place is still known for
its Belgian-style beer, one of which is brewed right on
the premises. Meals begin well with yellowfin-tuna tartar
or scallops with chorizo. Then come mussels and fries
congolaise, one of the few holdovers from Chambar's
early days. For something more exotic, try the spiced
lamb shank braised with figs, honey and cilantro. The
sweets are wonderful, especially the almond dacquoise
with whisky-and-bitters ice cream. The service is at once
warm and completely professional.
Open Monday to Friday noon to 2 pm, 5 pm to midnight, Sat-
urday and Sunday 11 am to 3 pm (brunch), 5 pm to midnight.
Licensed. Amex, Master Card, Visa. Book ahead. ♿

VANCOUVER　　　　　　　　　　　　**MAP 207**
CIBO
Moda Hotel　　　　　　　　　　　　　**$175**
900 Seymour Street
(604) 602-9570

Cibo is a down-to-earth Italian restaurant, specializing
in such things as carpaccio and octopus, followed by linguine with clams, tagliatelle, gnocchi alla romana,
salmon, osso buco and chicken with tomatoes and kale.
The best things on the menu are the chicken and the osso
buco. The oysters on the half-shell are indifferent and the
skirt steak is worse than most of its kind. The sweets,
however, are always attractive, especially the tiramisu and
the zabaglione. But Italian wine is really what the restaurant is all about. There's an expansive list of Amarones
and Bolgheris, all extremely expensive—there's only one
Bolgheri that the average person can afford, and it costs
71.00 a bottle.

Open Monday to Saturday 5 pm to 9 pm. Closed on Sunday.
Licensed. Amex, Master Card, Visa. &

VANCOUVER   MAP 207
CINCIN
1154 Robson Street   **$200**
(604) 688-7338

Cincin has lost some of its *panache* in the last year or two,
but it's still as expensive as ever. Andrew Richardson
cooks modern Italian dishes on his wood-fired oven and
if he's on his game he's good. Try his line-caught albacore
tuna tartar with lemon, radish and small greens or his
local octopus salad with Iberican chorizo. But his carpaccio with thyme and black pepper is merely dull and his
flying squid grilled over alder with barlotti beans little
more than a curiosity. As for the sablefish with maple,
honey and mustard, it has little of its old magic. Nowadays you come to Cincin for its wines. They have a fabulous collection of old barolos and several wonderful
ornellaias from Bolgheri. If you can't afford any of these,
ask for a bottle of Louis Martini cabernet sauvignon. It
costs only 11.00 a glass.
Open Monday to Friday 11.30 am to 3 pm, 5 pm to 11 pm,
Saturday and Sunday 5 pm to 11 pm. Licensed. All cards. Book
ahead if you can.

VANCOUVER   MAP 207
CIOPPINO'S   ☆☆☆
1133 Hamilton Street   **$290**
(604) 688-7466

At Cioppino's they cook in the northern-Italian style,
and every table has been full six days a week for as long
as anyone can remember. Perhaps that's because Pino
Posteraro is on the floor, and often in the kitchen, every
night. Cooking is what the place is all about, cooking and
fresh local produce. For instance, the prosciutto di Parma
is made with prosciutto that's been aged 24 months. (If
you prefer, you can have Iberican ham, cut from the black

Iberican pig, for 85.00.) If you can't afford that, and who can, ask for the calamari, made with tender young squid. It's a beautiful dish. Then there's Pacific octopus (surprisingly tender) and saltspring mussels. The lobster may be a simple dish, but it's perfect. After that there's sablefish, rack of lamb, wild boar, osso buco and even Dover sole—an unexpected pleasure. The wine-list offers a dozen or so reds and a dozen or so whites. The top price on the list is 4000.00 for a bottle of sassicaia—there are five to choose from, as well as six solaias and twelve ornellaias. (If you turn the page, you'll find that they have no fewer than 27 grappas.) These are the exceptions; there's good drinking at all prices.

Open Monday to Saturday 5.30 pm to 10.30 pm. Closed on Sunday. Licensed. All cards. Valet parking. Book ahead if you can. &

VANCOUVER   **MAP 207**
CRAVE
3941 Main Street   **$125**
(604) 872-3663

Crave is a small, smart bistro on Main Street at 22 Avenue. It has an attractive menu, agreeable service and low prices. We like to start with the shrimps. The shrimps are lightly battered with a dipping sauce of sweet-chilli mayo. (The tempura of Ahi tuna and the dungeness crabcakes are both less exciting than the shrimps.) If you prefer, you can have Pacific mussels, steak frites or, indeed, a whole roasted chicken. There are only about a dozen wines, but there are several beers, some local, some imported. Look for the Kronenburg from France or the Erdinger, a wheaten beer from Germany.

Open Tuesday to Friday 11 am to 10 pm, Saturday 9 am to 10 pm, Sunday 9 am to 9 pm. Closed on Monday. Licensed. Amex, Master Card, Visa. No reservations. &

The map number assigned to each city, town or village gives the location of the centre on one or more of the maps at the start of the book.

VANCOUVER MAP 207
DIVA AT THE MET ☆☆
645 Howe Street **$175**
(604) 602-7788

Diva at the Met got a new chef last October, and already there have been some changes. On the regular à la carte they now offer dishes designed to compete with the food trucks, ninety of which are now operating in the city. The best of these is the Thai-style chicken curry, which has no equal that we know of. The rest of the à la carte now tastes better than it used to, especially the hamachi with avocado, the flying-fish roe and the humboldt squid. After that there's wild coho salmon, but the salmon is often disappointing. You'll usually do better with the black cod with apple purée and even with the tortellini with foraged mushrooms. There's a sauvignon blanc from Stag's Hollow, a cabernet sauvignon from Sandhill and a Lafite premier grand-cru for 1500.00. If you prefer to drink by the glass you'll have a wide choice, starting with a likeable pinot noir from Joie Farm for 63.00. Read about the Lafite and buy the Joie Farm.

Open Monday to Friday 11.30 am to 2.30 pm, 5.30 pm to 9.45 pm, Saturday and Sunday 5.30 pm to 9.45 pm. Licensed. Amex, Master Card, Visa. Free valet parking.

VANCOUVER MAP 207
DON FRANCESCO ☆☆
860 Burrard Avenue **$150**
(604) 685-7770

Don Francesco isn't crowded or noisy, like so many successful restaurants. It's quiet and well lit, with widely-spaced tables, stiff white napkins and highly polished glasses. The menu is, of course, Italian and it's broadly familiar. Not that there are no surprises. The calamaretti is one such. Calamaretti are baby squid and they're served here with sweet capers, tomatoes and extra-virgin olive-oil. The ruby trout with lemon, parsley and olive-oil is another. The list of barolos—six of them, all priced at about 150.00 a bottle—is still another. If you want to see the kitchen at its best, ask for a bowl of wild-mushroom soup, made with a beautiful rich stock. The pasta is all perfect, the greens delicate and wonderfully fresh. The fish is all simply grilled. The veal is pounded until it's fork tender and then grilled. As for the service, it's perfect too. *Open Monday to Friday 11.30 am to 5 pm (lunch), 5 pm to 11 pm (dinner), Saturday and Sunday 5 pm to 11 pm. Licensed. All cards. Book ahead.* &

VANCOUVER   **MAP 207**
LA GHIANDA
2083 Alma Street   **$60**
(604) 566-9559

La Quercia (see below) is the oak, Ghianda the acorn in Italian. This is a licensed Italian deli and restaurant operating in the Point Grey district of Vancouver. The menu changes daily but always has a fine selection of soups, salads, pastas and sandwiches. For 10.00 you get your choice of three pastas, three paninis and three main dishes. Everything is authentic Italian. At noon you can have orecchiette with gorgonzola and walnuts, grilled fennel sausages or grilled trout. The sandwiches, served on house-made ciabatta, are rich and massive. We like the veal with tuna sauce and the lamb panini, both of which cost around 10.00. *Note:* as this edition went to press, we received reports that the restaurant might be planning to close. Call before you go.
Open Tuesday to Saturday 11 am to 9 pm. Closed on Sunday and Monday. Licensed. Master Card, Visa.

VANCOUVER   **MAP 207**
GO FISH
1505 W 1 Avenue   **$45**
(604) 730-5040

Go Fish is a small shack on Fisherman's Wharf overlooking False Creek, within easy walking distance of Granville Island. It has outdoor seating on a heated patio, which is fine unless it rains. They serve surprisingly complex dishes like Pacific salmon with side-stripe-shrimp mayonnaise, Japanese pickled cucumber and organic greens on a fresh Tartine Bakery bun. The salmon comes with Pacific Rim coleslaw, which is one of their signature dishes. Of course there's also halibut and chips in a beer batter with thick-cut potato fries. As for the oyster po'boy sandwich, everybody seems to love it. When things get really busy, the staff can sometimes be quite rude. Pay no attention.

Open Tuesday to Sunday 11.30 am to 6.30 pm. Closed on Monday. No liquor. Master Card, Visa. No reservations. &

VANCOUVER   **MAP 207**
HAWKSWORTH   ☆☆☆
Hotel Georgia   **$180**
801 W Georgia Street
(604) 673-7000

When he first opened at the Georgia Hotel, David Hawksworth, in spite of all the years he spent at West, still had things to learn. Well, he's learned them. His restaurant now has nearly every important virtue. The menu is lively and interesting, offering as it does things like charred hamachi salad, caramelized squid with chorizo, smoked salmon and saffron, pork belly with Japanese mustard, Lois Lake steelhead trout, Pacific halibut and sablefish with pickled shiitake, crisp yam and pea-shoots. It's true, the curried lamb doesn't compare with the lamb stews schoolboys used to eat years ago. The lamb isn't the same, but Hawksworth plays all the cards in his hand—cauliflower, raita and pakoras—to make his lamb a dazzling dish. The chef works with a remarkable variety of textures and his flavours are all clear and colourful. Hawksworth has a big list of open wines and they all speak for themselves. Try the Little Farm riesling from the Simulkameen or the Starmont chardonnay from Napa and judge for yourself. If you're drinking by the bottle, ask for the pinot noir from Joie Farm. It costs 98.00 but it's lovely.

Open Monday to Friday 1130 am to 2 pm, 5.30 pm to 11 pm,
Saturday and Sunday 10.30 am to 2.30 pm (brunch), 5.30 pm
to 11 pm. Licensed. All cards. Valet parking. Book ahead.

VANCOUVER   **MAP 207**
JAPADOG   🖐❧
530 Robson Street   **$25**
(604) 569-1158

The first Japadog was opened a few years ago by a Japanese couple who came to Canada with the idea of creating
a street stand selling dogs Japanese-style. They started by
working alone, then added one helper, then another, then
several more. Eventually they had five locations in Vancouver and 30 employees. One of these, the one on Robson Street, is a full-service restaurant. The Japadogs all
marry Canadian and Japanese traditions of street food.
Canadian hotdogs are good, but (as we've said before)
Japanese hotdogs are better. Ask for their top-of-the-line
okinomi dog, which is made with a gourmet kurobuta
wiener, bonita flakes, fried cabbage, Japanese mayonnaise
and a special okinomiyaki sauce. Most people also like
the oroshi dog, which comes with bratwurst, grated
radish, green onions and soy sauce.
Open daily noon to 7.30 pm (later on weekends). No liquor, no
cards. No reservations.

VANCOUVER   **MAP 207**
LIN   ✮✮
1537 W Broadway   **$110**
(604)733-9696

Yu Miao is now turning out almost 200 *xiao long bao*
dumplings every day. It was this that first drew our attention to Lin. Originally, almost all of her clients were
Chinese, but the word is now out and everyone is going
there. Her vegetable dishes are all special, but our
favourite is the Shanghai Malantou with pressed tofu.
You should also try the braised eggplant, the pea-shoots
with garlic and the smoked-tea duck. Right now, Lin is

facing stiff competition from the Shaolin Noodle House at 656 W Broadway (telephone (604) 873-1618).

Open Monday and Wednesday to Sunday 11 am to 3 pm, 5 pm to 10 pm. Closed on Tuesday. Licensed. Master Card, Visa. &

VANCOUVER   **MAP 207**
MAENAM THAI   ☆
1938 W 4 Avenue   **$115**
(604) 730-5579

Maenam, we think, is the best Thai restaurant in Vancouver. The chef, Angus An, takes traditional Thai dishes and adjusts them to make the most of the fresh organic produce available to him. He starts his lunch with steamed mussels with lemon grass and Thai basil, green curry of halibut cheeks, chicken salad with pomelo and grilled squid with green mango—all magic in An's hands. The dinner menu is more elaborate. There's red curry of duck, stir-fried short-ribs with wild ginger and stir-fried aubergine with Thai basil. The specialty of the house is eight-spice fried fish with caramelized tamarind and palm sugar. There are several wines on the list, but beer goes best with the food.

Open Monday 5 pm to 10 pm, Tuesday to Saturday noon to 2.30 pm, 5 pm to 10 pm (later on Friday and Saturday), Sunday 5 pm to 10 pm. Licensed. Amex, Master Card, Visa. &

VANCOUVER   **MAP 207**
MARKET   ☆
Shangri-La Hotel   **$175**
1115 Alberni Street
(604) 695-1115

Market made a good beginning when it opened in 2009, but since then it's lost a lot of its original polish. Try the snapper if you want to see what we mean. The fish comes in a lively broth, but it's seriously overcooked. The warm chocolate cake may be made with the best chocolate, but it's been left in the oven far too long. Overall, however, the menu is as impressive as ever. Dinner begins with

Kusshi oysters on the half-shell, steelhead sashimi, beef tartar and a fine homemade soup. The grilled lamb and beef that come next are both local, which is certainly no hardship. But what you really come to Market for nowadays is the stunning wine-list, with its pages of chardonnays and cabernet sauvignons. Prices are extremely high though and you won't be drinking a Mouton-Rothschild unless you have 3000.00 in your pocket. There are some cheaper wines, of course, but not many.

Open Monday to Friday 11.30 am to 2.30 pm, 5 pm to 11 pm, Saturday and Sunday 11 am to 3 pm (brunch), 5 pm to 11 pm. Licensed. Amex, Master Card, Visa. Book ahead. &

VANCOUVER   **MAP 207**
OAKWOOD
2741 W 4 Avenue   **$140**
(604) 558-1965

Oakwood is typical of its kind—dark and crowded but warm and friendly. Its noon-hour menu is extremely small, but it expands in the evening. Pork belly with scrambled eggs and asparagus omelette give way to fried octopus, seared tuna, beef tartar, halibut cheeks and fat-iron steak. Mike Robbins' eggs all come from Rabbit River Farms and his chickens are all grass-fed. His tuna benedict comes with house-made hollandaise and his scrambled eggs are as big and buttery as they are at Wildebeeste (see below). His seafood is all sustainable and ocean-wise. His lemon-meringue pie is made with a whole lemon curd and madeleine pastry, his Nanaimo bars are made into a custard. The wine-list is tiny, but it features Joie Farm's noble blend by the glass. What more could one ask?

Open Monday to Friday 5 pm to 10 pm, Saturday and Sunday 10 am to 2.45 pm (brunch), 5 pm to 10 pm. Licensed. Amex, Master Card, Visa. No reservations. &

Every restaurant in this guide has been personally tested. Our reporters are not allowed to identify themselves or to accept free meals.

VANCOUVER   MAP 207
PASTIS   ☆
2153 W 4 Avenue   **$140**
(604) 731-5020

Pastis is a typical bistro, and it serves both lunch and dinner. It's not cheap, and most of the appetizers sell for
nearly as much as the main courses. Still, the steak tartar
is perfect and so are the sautéed sweetbreads with pumpkin, sage and foie gras. The fish is all well prepared, especially the wild salmon and the Arctic char with barley
and black-trumpet mushrooms. The cassoulet is a great
dish, filled as it is with confit of duck, Toulouse sausage
and braised white beans. Finish with an apple tarte tatin
or a lemon crème anglaise. The wine-list is mostly French
and it's very well chosen.
Open Tuesday to Friday 11.30 am to 2 pm, 5.30 pm to 10.30
pm, Saturday and Sunday 11 am to 2 pm (brunch), 5.30 pm to
10.30 pm. Closed on Monday. Licensed. Amex, Master Card,
Visa. Book ahead if you can. ♿

VANCOUVER   MAP 207
THE PEAR TREE   ☆☆
4120 E Hastings Street **$125**
Burnaby
(604) 299-2772

Scott and Stephanie Jaeger spend the money they save on
rent—this is a low-rent district—on the food they serve
in their restaurant. They offer a table d'hôte, with or
without wine pairings, five days a week. There's also an
à la carte that starts with prawn cappuccino made with
dashi custard and local prawns and goes on to a braised
Peace River lamb shank served with a risotto of roasted
pears—pears find their way into almost everything Scott
Jaeger makes. There's also braised beef short-ribs with
crisp potatoes, a mushroom purée and local salsify. For
sweet there's a tangy lemon tart and an orange-chocolate
sorbet. They have a good wine-list and excellent service.
Open Tuesday to Saturday 5 pm to 11 pm. Closed on Sunday

and Monday. Licensed. All cards. &

VANCOUVER   MAP 207
PHNOM PENH
244 E Georgia Street   **$90**
(604) 682-5777

Phnom Penh is a family-run operation serving first-class
Vietnamese and Cambodian food at very affordable
prices. Over the years it's often been called the best Asian
restaurant in the city. The tables are close together and
almost always full. Chances are, you'll have to wait on
the street to get a place inside. The interior is neat and
trim, and if you can't wait go to the front desk and give
them your order to take away. There are said to be 200
dishes on the menu, all served with such Asian spices as
cilantro, lemon grass and chilli. Our favourite is the butter beef, which is the Cambodian answer to carpaccio. It
comes to the table barely steamed with a soy-lime dressing and a liberal sprinkling of fried shallots and cardamom. We also like and admire the hot-and-sour soup,
the garlic squid, the rolls stuffed with prawns and the papaya salad, made with papaya and carrots tossed in a spicy
citrus dressing topped with peanuts, mint and cardamom
The rice pudding with fruit is an exotic dish that goes
well with any of the moo milkshakes.
*Open daily 10 am to 10 pm. Licensed. Amex, Master Card,
Visa. No reservations.*

VANCOUVER   MAP 207
LA QUERCIA   ★★
3689 W 4 Avenue   **$150**
(604) 676-1007

In 2009 this place was named the best new restaurant in
Vancouver—and it was. They still have excellent service,
fair prices and outstanding food. Their carpaccio of beef
comes with the best shaved parmesan cheese and shredded arugula, their scallops are pan-seared in a reduction
of raisin and port. Venison is either pan-seared or roasted

and finished with chocolate. Their lamb's neck is a great, hearty peasant dish seldom seen outside rural Italy. There's also a tasty chicken-liver pâté and a great deboned rabbit wrapped in prosciutto and served on a bed of puréed celeriac. Toffee pudding is the best of the sweets, though some prefer the apple strudel with raisins and pine-nuts.

Open Tuesday to Sunday 5 pm to 10 pm. Closed on Monday. Licensed. Master Card, Visa. Book ahead.

VANCOUVER   MAP 207
RANGOLI
1488 W 11 Avenue   **$75**
(604) 736-5711

Vij's Rangoli doubles as a market and a restaurant, selling ready-to-eat Indian dishes and freshly roasted and ground Indian spices, as well as eat-in dishes that are almost as good as Vij's (see below) and a lot cheaper. There are several eat-in dishes, especially at noon: pakoras with dal, lamb and beef kebabs with tamarind chutney, marinated chicken with sprouts, pulled pork with sour-cream chutney and beef short-ribs in kalonji curry. They all come with hot naan.

Open daily 11 am to 10 pm. All cards. No reservations. &

VANCOUVER   MAP 207
SHANGHAI RIVER
7831 Westminster Highway   **$85**
Richmond
(604) 233-8885

When it comes to the pork-filled dumplings known as xiao long bao, the Shanghai River runs head to head with the celebrated Lin (see above). They also make superb Peking duck, black-vinegar spare-ribs with pine-nuts and pork belly with preserved mustard greens. The service problem, hasn't gone away, as we once believed. It's worse.

Open daily 10.30 am to 3 pm, 5.30 pm to 10.30 pm. Licensed. Master Card, Visa. Book ahead. &

TABLEAU   ★★
1181 Melville Street   **$125**
(604) 639-8692

If you want to find out how good the cooking at Lumière used to be, come to Tableau on Melville Street. Marc-André Choquette, who used to work at Lumière, opened the place after Lumière closed. In its early days, Tableau was called Voya and served as a dining-room for the Loden Hotel, an upscale boutique hotel next door. But now, with a brand-new name, the restaurant is on its own. The menu is limited but exciting, offering things like steak tartar, tuna niçoise, grilled squid, dungeness crab and Kusshi oysters on the half-shell, followed by steelhead trout with quinoa and lemon, steak frites and charcuterie with cheese. The cooking is superlative and the service is excellent. The wine-list is full of good drinking—just look for either the Pfaffenheim gewurztraminer or the barbera d'Alba from Bratiasiola. Nothing at Tableau, except the Kusshi oysters, is expensive, and that's part of the pleasure. (Lumière was very expensive indeed.)
Open Monday to Thursday 11.30 am to 2.30 pm, 5 pm to 10.30 pm, Friday 11.30 am to 2.30 pm, 5 pm to 11 pm, Saturday 5 pm to 11 pm, Sunday 11.30 am to 2.30 pm (brunch). Licensed. Amex, Master Card, Visa. Book ahead if you can. Valet parking. &

THE TRUFFLE HOUSE
2452 Marine Drive   **$125**
West Vancouver
(604) 922-4222

The Truffle House is a popular boutique restaurant that serves mainly truffle-infused dishes. It's a tiny place with only a few tables and chairs. They serve brunch on Saturday and Sunday and dinner on Friday and Saturday. At noon they have a marvellous onion soup, quite the best in the city. The place is packed early in the day for a breakfast of two-egg omelettes with wild mushrooms and black truffles. For dinner they start with truffle gnocchi, a warm scallop-and-spinach salad and dungeness and snow crab with a lemon-and-tarragon aioli, followed by a risotto of wild mushrooms and truffles and roasted sablefish marinated in maple and soy. Afterward there's a variety of crêpes and a really good tarte tatin.

Open Monday to Thursday 8 am to 11 am (breakfast), 11 am to 3 pm (lunch), Friday 8 am to 11 am, 11 am to 3 pm, 5 pm to 9 pm, Saturday 8 am to 3 pm (brunch), 5 pm to 9 pm, Sunday 8 am to 3 pm (brunch). Licensed. Master Card, Visa. No reservations. Book ahead.

VANCOUVER   **MAP 207**
VIA TEVERE
1190 Victoria Drive   **$45**
(604) 336-1803

Via Tevere is named for the street in Naples where the owners grew up. They offer Neapolitan-style pizzas made in a wood-fired brick oven. Our favourite is the Girasole, a white-based pizza made with panna, parmesan, prosciutto, fresh corn and basil. They bring a variety of infused oils to add to your pizza, and if you order the arula salad as well, you can put it on top of your pizza and eat them both together. The heritage building is softly lit, which makes this an ideal place for a meaningful date. The wood-fired onion means quick service and that's what you get.

Open Tuesday to Thursday 5 pm to 10 pm, Friday and Saturday 5 pm to 11 pm, Sunday 5 pm to 10 pm. Closed on Monday. Licensed. Master Card, Visa.

VANCOUVER   **MAP 207**
VIJ'S   ☆☆
1480 W 11 Avenue   **$150**
(604) 736-6664

Vij's is not just a restaurant; it's an experience. Vikram

Vij doesn't cook Indian pure and simple. He uses Indian spices and creates every dish out of his imagination. The service is the best we can remember, and if you have to wait for a table—they take no reservations—they bring you *amuse-bouches* that help to while away the time. When you finally get to sit down, it's a good idea to ask for an appetizer of spicy pork belly and follow that with lamb popsicles, served with turmeric spinach or rice. The Rajistani goat curry is good too and so is the black cod with yogurt and tomato. There's always plenty of naan; if you want more, just ask for it. The pistachio kulfi with mango is a great way to finish any meal. There are many local wines on offer, but beer goes better with most of Vij's dishes, and of course it's cheaper.

Open daily 5.30 pm to 9.30 pm. Licensed for beer and wine only. All cards. No reservations. ⚊

VANCOUVER   **MAP 207**
WILDEBEEST   ☆
120 W Hastings Street   **$115**
(604) 687-6880

Wildebeest is all brick and grey paint. It's in a run-down part of town across the street from the old Woodward's building, and by the time you get a seat you're probably prepared to be unhappy. If that is so, get ready for a surprise, because the menu is astonishing and the food that comes from the open kitchen electrifying. In the evening they offer Sawmill Bay oysters with elderberry wine, lamb tartar, veal neck, Humboldt squid and Fraser Valley lamb. Actually, it's almost more fun to come for brunch and have croque Madame, smoked-cheddar bierwurst, pork jowl with a poached egg, a dish of foraged greens or, best of all, scrambled eggs with bone marrow. The marriage of big, buttery scrambled eggs with the haunting flavour of bone marrow is something to remember. They'll give you a big glass of fresh-squeezed orange-juice for 4.00, but if you come for dinner you'll probably want a glass of sauvignon blanc from the Loire or a half-bottle of beaujolais villages, or maybe a glass of apple

cider or one of the five draft beers. (They also have some fine old port and an excellent Pedro Ximenez sherry. Nothing is expensive.
Open Monday to Friday 5 pm to midnight, Saturday and Sunday 10 am to 2 pm (brunch), 5 pm to midnight. Licensed. Amex, Master Card, Visa. No reservations. ♿

VANCOUVER
See also GIBSON'S.

VIBANK, Saskatchewan   (MAP 160)
THE GROTTO   ☆
101 2 Avenue   **$115**
(306) 762-2010

Located about 30 miles east of Regina, the Grotto occupies the premises of an old convent. Here they offer fresh Mexican dishes as well as several southern barbecues. On Wednesday and Friday they serve a variety of tacos, tamales, smoked ribs and street-style corn. On Saturday it's southern-style barbecues like Carolina ribs, pecan-smoked breast of duck, smoked prime-rib steak and their special show-stopper, which is the Texas Platter. The Texas Platter is a huge tray piled high with brisket, ribs, chicken, baked beans and corn-bread. Dinners end with a chocolate flan, mango-and-pineapple pie or a piece of *tres-leches* cake. You have to book ahead because often all the tables are booked for several weeks at a time.
Open Tuesday 9 am to 2 pm, Wednesday and Friday 9 am to 9 pm, Saturday 5 pm to 9 pm. Closed on Sunday, Monday and Thursday. Licensed. Master Card, Visa. You must book ahead.

VICTORIA, B.C.   MAP 209
THE BLACK OLIVE
739 Pandora Avenue   **$150**
(250) 384-6060

The Black Olive is casual and unpretentious. It's run by Demetros Psyllakis (known as Paul), and he often stops at your table to have a glass of wine and a chat. Many of his dishes are made with the cold-pressed Kastamonitsa olive oil that he imports from his native Crete. Lunch is a substantial meal that may involve a cioppino with salt-spring mussels, scallops, prawns and cilantro or perhaps a vegetarian risotto made with wild mushrooms, artichokes, leeks and fresh tomatoes. In the evening they'll marinate their squid in the house olive-oil and garnish them with sweet onions. Paul is fond of lamb and serves it often, either with rosemary and a red-wine demi-glaze or slow-cooked with tomato and lemon. But there have been a number of turnovers in the kitchen recently, with the result that chefs unfamiliar with the menu have made occasional mistakes. The service, however, has always been good.

Open Monday to Friday 11.30 am to 2.30 pm, 5 pm to 10 pm, Saturday 5 pm to 10 pm, Sunday 5 pm to 9 pm. Licensed. All cards. &

VICTORIA   MAP 209
BRASSERIE L'ECOLE   ☆☆
1715 Government Street   **$135**
(250) 475-6260

This place is supposed to be a Parisian-style bistro, but actually it's more elegant than most Parisian bistros and the cooking is, if anything, better. The menu reflects Sean Brennan's desire to use local products cooked in the French country style. It's chalked up on a blackboard and changes regularly, but it always features steak with fries and usually offers oysters and mussels as well. The oysters on the half-shell are about the best in town, but they also offer an endive salad and braised pork belly in a broth of white wine. For sweet, if you're tired of crème brûlée, ask for the tarte tatin. It's a good one. There's a great little wine-list.

Open Tuesday to Saturday 5.30 pm to 11 pm. Closed on Sunday and Monday. Licensed. Master Card, Visa. No reservations. &

If you use an out-of-date edition and find it inaccurate, don't blame us. Buy a new edition.

VICTORIA
CAFE BRIO
944 Fort Street
(866) 270-5461

MAP 209
☆☆
$125

Silvia Marcolini and Greg Hays first became known at the legendary Herald Street Café, where they established a reputation for good food at reasonable prices, modest wine markups and good, knowledgeable service. They now work on Fort Street at the Café Brio, where the cooking has always been outstanding, though the prices are a bit higher than they used to be. If you can't get a table on the patio and have to eat inside, you'll need a flashlight to read the menu. It's a good idea to start with mussels—either the mussel soup (eco-farmed on Salt Spring Island) or the plain mussels and fries. (There are other good soups too, among them the cauliflower and the squash.) The best of the main courses—it's brilliant—is the slow-cooked braised pork. They make a fine granduja semifreddo too, though it's very rich. Their list of wines from the Okanagan and Vancouver Island is probably the best in Victoria.
Open daily 5.30 pm to 10 pm. Licensed. Master Card, Visa.
&

VICTORIA
CHOUX CHOUX CHARCUTERIE
830 Fort Street
(250) 382-7572

MAP 209
☞
$45

Almost hidden on Antique Row in downtown Victoria, Choux Choux is an old-world deli with the best gourmet meat products in town. The deli case has an impressive array of terrines, pâtés and rillettes. American visitors will find that they also carry haggis, a Scottish delicacy that's not for sale in the U.S. The best thing they do is the pâté of foie gras with truffle oil. They also have the French sausages needed to make an authentic cassoulet at home. If you get there early, you may find some of the *plat du jour* left. There's always soup and the *plat du jour* might be a smoked-chicken-and-brie baguette with a lovely fresh organic green salad.

Open Tuesday to Friday 10 am to 5.30 pm, Saturday 10 am to 5 pm. Closed on Sunday and Monday. No liquor, no cards. No reservations.

VICTORIA · MAP 209
DEVOUR
762 Broughton Street · **$90**
(250) 590-3231

Devour is a tiny place with five tables for two. They serve their wine in toothbrush glasses and their cider in a bottle. They have a very small wine-list that lists four red wines and four white. The best of these are a Sandhill chardonnay and a surprising pinot noir from Kim Crawford. The menu is lively and interesting. It starts with a Moroccan version of chicken pastilla and offers two baguettes, one of crab and avocado, the other of spiced meat-loaf. There's a nice beef stroganoff with spaetzle and sour cream, and a colourful flank steak with grapefruit. In the evening they have Ahi tuna, lamb tarts with caramelized onions and a spiced chicken mole. The meal ends well with a flourless-chocolate brownie.

Open Monday to Wednesday 8 am to 4 pm, Thursday and Friday 8 am to 9 pm. Closed on Saturday and Sunday. Licensed. Master Card, Visa.

VICTORIA · MAP 209
FOO
769 Yates Street · **$45**
(250) 383-3111

Foo is at the corner of Yates and Broughton, facing a hotel parking-lot that Foo's customers are not allowed to use. Here they serve Asian street food at bare tables that encircle the room. Everything is very cheap and the counter service is very crisp. The menu is written up on big blackboards and few things ever change. There's always some red coconut curry, butter chicken, octopus salad glazed with sweet chilli, caramelized chicken, sweet-and-sour pork belly and tuna tataki with soba noodles. The last two are our favourites, but they never put a foot wrong with any of their dishes. There are no wines or spirits and only two beers, Driftwood ale and White Bark wheat beer, both of them brewed locally. We usually ask for the ale, but whatever you ask for you'll be glad. We love Foo.

Open Monday to Saturday 11.30 am to 10 pm, Sunday 11.30 am to 9 pm. Licensed for beer and wine only. Master Card, Visa. No reservations. &

VICTORIA

MAP 209
★★★
$165

MATISSE
512 Yates Street
(250) 480-0883

Matisse occupies a quiet dining-room on Yates Street, where everybody feels warm and comfortable. There are old-fashioned graphics on the menu and crisp, fresh table-cloths on every table. The menu is inviting. It offers things like foie gras de canard in a pineau-des-charentes jelly, sautéed Arctic char and rack of fresh Australian lamb. The lamb is about as good as it gets, and the foie gras is a lively variation on a familiar theme. Dinner usually ends with something like bavarois au citron with red fruit, a beautiful dish. The wine-list is ambitious and rises to a Mouton-Rothschild (1050.00 for a bottle of the 1985). But if you settle for a white wine, you can have a bottle of mâcon chardonnay for just 60.00. Matisse has been underrated for years. It's now time that it was taken as seriously as it deserves.

Open Wednesday to Sunday 5.30 pm to 10 pm. Closed on Monday and Tuesday. Licensed. Amex, Master Card, Visa. &

This is a guide to Canadian restaurants from coast to coast—the first ever published and the only one of its kind on the market today. We accept no advertisements. Nobody can buy his way into this guide and nobody can buy his way out.

VICTORIA   **MAP 209**
PRIMA STRADA
2960 Bridge Street   **$90**
(250) 590-4380

Prima Strada has recently been awarded the Verace Pizza
Napoletana or True Pizza of Naples Award, which means
that they make their pizzas as they've been made in
Naples for hundreds of years. Only a handful of restaurants in Canada have won this award. We think the pizzas
at this location are even better than those at 230 Cook
Street (telephone (250) 590-8595). Prima Strada uses
great local produce and their thin-crust pizzas are much
the best in Victoria. Try the pizza funghi, which is topped
with roasted mushrooms and onions, porcini cream and
thyme. We think you'll agree.
Open Tuesday to Saturday 11 am to 9 pm. Closed on Sunday
and Monday. Licensed. Master Card, Visa. &

VICTORIA   **MAP 209**
SHINE CAFE
1548 Fort Street   **$45**
(250) 595-2133

Shine is a great place for both breakfast and brunch. For
one thing, they're very good with omelettes. Try the Seventh Heaven or the Tree Planter, which is stuffed with
spinach, mushrooms, yams, avocado, brie and basil. At
noon they also have several soups, salads, burgers and
sandwiches. We once had a daily special of magret de canard eggs benedict, but the regular menu is equally imaginative. Don't miss the so-called Rabbie Burns, which is
made with maple caramelized red onions and bacon. The
original location is here on Fort Street, but they now have
a branch that's more convenient for tourists. It's at 1320
Blanshard Street (telephone (250) 595-2134). Both cafés
have the same menu.
Open daily 8 am to 3 pm. Licensed. Master Card, Visa.

Nobody but nobody can buy his way into this guide.

VICTORIA

STAGE
1307 Gladstone Avenue
(250) 388-4222

MAP 209
☆
$105

George Szasz sold Stage—his personal creation—to Graham Meekling in the fall of 2012, but so far there have been few important changes. This is still a funky little bistro specializing in small-portion presentations of fish, meat and vegetables. There are several salads as well—look for the tuna and the octopus—and several kinds of sausage—pork chorizo and Moroccan merguez. The best of the large plates are the seared sablefish, the Sooke trout and the fried octopus, though they also have an attractive treatment of mussels with coconut, cilantro and ginger. People often just ask for a plate of cheese and charcuterie, choosing from a list of eight meats and nine cheeses—three cow's milk, three sheep's milk and three goat's milk. There's a short list of wines, but if you want a half-bottle ask for the Blue Mountain pinot gris, which is a lot better than the Kettle Valley sauvignon from Naramata. There's one wonderful buy—a glass of ornellaia grappa for just 10.00, which is so cheap that it's often sold out. Call before you book.

Open daily 5 pm to midnight (earlier on Sunday and Monday).
Licensed. Master Card, Visa. No reservations. &

VICTORIA

IL TERRAZZO
555 Johnson Street
(250) 361-0028

MAP 209

$150

Look for Il Terrazzo in Waddington Alley, behind Willie's Bakery. It's crowded and the noise is overwhelming. They cook in the northern Italian style, which means brodeto di pesce to begin with or fried squid with cucumbers and cilantro, or perhaps seared scallops with smoked tuna. After that you may be tempted by the osso buco or the rack of lamb. The lamb, however, is tough and tasteless; better the roasted salmon with mango or the baked local halibut. The wine-list is large and comfortable, offering, among other good things, a Liberty School and a Joie Farm from Peter Lehmann. Take your pick.

Open Monday to Friday 11.30 am to 2 pm, 5.30 pm to 10 pm, Saturday and Sunday 5.30 pm to 10 pm. Licensed. Amex, Master Card, Visa. ♿

VICTORIA   MAP 209
ULLA
509 Fisgard Street   **$110**
(250) 590-8795

Ulla is located in a restored building at the corner of Fisgard and Store, where skid row ends and Chinatown begins. High ceilings, arched windows and contemporary art all give the place a gentrified air. Now in its fourth year, Ulla has a menu that features ethically-raised proteins, whatever that means. Presumably, albacore-tuna tataki in ponzu sauce and short-rib steaks in black-garlic jus. Reviewers all admire the semolina polenta, the beet salad and the lamb three ways. If elk is on the menu, be sure to ask for it. The recipes aren't all that startling, but the presentation is always beautiful. They take sweets seriously too, especially the poached apple with calvados.

Open Tuesday to Saturday 5.30 pm to 10 pm. Closed on Sunday and Monday. Licensed. Master Card, Visa. Book ahead.

VICTORIA   MAP 209
ZAMBRI'S   ☆
820 Yates Street   **$160**
(250) 360-1171

The new Zambri's is all steel and glass. The menu is Italian. It starts with tuna tartar and chilled octopus with tomato and goes on to penne with gorgonzola, tagliatelle with duck, shoulder of pork, lamb shanks and panna cotta with (too little) grappa. The cooking is country-style Italian. The flavours are bold, the helpings large. At times the cooking is brilliant, and the chilled octopus with fresh tomatoes is certainly a brilliant dish. The same is true of the thin-crust pizzas. At other times, however, Zambri's is merely pedestrian. The Cornish game hen, dry and thin on flavour, is such a dish. The veal is really young beef—milkfed veal is hard to find anywhere except in Montreal. The beef tenderloin with gorgonzola is a much better choice. There's a decent list of Italian wines, and they have an appealing chianti classico from Castello di Bossi for 60.00 a bottle.

Open daily 11 am to 3 pm, 5 pm to 10 pm. Licensed. Amex, Master Card, Visa. No reservations for lunch. &

VICTORIA
See also SALT SPRING ISLAND, SIDNEY.

VICTORIA-BY-THE-SEA, P.E.I. (MAP 39)
ISLAND CHOCOLATE COMPANY
7 Main Street
(902) 658-2320

This old general store has been completely renovated. The machines that produce the chocolates have been moved to the back and the front opened up for more tables. The chocolates are all made with Belgian chocolate stuffed with fresh fruit—strawberries, raspberries and cranberries, each in their season. We first heard of Linda Gilbert as a baker and she still bakes a lot of muffins, brownies and flourless tortes. She has espresso and cappuccino as well, both made from beans roasted right here on the Island. Three years ago the Gilberts organized a chocolate festival that's since become an annual event. It takes place on the third Saturday in September.

Open Monday to Saturday 10 am to 8 pm, Sunday noon to 6 pm from mid-June until early October. No liquor. Master Card, Visa. &

The price rating shown opposite the headline of each entry indicates the average cost of dinner for two with a modest wine, tax and tip. The cost of dinner, bed and breakfast (if available) is shown in parentheses.

VICTORIA-BY-THE-SEA (MAP 39)
THE LANDMARK CAFE
12 Main Street **$80**
(902) 658-2286

The Landmark is a fixture in the village of Victoria-by-the-Sea. The opening night in June is sold our every year; regulars come to celebrate the return from abroad of Eugene Sauvé and his family. Eugene himself has been here for 25 years and his son, Oliver, and his daughter, Rachel, now help in the kitchen. Not that Eugene needs help—he's as strong as a horse. He's a relaxed and friendly man and he cooks well. His menu seldom changes, though the specials vary with the seasons. Our favourites are the lobster roll packed with sweet, fresh lobster and the meat pies, which can be superb. The only complaint we've ever had was that Eugene doesn't put enough vegetables on the plate. But, vegetables or no vegetables, the Landmark is always fun.
Open daily 11.30 am to 8 pm from 1 June until Thanksgiving. Licensed. Master Card, Visa. Book ahead. &

WAINWRIGHT, Alberta MAP 211
THE HONEY-POT
823 2 Avenue **$95**
(780) 842-4094

We discovered the Honey-Pot in 1989. It had opened ten years earlier, when it began offering meals to the soldiers of Western Command. The soldiers were lucky to find such a place in a small Prairie town like Wainwright. The Honey-Pot has now been owned and operated by three generations of one family. Alex Heath is running the place today, with the help of his daughter, Michele. Alberta beef is what the kitchen does best. They tried ranch-raised elk a few years ago, but found the quality of the meat wasn't always up to scratch. The fish and chips, however, are surprisingly good and so is the Caesar salad. The vegetables are always fresh and there's a different homemade soup every day of the week except Sunday.

All the sweets are made in the kitchen, even the vanilla pudding called Foggy Bottom. The local Ribstone Creek beer is on tap and that's usually the thing to drink.
Open Monday to Saturday 11 am to 9.30 pm. Closed on Sunday. Licensed. Amex, Master Card, Visa. &

WATERLOO, Ontario

(MAP 96)
MASALA BAY ☆
3B Regina Street N **$85**
(519) 747-2763

Waterloo is the high-tech capital of Canada, home of the University of Waterloo, the Perimeter Institute of Theoretical Physics and the Steven Hawking Institute. Masala Bay is a small Indian restaurant where Dr. Hawking has been photographed with the proprietors. This is not surprising, because the food is good and very cheap. The best things come from the tandoor oven and the naan is superb. People write to us about the tikka and the aloo gobi. Actually, our favourite is the bhoona gosht or beef curry. There's a good buffet at noon, but the evening helpings are too large for comfort.
Open Monday to Thursday noon to 2 pm, 5 pm to 10 pm, Friday 11 am to 2 pm, 5 pm to 10.30 pm, Saturday 11.30 am to 2 pm, 5 pm to 10.30 pm, Sunday 6 pm to 9 pm. Licensed. All cards. &

WATERLOO

(MAP 96)
NICK & NAT'S UPTOWN 21 ☆☆
21 King Street N **$150**
(519) 883-1100

Nick is the chef, Nat the waiter. If you take a seat at the bar, you can watch them both at work. Every day they put on a *prix-fixe* dinner where you can have apple-and-onion soup and any one of a number of unusual salads, all made with local greens. There's also an à la carte that offers steak frites, pork chops, choucroute, and fresh fish. For vegetarians there's great ravioli, stuffed with a variety of seasonal ingredients.) Nick smokes his own sausages and serves them with pork chops braised in white wine. There's a decent wine-list that majors in wines from the Niagara Region.

Open Tuesday to Saturday 5 pm to 9 pm. Closed on Sunday and Monday. Licensed. All cards.

WATERLOO (MAP 96)
SOLE ☆
83 Erb Street W: Building 2 **$140**
(519) 747-5622

Sole is housed in a former cooperage factory, a heritage building that gives visitors a sense of what the city was once all about. The menu has been shortened this year, but they've kept their salads and most of their appetizers, as well as a variety of fish. In the evening the most exciting dish, we think, is the rosemary porchetta, a slow-roasted pork loin wrapped in pork belly and served with a parmesan risotto. The combination of the succulent loin with the rich, soft belly and the crackling rind makes the dish memorable. The steaks are good too and come with a delicate garlic mash. The fried potato cakes are done with chorizo, asiago cheese and sweet peas until they're crisp outside and light and fluffy inside. Our long-time favourite sweet is the carrot cake with pecans, and it's a better choice than the vanilla crème brûlée. There's an extensive list of beer and wine, and the carafes are all excellent buys.

Open Monday to Thursday 11.30 am to 11 pm, Friday 11.30 am to midnight, Saturday 11 am to midnight, Sunday 11 am to 9 pm. Licensed. All cards. ♿

WELLINGTON, Ontario (MAP 142)
EAST & MAIN
270 Main Street **$150**
(613) 399-5420

East & Main is a relative newcomer to this area, but already it's packed at all hours, and you should book ahead. There are good reasons for its success. The cooking is good, the portions ample, the service attentive. The wine-list offers twenty local whites and twenty local reds. You can start dinner with gravlax cured in vodka and go on to braised lamb shanks with zinfandel or cider-brined pork tenderloin with red cabbage The best of the sweets is either the chocolate torte or the blueberry streusel cake. *Open Monday and Thursday to Sunday noon to 2.30 pm, 5.30 pm to 9.30 pm. Closed on Tuesday and Wednesday. Licensed. Master Card, Visa. Book ahead.*

WHISTLER, B.C.   **MAP 214**
ALTA
4319 Main Street: Site 104   **$175**
(604) 932-2582

Alta is offering good cooking at a reasonable cost in a town known everywhere for its astronomical prices. Nicholas Cassettari is a strong believer in locally-sourced ingredients. His water is drawn from a well outside the door. His beers come from a brewery down the street. His signature sweet is made from local fruit served with sour-cream ice cream. He starts with elk tartar and duck-liver parfait, and his mains are maple-glazed pork cheeks and beef short-ribs, both of which are often better than the Ahi tuna. All his wines are organic. Best of all, he offers a three-course table d'hôte for just 39.00 a head, though of course you'll pay more than that on the à la carte.
Open daily 5.30 pm to 8.30 pm (longer hours in winter). Licensed. Amex, Master Card, Visa. Book ahead. &

WHISTLER   **MAP 214**
                                       ☆☆
ARAXI
4222 Village Square   **$200**
(604) 932-4540

Gordon Ramsay called Araxi the best restaurant in Canada. That's hardly true, and several of its creations are definitely over the top. But the menu does touch most of the important bases. For instance, the raw bar serves six varieties of oyster and five sushis. There are 9000 bottles of wine in the cellar, many of them priced within the means of the average diner. Most things on the menu are fairly priced too. For instance, grilled red tuna can be had for just 29.50, which is cheap for Whistler. Almost everything on the menu (with the exception of the lobster and some of the cheeses) is grown locally. This includes the dungeness crab and the breast of duck, which comes from Yarrow Farms. The steaks are as good as any in the province. The short list of sweets offers poached Okanagan pears and valhrona chocolate. The best of the cheeses come from Salt Spring Island.

Open daily 11 am to 11 pm from 1 June until 30 September, daily 5 pm to 11 pm from 1 October until 31 May. Licensed. All cards. Book ahead if you can. &

WHISTLER   MAP 214
BEARFOOT BISTRO   ☆☆
4121 Village Green $350
(604) 932-3433

The Bearfoot Bistro gets bad press from time to time, but we've never found anything to criticize. The service is no slower than one would expect for dishes that require so much last-minute preparation. Prices are high, of course, but cooking of this quality always costs money. André St.-Jacques runs a very tight ship and he makes few mistakes. In Melissa Craig he has one of the best chef in the business. If you order the three-course table d'hôte you'll get a superb meal. There's yellowfin tuna with grilled octopus and Israeli couscous. There's breast of duck with cabbage, chestnuts, honey and brown butter. There are several amazing vegetarian dishes. If you want the nitro ice cream you'll have to pay a *supplément* of 20.00 for it, but there are many other good things to be had. In the wine-cellar there are no fewer than 1100 labels. There's a lot to enjoy here.

Open daily 5.30 pm to 1 am from 1 May until 15 December (shorter hours in winter). Licensed. All cards. Book ahead. &

WHISTLER
RIMROCK CAFE
Highland Lodge
2117 Whistler Road
(877) 932-5589

MAP 214
★★
$200

Rolf Gunther is still in charge of the kitchen at the Rim-rock and everyone is happy with his cooking. Seafood has always been his strong suit, though recently he's be-come interested also in game. Fish and shellfish (including lobster) come in regularly by truck from Vancouver. Oysters are now on the menu and the sablefish crusted with macadamia nuts and the halibut with prawns and tuna are both always cooked to perfection. The same is true of the steak and the lamb. The wines are expensive, but the sticky-toffee pudding is not.
Open daily 5 pm to 9.30 pm (shorter hours in winter). Licensed. All cards. Book ahead if you can.

WHISTLER
SPLITZ GRILL
4369 Main Street: Unit 104
(604) 938-9300

MAP 214
$60

The Splitz Grill never seems to change. Their hamburg-ers are always good, and bison is the current favourite. The burgers come with at least twenty different toppings. There's also a huge choice of ice creams and an incompa-rable chocolate milkshake. The children's menu offers hot-dogs and chicken fingers for about 6.00 a time. The service is cafeteria-style and there's a big room at the back if you don't want to eat in the car. You'll find Splitz in the Alpenglow Hotel, not far from the centre of town.
Open daily 11 am to 9 pm from 1 May until 30 November, daily 11 am to 10 pm from 1 December until 30 April. Licensed for beer and wine only. Master Card, Visa.

We accept no advertisements. We accept no payment for listings. We depend entirely on you. Recommend the book to your friends.

WHITBY, Ontario　　　　　　　　　　　**(MAP 202)**
NICE BISTRO　　　　　　　　　　　　　　　☆
117 Brock Street N　　　　　　　　　　**$110**
(905) 668-8839

It's more than twenty years since Bernard Alberigo and his wife, Manon, opened this bistro in Whitby. They've worked hard and kept their standards high, and we've never heard a word of criticism. Everybody likes the place. The menu aims to marry Canadian produce like maple syrup with French recipes. You'll find some of the best things among the daily specials on the chalkboard—the soup of the day, the country-style pâté and the snails in garlic butter. Of course, they also have steak frites, moules marinière and steak au poivre. Nice isn't far from Italy and so it's no surprise to find tortellini stuffed with spinach and figs on the menu. On Tuesday night they offer all the mussels you can eat. The rest of the week there's a four-course table d'hôte for 30.00 a head (39.99 on jazz nights). The cheeseboard is ambitious and well maintained. Manon is in charge of the sweets, and the wine-list is always full of good buys.
Open Tuesday to Saturday 11.30 am to 3 pm, 5.30 pm to 10 pm. Closed on Sunday and Monday. Licensed. Amex, Master Card, Visa. ♿

WHITEHORSE, Yukon　　　　　　　　*MAP 216*

There's a new restaurant in Whitehorse this year. The Wheelhouse at 2237 2 Avenue: Unit 170 (telephone (867) 456-2982) is a stunning place to look at. The menu is short and features local produce (elk cannelloni, bison short-ribs and almond-crusted halibut). The cooking is consistent, but the service is pretty rough. The Cork and Bull at 103 Main Street (telephone (867) 633-3305) is a steak house. It's been open for a couple of years, but its cooking is no match for that at the Wheelhouse. The Baked at 100 Main Street (telephone (867) 633-6291) is a bakery, as the name implies. They have long lineups at the door, but it's a great place for breakfast, and at noon they have big, healthy sandwiches. The Sanchez Cantina at 211 Hanson Street (telephone

(867) 668-5858) claims to have the only authentic Mexican food in the Yukon. Orlina Sanchez makes nearly everything from scratch. Her tacos and her enchiladas are good, but don't try her chicken. The Burnt Toast Café at 2112 2 Avenue (867) 393-2605) is a quirky little place with good cooking. Their coffee is roasted locally and most people find it fun. The Wheelhouse is open daily for dinner in summer, but has shorter hours in winter; the Cork and Bull is open for dinner from Tuesday to Saturday; Baked is open daily for breakfast and lunch, the Sanchez Cantina is open for lunch and dinner every day but Sunday, Burnt Toast is open every day but Monday for lunch, every day but Sunday and Monday for dinner. They're all licensed and all take most cards.

WHITE LAKE, Ontario
CASTLEGARTH
90 Burnstown Road
(613) 623-3472

MAP 217

$150

Matthew and Jennifer Brearley make the best of their unlikely location—Castlegarth is an hour's drive from Ottawa, the nearest city. But the two chefs (both graduates of the Stratford Chefs School) have stayed true to their belief that everything should come straight from the garden to the table. (The family farm down the road makes it possible to serve tomatoes on the vine and just-picked beans.) The house, which is right in the middle of the village, has no frills, but it seats 30 people in comfort. The menu changes frequently, and during the year there are some special occasions. Not long ago, Robbie Burns Day brought a salad of brussels sprouts with haggis and rabbit sausage with pickled rutabaga. At other times they offer things like seared quail with butter-braised cabbage, wild-rice pancakes and onions with hawthorn honey. The coffee is marvellous.
Open Wednesday to Sunday 5.30 pm to 10 pm. Closed on Monday and Tuesday. Licensed. Master Card, Visa. &

If you use an out-of-date edition and find it inaccurate, don't blame us. Buy a new edition.

WINDSOR, Ontario
TOSCANA
3891 Dougall Avenue
(519) 972-5699

MAP 218

☆

$115

Jonathan Reaume once described himself as "one of the most accomplished chefs in Metro Detroit." If you can forgive him for that remark, you'll find that indeed he is a remarkably good chef over a wide range of dishes. The menu is supposed to be Italian, and it does include such Italian staples as veal and pasta. (Some people come here once or twice a week for the pasta.) There are also several interesting salads. Jonathan has no patience with regional cuisine. He has (or claims to have) suppliers from all over the world. His lamb, for instance, comes from Colorado. His chicken, at least, is free-run and organic. He's good with fish and offers several vegetables every day. His calf's liver is carefully cleaned and lightly cooked; his beef is always tender. Then there's a big list of wines from the Old World and the New, a good many of which are offered by the glass as well as the bottle.

Open Monday to Friday 11.30 am to 2.30 pm, 5 pm to 10 pm, Saturday 5 pm to 10 pm. Closed on Sunday. Licensed. Amex, Master Card, Visa. ♿

WINNIPEG, Manitoba
BISTRO DANSK
63 Sherbrook Street
(204) 775-5662

MAP 219

☞

$90

Josef Vocadlo started the Bistro Dansk many years ago; nowadays the place is run by Josef's son, Paul. The restaurant hasn't changed much since it opened, and it still has its Danish menu, with a few Czech dishes to give it variety. Start with the herring and go on to the frikadeller, the kylling (half roasted chicken stuffed with apricots and walnuts), the veal tenderloin stuffed with ham and cheese, the pan-fried rainbow trout or the pork tenderloin sautéed in garlic with sweet-and-sour cabbage. With your dinner, ask for a bottle of Mondavi Woodbridge, which costs almost nothing. Indeed, everything at Bistro Dansk is spectacularly cheap.

Open Tuesday to Saturday 11 am to 2.30 pm, 5 pm to 9 pm. Closed on Sunday and Monday. Licensed. All cards. Book ahead.

WINNIPEG MAP 219
EAST INDIA COMPANY ☆
349 York Avenue **$75**
(204) 947-3097

This is one Indian restaurant where nobody has to apologize for the décor or, for that matter, for anything else. The dining-room is bright and cheerful. It has a big buffet table that starts with salads and yogurts, goes on to tandoori chicken and such things as mussels, shrimps and whole fish. There are vindaloos on order and a variety of vegetarian dishes. The dessert table has a number of custards, of which we think the mango is the best. There are a few wines on offer and a couple of Indian beers. When it comes to value for money, no restaurant in the city can compare with the East India Company.

Open Monday to Friday 11 am to 2 pm, 5 pm to 10 pm, Saturday 5 pm to 10 pm, Sunday noon to 8 pm. Licensed. Amex, Master Card, Visa. Book ahead if you can. ♿

WINNIPEG MAP 219
MISE
842 Corydon Avenue **$110**
(204) 284-7916

Mise used to occupy the basement of an office building; then it moved up-market to a former furrier's store. It now has a beautiful bar, a well-appointed dining-room and an outdoor terrace. It also has a big menu, good cooking and excellent service. There's tender calamari to start with, a vegetable tempura and a cranberry brioche. Main courses steer a middle course between pasta and Prairie steak house. There's pancetta and salmon with rosemary, angel-hair pasta and confit of duck with soy sauce. Some dishes just don't work—bouillabaisse, for example, with clams, a nondescript broth and a cookie spread with saffron butter. The sweets, however, are usually very good, especially the fruit pies and the lemon mousse. There's a decent, fairly-priced wine-list.

Open Tuesday to Saturday 5 pm to 10 pm, Sunday 10 am to 2 pm (brunch). Closed on Monday. Licensed All cards. &

WINNIPEG **MAP 219**
NORTH GARDEN 🖐
33 University Crescent: Unit 6 **$60**
(204) 275-2591

The North Garden is actually in south Winnipeg and it has no garden. But it's popular with Chinese students and faculty from the nearby University of Manitoba, and rightly so because they have a great variety of authentic szechuan and cantonese dishes. Dim sum is offered in steamer baskets every day until 4 o'clock. This is by far the best dim sum to be had in Winnipeg. They also have lobster and crab at market prices, and the place is crowded every evening during the school year. After about 9 o'clock, however, things become quieter and the service improves.

Open Monday to Thursday 10 am to midnight, Friday and Saturday 9 am to 1 am, Sunday 10 am to midnight. Licensed. All cards. Book ahead if you can. &

WINNIPEG **MAP 219**
THE PALM ROOM ☆
Fort Garry Hotel **$125**
222 Broadway Avenue
(204) 942-8251

The Fort Garry Hotel was built in 1913. Later taken over by the C.N.R., it was eventually allowed to fall into disrepair. A few years ago, it was restored by Richard Bel and Ida Albo and turned into a grand hotel with a period dining-room. The menu at the Palm Room, as it's called, is that of a road-house, presented in high style. In the evening you dine on gravlax, roast chicken and pecan pie, all to the gentle music of a string quartet. On Sunday they put on a magnificent buffet, for which they earn a star in this guide. It costs 55.00 (35.00 for seniors, 25.00 for children from six to twelve and nothing for children under six). There's a massive array of eggs, pancakes, roasts, pastries, tarts and tortes, as well as a fine selection of whiskies. If you want to recover from all this excess, the hotel operates a Turkish-style spa.

Open Monday to Thursday 11 am to midnight, Friday and Saturday 11 am to 1 am, Sunday 10 am to 1 pm (brunch), 3 pm to 11 pm. Licensed. All cards. Book ahead for Sunday brunch. &

WINNIPEG   MAP 219
PEASANT COOKERY
283 Bannatyne Avenue: Unit 100   **$100**
(204) 989-7700

Peasant Cookery is the new name for Oui, which in turn was a downscale version of the lavish steak house that used to be known as 529. The word *peasant* can be taken to apply to a rural truck-stop or perhaps to a minimalist take on pub grub—or even to an upscale tease about the place as a whole. There are good things to be had here, as well as dishes to be avoided at all costs. The menu looks as if it had been drawn up by a committee that had more than one idea, but no single vision. With care, one can navigate the list, which starts at tourtière (cheap at 17.00) and rises to cold cuts (also cheap at 16.00). The burger on a bun is pretty bland—better the butter-lettuce salad. There are pork schnitzels and short-ribs, but no bangers and mash. Look around and order with care.

Open Monday to Friday 11.30 am to 11 pm, Saturday 5 pm to midnight, Sunday 5 pm to 10 pm. Licensed. All cards. &

This is a guide to Canadian restaurants from coast to coast—the first ever published and the only one of its kind on the market today. Every restaurant in the guide has been personally tested. Our reporters are not allowed to identify themselves or to accept free meals.

WINNIPEG

MAP 219

RAE & JERRY'S
1405 Portage Avenue   **$100**
(204) 783-6155

Rae & Jerry's takes you back more than 50 years to 1957, the year the place opened. Very little has changed since then. They still have thick red carpets on the floor and deeply cushioned booths. The bar still treats martinis as if they were a fashionable cocktail. The kitchen still caters to people—of all ages and incomes—who want roast beef or beefsteak. The steaks are all good—surprisingly good. There's a fine pecan pie, as well as a coconut-cream pie and bread pudding. They have some good cabernets from Australia and several good malbecs from Argentina. The wines are all fairly priced and so is the food.
Open Monday to Saturday 11 am to 11 pm, Sunday 11 am to 8.30 pm. Licensed. Amex, Master Card, Visa. Book ahead if you can. &

WINNIPEG   MAP 219

LA SCALA
725 Corydon Avenue   **$125**
(204) 474-2750

Perry Scaletta has run La Scala for over twenty years. It's always had an Italian menu with touches here and there of fusion cuisine. But to enjoy the place to the full you have to know what to order. That means dumplings, which are Chinese in concept but ethereal on your plate. It means seafood linguine and penne with spicy sausage. Best of all, it means penne with garlic and tomatoes, chillies and red and green peppers. Main dishes run from osso buco and cioppino to veal scaloppine and rib steak with black beans. The wine-list is large and features cabernets from Italy and Australia. The service is competent, the prices reasonable.
Open Monday to Friday 11.30 am to 1.30 pm, 5 pm to 11 pm, Saturday and Sunday 5 pm to 11 pm from 1 May until 31 August, Monday to Thursday 5 pm to 8.30 pm, Friday and Sat-

urday 5 pm to 10 pm from 1 September until 30 April. Closed on Sunday in winter. Licensed. All cards.

WINNIPEG
SYDNEY'S AT THE FORKS
1 Forks Market Road
(204) 942-6075

MAP 219
★★
$175

There's no better place to dine in Winnipeg than Sydney's at the Forks. That said, you need to know that getting there is not easy. Sydney's is part of the Forks Market, which is basically a congeries of junk. But once you're seated, you'll find yourself in an island of wood and stone, all designed in the best of good taste. The dining-room is quiet and you can hear your companion if she (or he) has something to say. Dinner costs 55.00 a head, for which they give you an interesting soup (parsnip and toasted almond, perhaps), an appetizer of wild scallops or a saffron-roasted corn samosa and a main course of shrimps poached in butter—though for the shrimp you'll have to pay a *supplément* of 21.00. There's an impressive wine-list that extends from old barolos to a number of big super-Tuscans. If you have money to burn, there's a Pétrus for less than 350.00, which for a Pétrus is a really good buy. Lunch, of course, is cheaper, featuring things like a high-end BLT or a ricotta gnocchi. Everybody in the restaurant, however, whether you come for lunch or for dinner, is treated as a somebody, which is nice, especially if you aren't. There's plenty of free parking at a distance; if you park close to the restaurant, however, you have to pay.

Open Monday 5 pm to 9 pm, Tuesday to Friday 11.30 am to 2 pm, 5 pm to 9 pm, Saturday 5 pm to 9 pm. Closed on Sunday. Licensed. All cards. Book ahead. &

This is a guide to Canadian restaurants from coast to coast—the first ever published and the only one of its kind on the market today. We accept no advertisements. Nobody can buy his way into this guide and nobody can buy his way out.

WINNIPEG
TRE VISI
173 McDermot Avenue
(204) 949-9032

MAP 219

$110

The original Tre Visi is in a shabby district, but inside everything is warm and comfortable. The creation of the chef-owner, Giacomo Appice, it has the best Italian kitchen in Winnipeg. They have a variety of cured meats and marinated vegetables. They have some amazing pastas—just try the capellini with roasted red peppers and saffron cream. They do a fine piccata of veal in white wine as well, and their saltimbocca of pork has few equals. If you don't feel like another zabaglione marsala, ask for the chocolate ganache instead. Recently, Tre Visi has opened a second restaurant at 926 Grosvenor Avenue (telephone (204) 475-4447). It has a similar but smaller menu that emphasizes pasta, but they don't take reservations.

Open Monday to Wednesday 11.30 am to 2.30 pm, 5 pm to 9 pm, Thursday and Friday 11.30 am to 2.30 pm, 5 pm to 10 pm, Saturday 5 pm to 10 pm. Closed on Sunday. Licensed. All cards. Book ahead. &

WOLFVILLE, N.S.
BLOMIDON INN
195 Main Street
(877) 542-2291

MAP 220
☆☆

$175 ($360)

Sean Laceby is in charge of the kitchen here; his brother, Michael, is the *sommelier.* (Another brother, Rob, runs the Amherst Shore Country Inn.) All three are the children of Jim and Donna Laceby, who are both still very much around. Michael has built up a remarkable list of Canadian and imported wines, among which is the wonderful Benjamin Bridge Nova 7, raised nearby in the Gaspereau Valley. Michael will warn drinkers that the 2011 vintage doesn't match the 2010, but it's good enough to transform any dinner. Dinners begin with one of three soups or a salad. Sean makes much of Annapolis Valley fruit in his salsas, a trick that works especially well with scallops. He also has fresh Atlantic salmon, braised lamb shanks and a fine treatment of well hung filet mignon—five ounces for just 26.95. As for his lobster tails, you won't be able to match them for quality anywhere within a hundred miles.

Open Monday to Friday 11.30 am to 2 pm, 5 pm to 9.30 pm, Saturday and Sunday 10 am to 3 pm (brunch), 5 pm to 9.30 pm. Licensed. Master Card, Visa.

WOLFVILLE   **MAP 220**
CELLAR DOOR   ☞
Luckett Vineyards   **$50**
1293 Grand Pré Road
(902) 542-2600

Pete Luckett made an instant success of his grocery stores, which he calls Pete's Frootiques. He then opened a vineyard called Luckett's. That was in 2010 and the Luckett Vineyards were rated the top tourist attraction in Wolfville just two years later. The wines are still young, of course, but the restaurant offers spectacular views of Minas Basin and Cape Blomidon. The Cellar Door itself is reserved for private parties, but the outside patio has seating for ordinary travellers. Here you can have a soup, a sandwich (Italian ham with figs, say) and a salad (patty-pan squash with chanterelles, perhaps). They also have cheese-and-charcuterie platters, as well as one or two excellent sweets. The German tasting varietal, Ortega, is the best of the wines on offer, though it's often sold out. Good news—they have a red telephone booth from which you can call anyone in North America free of charge.

Open daily 10 am to 5 pm from 1 June until 31 October. Licensed. Amex, Master Card, Visa. Book ahead if you can.

Where an entry is printed in italics this indicates that the restaurant has been listed only because it serves the best food in its area or because it hasn't yet been adequately tested.

WOLFVILLE
FRONT & CENTRAL
117 Front Street
(866) 542-0588

MAP 220
★★★
$150

David Smart, the former chef of Tempest, has now put his seal of approval on the restaurant he took over from Michael Howell. His menu, however, is more adventurous than Howell's. He likes to work with small plates and you're expected to order three of these in an evening. His menu offers things like a risotto of mushrooms and barley, a paella of seafood and sausage, breast of duck with hukirei turnip, savoury granola and apple purée, gnocchi with oyster mushrooms, kale, maple and ginger, ravioli of peas and ricotta and, most inviting of all, sour-cream ice cream with lemon, peas and Maldon sea salt. The service is attentive and very knowledgeable.

Open Tuesday to Sunday 5 pm to 9 pm from early May until late October, Wednesday to Sunday 5 pm to 9 pm from late October until early May. Closed on Monday in summer, Monday and Tuesday in winter. Licensed. Amex, Master Card, Visa. Book ahead if you can.

WOLFVILLE
THE PRIVET HOUSE
406 Main Street
(902) 542-7525

MAP 220
★★
$100

Jamie Smye and Liisa Sellors, originally from Ontario, first moved to Newfoundland and then to Wolfville, taking over the location once owned by Acton's. They're interested in using regional produce whenever they can, like so many other restaurants in the area. But they cook better than most. Try their squid, served with aioli and a Korean-style sauce. It's fantastic. The halibut too is well served with dulse tapenade and sum me vegetables in cream. Our favourite sweet is the lemon tart brûlée, an interesting take on crème brûlée. The wine-list, once full of nothing but familiar wines, is getting better.

Open Tuesday to Saturday noon to 3 pm, 5 pm to 9 pm. Closed on Sunday and Monday. Licensed. All cards. &

WOLFVILLE
See also GRAND PRE.

WOODSTOCK, N.B.
HEINO'S
John Gyles Motor Inn
Highway 165
(866) 381-8800

MAP 221

$75

This is one of our favourite restaurants, and we travel hundreds of miles each year to have dinner here. The place is so genuine, so honest, so cheap. Heino Toedler cooks German, as everyone knows. That means gulyasuppe, fried onions, sausages, spaetzle, red cabbage, schnitzels, lachsfilet (salmon) and bienenstich cake. We keep coming back for Heino's potato pancakes, but what the restaurant is really all about is its bratwurst, debreziner, knackwurst and weisswurst. (Weisswurst or white sausage is made with fried veal.) That and sauerbraten, zigeuner schnitzel, jaeger schnitzel and farmer's schnitzel. The sausages cost about 15.00, the schnitzels about 20.00, and they all come with German beer. (Heino should add more German wines; until he does, just ask for a glass of beer.) To get to Heino's, take Exit 200 from the Trans Canada a few miles south of Woodstock, turn left at each of two stop signs and proceed a few hundred yards to the north. The John Gyles is at the top of a hill on the west side of the road.
Open Monday to Saturday 5 pm to 9 pm, Sunday 5 pm to 8 pm. Licensed. Amex, Master Card, Visa. &

WOODY POINT, Newfoundland
THE OLD LOFT
Water Street
(709) 453-2294

(MAP 164)

$90

The Old Loft has never pretended to be a gourmet restaurant. But they'll give you a generous helping of traditional Newfoundland food at a very low price. That means that you'll have a bottle of Heinz ketchup on the table and gravy with everything on your plate. Not that it's hard to enjoy an open-face turkey sandwich piled high with meat and stuffing and covered with gravy. The fries are hand-cut and perfectly cooked, the onion rings are big and delicate. Both cod and halibut are caught locally and pan-fried in the kitchen. The salmon is farmed but nicely served with dill. The moose wellington has wonderful pastry. Pastry is what the Old Loft is really all about. Clarice Bursey is a keen baker, but it's her mother, Rose, who makes the irresistible pastry and the partridge-berry pies. The Old Loft is on the second floor of an old fish-house, so you have to climb stairs to get in. When you get there, you'll find that the place is rather dark, which makes it hard to enjoy the artwork. Woody Point is on the south arm of Bonne Bay in Gros Morne National Park. It was settled more than a hundred years ago, and the big old house and garden have been lovingly cared for ever since. To get there, turn off Highway 431 on the road to Trout River. The Old Loft is right on the highway.

Open daily 11.30 am to 9 pm from Victoria Day until Thanksgiving. Licensed for beer and wine only. Amex, Master Card, Visa.

YARMOUTH, N.S.

MAP 223

OLD WORLD BAKERY
232 Main Street
(902) 742-2181

$40

In spite of the recent cancellation of ferry sailings between Yarmouth and Bar Harbour, Tony and Nova Papadogiorgakis are carrying on at the bakery as if nothing had happened. Their breads and pastries are as good as ever. Their huge muffins are good enough to take home. (They come with cheese, cranberry, lemon, blueberry, bran, cinnamon, dates, apples and oranges.) They make rye, whole-grain, sourdough and sweet-potato bread. There's also a homemade soup every day and big, filling sandwiches, of which our favourite is the smoked lamb. (The lamb, like the turkey and the sausages, is smoked on the premises.) The coffee is fairly traded and it's always great.

Open Tuesday to Friday 7 am to 6 pm, Saturday 7 am to 5 pm. Closed on Sunday and Monday. No liquor, no cards. ♿

YARMOUTH
See also MIDDLE WEST PUBNICO.

YELLOWKNIFE, N.W.T.	**MAP 224**
BULLOCK'S BISTRO	☆
3534 Weaver Drive	**$130**
(867) 873-3474	

Everybody likes Bullock's. It used to be a working fish shack, and it's always been here—small, crowded, noisy and expensive. The chairs are rickety, the tables carved with old initials, the service easy-come, easy-go. But the fish is about as fresh as it gets. Most of it comes from Great Slave Lake—whitefish, cod, pickerel and trout are always on the menu. Renata serves all the fish grilled, pan-fried, poached, blackened Cajun-style or deep-fried in a beer batter. Meals all come with warm sourdough bread and a slab of butter. If you want something to drink, help yourself from the cooler—there's always plenty of beer and a couple of wines in there.

Open Monday to Saturday 11.30 am to 9 pm. Closed on Sunday. Licensed. Master Card, Visa. Book ahead if you can.

YELLOWKNIFE	*MAP 224*
WILDCAT CAFE	
3904 Wiley Road	*$95*
(867) 873-8850	

It's sad to see that Pierre LePage is no longer active in Yellowknife. He was a fine chef with big dreams. The Wildcat is not in any sense his restaurant, but it has recently reopened after being closed for two long years, and it's a place our readers should know about. It's housed in an old log shanty near the Pilot Monument in the old town, and has long tables inside and out. The bison burger and the whitefish are both good, and so are the bannock, the kale and the fennel slaw. Gluten-free beer is served cold in an old tin cup, and the coffee is strong. It's still too soon to say exactly when it'll be open, but it has a licence and takes most cards. Further reports needed.

We will soon be preparing the next edition of this guide. To do that, we need the help of our readers, many of whom routinely send us information and comments on restaurants that interest them, whether or not they are already in the guide. Please address us by mail at 145 Spruce Street: Suite 205, Ottawa, Ontario K1R 6P1, by fax at (613) 238-3275 or by e-mail at oberon@sympatico.ca

First published July 1971. Reprinted September 1971, November 1971, January 1972. Second edition published June 1972. Reprinted July 1972. Third edition published June 1973. Reprinted July 1973. Fourth edition published June 1974. Fifth edition published June 1975. Book-of-the-Month Club edition published July 1975. Sixth edition published June 1976. Seventh edition published June 1977. Eighth edition published June 1978. Ninth edition published June 1979. Tenth edition published June 1980. Eleventh edition published June 1981. Twelfth edition published June 1982. Thirteenth edition published June 1983. Fourteenth edition published June 1984. Fifteenth edition published June 1985. Sixteenth edition published June 1986. Seventeenth edition published June 1987. Eighteenth edition published June 1988. Nineteenth edition published June 1989. Twentieth edition published June 1990. Twenty-first edition published June 1991. Twenty-second edition published June 1992. Twenty-third edition published June 1993. Twenty-fourth edition published June 1994. Twenty-fifth edition published June 1995. Twenty-sixth edition published June 1996. Twenty-seventh edition published June 1997. Twenty-eighth edition published June 1998. Twenty-ninth edition published June 1999. Thirtieth edition published June 2000. Thirty-first edition published June 2001. Thirty-second edition published June 2002. Thirty-third edition published June 2003. Thirty-fourth edition published June 2004. Thirty-fifth edition published June 2005. Thirty-sixth edition published June 2006. Thirty-seventh edition published June 2007. Thirty-eighth edition published June 2008. Thirty-ninth edition published June 2009. Fortieth edition published June 2010. Forty-first edition published June 2011. Forty-second edition published June 2012. Forty-third edition published June 2013. Forty-fourth edition published June 2014.